Praise for *Magick Made Easy...*

M000103945

"Patricia Telesco is a four-star spiritual chef and in Magick Made Easy *she skillfully blends inspiring insights with useful examples and an impressive list of thoroughly researched, easily available ingredients. With this helpful book, anyone—novice or adept—can create personal magick that nourishes the soul."*

—High Priestess Phyllis Curott, J.D., author of *Book of Shadows*

"An undaunting and friendly introduction to magick, full of common sense and with a useful list of correspondences."

—Starhawk, author of *The Spiral Dance*

*"*Magick Made Easy *provides a simple, direct, first step into the world of Wicca for those who are curious about witchcraft but unsure where to start. A well-stocked reference text and an introduction to spellcrafting basics that is easy to relate to."*

—Francesca De Grandis, author of *Be a Goddess! A Guide to Celtic Spells and Wisdom for Self-Healing, Prosperity, and Great Sex*

"Hurray for Patricia Telesco and Magick Made Easy! *There are no obscure ingredients to buy, and absolutely no guesswork. With this book, even the Scarecrow could meet with magickal success!"*

—Dorothy Morrison, author of *Everyday Magic*

"If you have been hungering for a book that makes magick easy to understand and use, this is your lucky day! Magick Made Easy *is a supernatural feast of fun, filled with spellcraft secrets and folk magick fundamentals. Premier kitchen witch Patricia Telesco shows you how to make powerful magick with the ordinary things around your home or workplace. Delightful, empowering, and highly recommended,* Magick Made Easy *is the perfect book for the twenty-first-century witch!"*

—Sirona Knight, author of *Love, Sex, and Magick, The Shapeshifter Tarot*, and Contributing Editor for *Magical Blend* magazine

"I found Magick Made Easy *to be a practical and resourceful guide to folk magick and lore. It is written with warmth and is sure to be a delight for the beginner."*

—Raven Grimassi, author of *The Wiccan Mysteries*

"This book really does make magick easy and understandable and user-friendly! Patricia Telesco makes us understand that we all perform simple magickal acts each day, but rarely do we think about it. Thank you, Trish, for clear explanations and inspired insights that make magick and wonder accessible to everyone!"

—Frank and Cate Dalton, organizers of CraftWise

MAGICK MADE EASY

Also by Patricia Telesco

365 Goddess
Goddess in My Pocket
Kitchen Witch's Cookbook
Wishing Well: Empowering Your Hopes and Dreams
The Herbal Arts
Your Book of Shadows
Seasons of the Sun
The Language of Dreams
Victorian Grimoire
Futuretelling

PATRICIA TELESCO

MAGICK MADE EASY

Charms, Spells, Potions, and Power

HarperSanFrancisco

A Division of HarperCollinsPublishers

HarperCollins books may be purchased for educational, business, or sales promotional use. For information please write: Special Markets Department, HarperCollins Publishers, Inc., 10 East 53rd Street, New York, NY 10022.

HarperCollins Web Site: http://www.harpercollins.com

HarperCollins®, ▨ ®, and HarperSanFrancisco™ are trademarks of HarperCollins Publishers Inc.

FIRST EDITION

Designed by Laura Lindgren and Celia Fuller

Library of Congress Cataloging-in-Publication Data
Telesco, Patricia.
    Magick made easy : charms, spells, potions & power / Patricia Telesco. — 1st ed.
      p.   cm.
    Includes bibliographical references and index.
    ISBN 0–06–251630–2 (paper)
    1. Magic.   I. Title.
  BF1611.T45 1999
  133.4'3—DC21   99–28515
                                                    CIP

99 00 01 02 03 ❖ RRD(H) 10 9 8 7 6 5 4 3 2 1

*To anyone, anywhere, who has ever wanted
a little more magick in his or her life, and to all
the people who have made my life so magickal!
and
To WADL. This organization provides support,
education, and other ongoing efforts to protect everyone's
right to religious freedom. Visit their website at
http://members.tripod.com/~Elderpaths/WADLhome.html.*

CONTENTS

Contents

ACKNOWLEDGMENTS

To the elders, teachers, guides, family, friends, and readers who have helped make the path of magick a little easier, fun, and fulfilling for me, this book is my note of thanks. Specifically I'd like to extend my appreciation to A. J. for ongoing cyber support, the folks at CraftWise, who have become my extended family, Jennie for her efforts to get good books into the market, Sirona and Dorothy for being reassuring, Colleen for her artistic vision, David and Blythe for research assistance, and David H. for fantastic insights and tweaking the pages of this book to perfection.

There are many more people who have touched my spiritual life deeply, some whose names I never learned. To all of you, I extend this prayer: May your path be smooth and filled with sunlight, may your days be long and filled with joy, and may the years ahead find you growing toward Spirit, with magick as an ever sure companion.

Yours in the moonlight and the shadow of a star.

Trish

INTRODUCTION

The real magic is enthusiasm.
NORMAN VINCENT PEALE

Magick: the word conjures images of an enchanted time filled with court mages and mythical creatures. Although it seems that our technologically driven society has all but lost sight of magick's bewitching spark, I am happy to tell you that the god/dess is still alive and magick is, indeed, afoot! All around the world right now people just like you are casting spells, making amulets, meditating, and performing rituals to improve finances, ease troubled relationships, spice up their love lives, and tone down negativity.

Everyday folks, in all walks of life, have rediscovered magickal ideals and practices as a way of coping with chaos and satisfying their spirits, and you can too. Now, before the idea of working magick puts you off, relax. Think of spells, charms, and rituals as similar to detailed prayers to which you add some old-fashioned willpower, symbolic components, and actions to emphasize your desire. By so doing, you put your needs and goals before the Sacred Powers, then support that "prayer" with magickal energy and concrete efforts. This combination encourages active participation in making your present and future happier and more fulfilling.

Sound complicated? I promise that by the time you're finished reading this book, it won't seem that way at all. Magick is quite natural, and it's something we all have available to us. If you've recently discovered an interest in magick, Wicca, and other emerging metaphysical lifestyles, *Magick Made Easy* can answer a lot of those nagging questions that come up in the light of a whole new way of thinking.

In fact, the main goal of *Magick Made Easy*, and particularly Part One, is to do exactly what the title says—to make magick easy for you! How? By familiarizing you with the basic art of folk magick—its methods and tools—and then helping you feel more at ease with those methods and tools. And why folk magick? Because, by its nature, folk magick is pragmatic, simple, straightforward, and unassuming and therefore well suited to our busy lives.

See, our ancestors didn't have a lot of time for complex or meaningless procedures. Instead, they brought spirituality together with daily living, using creativity and inspiration to make magick out of everyday circumstances and objects. To me, this seems like the perfect combination for modern magick too.

Part Two is a list of potential components you can use in developing your own spells, meditations, rituals, pathworking exercises, charms, and visualizations. This list includes no Shakespearean elements—no tongue of dog, no eye of newt, and no "toil and trouble." Instead, *Magick Made Easy* lives up to its claim by listing components found readily in and around the sacred space of home, including your coffeepot, various edibles, the telephone, pantry spices, your computer, and even the toilet! These items become the ingredients for your magickal recipes. Better still, they are already saturated with personal energy and meaningfulness, so they work better for any type of magick you hope to create.

In a society in which everyone juggles several responsibilities at once, this approach holds tremendous merit. It advocates looking at our personal environment differently, seeing the magickal potential and possibilities in everything—most important, seeing this potential in yourself. See, even without the bells and whistles—without the trappings or any components whatsoever—*you* are the magick. Spiritual energy lies inside each one of us just waiting to be expressed. This book will help you find the right mediums and methods through which to express your own form of magick.

Think of *Magick Made Easy* as a course in mystical cookery. In the pages of this book you can examine various ways of baking up magickal energy just right, considering the implements and components you have available, your tastes, and the goal at hand. By measuring this information against your personal vision, then mixing and mingling these things in personally meaningful ways, the outcome is bound to be more satisfying, more transformational, more life-affirming, and more powerful. So make life and magick a little easier, beginning right here and now. Put on those ruby slippers and turn the page!

PART ONE

OFF

to

"OZ"

CHAPTER 1

Common Questions About Magick

The visible is, for us,
the proportional measure of the invisible.
OLD MAGICKAL CREED

Although science seeks to unravel the mysteries of the universe, magick practitioners revel in them. We perceive these gaps in concrete data as the perfect opening through which spiritual truths can sneak and touch our reality. The world of the modern metaphysician is, after all, like Oz to our mundane Kansas—a place filled to overflowing with wonders, potential, and possibilities. One of them is the very viable possibility that humans are much more than simple flesh and blood, that we are, instead, beings of soul, and power, and magick!

Some people think such talk is nothing more than superstitious prattle. Others regard the human soul and magick as part of the supernatural world, and as such seemingly separate, inaccessible, and incomprehensible to most humans. I, and thousands of other people in the world today, disagree with both of these outlooks wholeheartedly. We see both the soul and its inherent magick as a birthright and as an important part of humankind's makeup. *Magick Made Easy* builds on this premise, recognizing that this birthright affects different people in very different ways. Exactly how it transforms each individual's present into a more fulfilling and empowering future depends a lot on

3

personal vision and how he or she perceives this enigmatic thing called "magick."

For those of you who have already been exposed to the world of magick, some of the information in this chapter may be a review. I suggest you scan it anyway. I think you'll find some fresh perspectives in here that will augment or facilitate your continuing studies.

For the newcomers reading this who might be anxious to dive in headfirst and get started on spellcraft or other processes, I'm a great advocate of testing the waters. Consequently, this chapter focuses on the "abouts" rather than the "how-tos" of magick. In the following pages you can get your astral feet wet by examining the answers I've given to the most common questions people ask about magick and how the whole thing works.

As you read, please know that my vision of magick and spirituality is not the only way to approach this topic successfully—it's just the way that works for me and one that seems to have helped my students over the years. To embark on this adventure with me as a teacher, however, you must first be willing to follow some rules I give to all my students:

Auntie Trish's First Rule of Magick

A true magician is his or her own priest,
priestess, guru, psychic, or shaman.

Don't let anyone or anything else take over this important job in your life.

Wait a minute. Don't go getting all nervous on me now. You already fulfill this role every day simply by making choices. You sort out good from bad, action from inaction. Now you're just going to take it one step farther into your spiritual life. Right here and now I want you to start trusting your instincts about what's wholly right for you—don't just take my word for anything—then act accordingly. After all, I can only share with you what I've experienced. Ultimately, it will be up to you to decide if the glimmers of "truth" I've gathered over the years can be successfully adapted and applied to your life and reality.

What Is Magick?

I must confess that I've always hated the "M" word. This is because the first thing that comes to most people's minds is a stage magician pulling a bunny out of a hat or Mickey Mouse as the sorcerer's apprentice with a rainbow of sparks flying out of his wand. Unfortunately, I don't have a better word to work with, so bear with me.

Real magick is not a stage illusion, and it's nothing like what the media has portrayed it as. Though I might wish I could reach into a hat and pull out whatever I need, twitch my nose and have a clean house, or hop on a handy broom to travel abroad (I hear brooms get great mileage), this is not modern magick as we know it. And, unfortunately, these portraits do little to help us clarify what constitutes magick as a mystical, spiritual procedure that makes sense in the workaday world around us.

So to define magick, let's first try looking to the dictionary. Here we discover that the root word for magick, *magi,* was a title given to priests in Persia who were skilled in sorcery. Consequently, the term *magick* implies occult competence, but don't let the word *occult* scare you off. This term originally meant a natural science that sought to uncover the secret mysteries of the mind and the world in which we live and then endeavored to apply that knowledge effectively. That pretty well describes what most modern practitioners of magick try to do!

Beyond this, we also know that the magi were considered learned, wise people who had the ability to produce amazing effects through the careful and responsible use of power. This, too, describes the modern magick practitioner. Even so, it leaves us with two unanswered questions: Where does this power come from? How does it produce such effects?

To answer those questions, we have to look at a secondary characteristic of magick, which is to bend and change. Through various techniques, discussed in this book, the magick user willfully gathers energy from the world around him or her, and sometimes from the expanse of the universe or the god/dess (the Sacred Parent/Divine Power behind all creation), and binds it into a strand of power. The resulting energy strand is then returned to the tapestry of life in a very specific, mindful way so it begins weaving a new pattern—a pattern that represents the meeting of a need or manifestation of a desire. In other words, the pattern is the magick in realized, tangible form.

This approach is based on the axiom that *energy cannot be created or destroyed, but simply changes shape.* Magick not only changes the patterns and cycles of life's tapestry, but also, in the process, transforms something within the magick user. Self-confidence improves, and the individual begins taking an active role in creating a personal destiny that's earth-friendly and conscious of universal laws in its design.

Mind you, these changes aren't always full of flash and fanfare. Folk magick, sometimes called kitchen magick, is simple and rather plain to the curious onlooker. It also follows natural patterns and progressions in its manifestation process. So although the components, words, and outcomes may not seem overly spectacular in folk traditions, the power is still there subtly bending and changing reality. With this in mind . . .

Auntie Trish's Second Rule of Magick

Magick doesn't have to be complicated, or the results ostentatious,
to be effective and transformational.

Now this lack of complication certainly doesn't limit the folk magician's creativity or sense of personal flair! Magick, by its very nature, is an art. There is an ingenious, aesthetic element to magickal procedures. This element comes from each individual's expression of his or her innermost essence in a unique manner. This is why you see so many "flavors" or "schools" of magick. Whether it's shamanism, Wicca, paganism, or Druidry, practitioners in these schools are each revealing their vision of magick by the personally meaningful methods they choose to use in creating it. This means that all magickal explorations begin with exploring yourself and your vision of spirituality on a very intimate level. Which brings us to Rule 3:

Auntie Trish's Third Rule of Magick

Magick users know themselves in truthfulness.

Know your abilities and limitations, accenting the positives and slowly working on the negatives. Know what you feel "at home" with, and never waver from that unless you feel guided to do so by Spirit or by a path that inspires the best in you.

Ah, but I've gotten sidetracked from answering the question at hand. Besides illustrating occult competence, bending energy, and being an art, what else is magick? In my classes I use various terms to describe and explain this elusive concept to students. Specifically, magick is:

- *Natural:* I can't stress enough the importance of getting away from the mind-set that regards magick as supernatural. It is just as natural as the birds and bees, except the "baby" produced is conceived in your mind and will.
- *Respectful:* Folk magick has a deep abiding respect for life and diversity. Without variety, growth, and change, magick becomes bland and stale. This is also true of our world. People are different. Their recipes for magick and spirituality are different—but it all makes for a wonderful blend and certainly keeps things interesting! Respect all paths to magick and the Sacred as having equal validity and all things in the world as potential tools for fine-tuning your spiritual quest, and you'll do just fine.
- *Tantalizing:* Folk magick can be quite addictive. Once you get a taste of spontaneous, heartfelt magick in action, it awakens the inner child in you who wants to get out and play some more! Be prepared to suddenly find yourself walking around the house, office, or supermarket with magick on your mind. Don't shut this part of yourself down out

of habit. Use it to explore, ponder, muse, and enjoy the world from the perspective provided by a truly appreciative, magickal eye.

- *Refreshing:* Unlike some types of magick that require many years of study just to learn the basic rituals, folk magick is first and foremost a vision-driven path: it is formed by your own environment, traditions, symbols, cultural background, familial lore, and the like. This releases a lot of the pressure you might feel in a more structured setting to perform or act a certain way, even if that "way" isn't wholly right for you. It also releases the awkwardness some people feel when they're baring their souls in a group setting.

   Folk magick practitioners frequently fly by the seat of their proverbial broomsticks, using inspiration for fuel and prevalent circumstances for motivation. Their path is often a solitary one by choice. In this kind of setting, everything boils down to you the practitioner, the Sacred, and the magick—no onlookers, and no judgmental voices other than those that come from your own heart about "right" and "wrong."

   To balance this statement, I should say that formalized forms of magick or group settings might be *good* for you. They just don't work for me. I've also discovered that folk magick is something nearly everyone relates to and learns fairly easily. Better still, it provides a good foundation for any type of magick tradition you might want to study in the future.

- *Enriching:* The exploration of magick not only brings us back in touch with ourselves and our spiritual nature, but it also connects us with others of like mind and the earth as a living symbol of greater truths. Once you begin studying magick, each day (and every moment in it) represents a whole new chance to learn and grow as a spiritual being and a member of humankind's family. Trust me when I say that after your spirit starts receiving magick's "water," it will thirst for more. This ongoing thirst acts as a strong motivation to always keep you seeking and moving forward, in both magick and life.

- *Unifying:* Magick definitely advocates global thinking in ways that might not be immediately evident. For example, in studying folk magick you'll come across approaches from all over the world, at least some of which you'll relate to and want to use. In these little gems of wisdom we begin to see that people are far more alike than they are different. We can then honor those similarities by respectfully adding tidbits of culturally inspired methods into our daily magickal practices.

- *Liberating:* Folk magick encourages us to be exactly who we are, just in a slightly different way. We continue in our roles in life, but now have at our disposal added dimensions. Ecologists continue to be ecologists, but may now choose to add an awareness of the moon's influences or other magickal methods to their work to improve the results and make the effort more fulfilling. Writers still write; they just enact a creativity spell or ritual before beginning, so that Spirit and magick flow through the work.

In summary, folk traditions advocate bringing that special spark of magick to anything and everything—from the bedroom to the supermarket to the office and every moment in between—until life itself becomes a joyful act of worship and is filled to overflowing with positive energy.

Can Anyone Work Magick?

Definitely. As you've probably guessed by now, I don't see magick traditions as elite clubs that only a few favored individuals can join, but the practice isn't necessarily *right* for everyone. By the time you're done reading this chapter, you should have a better understanding of what magick is and whether or not it's a suitable path for you.

From the get-go you should know that, like any other respected art form, the mastery of magick isn't instantaneous. It will take time, practice, and patience to use the techniques and resulting energies effectively. Our drive-through society has fostered the idea that someone can become adept at magick by attending one ritual, casting one spell, or reading one book. This is simply not the case (not even with this book), and it would be misleading you to tell you otherwise.

There is a pace and rhythm to both the process of learning magick and its manifestation. Because magick is driven by the vision and abilities of the practitioner, your ability to learn and use it effectively can't be determined by anyone else's clock. Don't try and "keep up" with anyone; don't try to push progress. Take magick one step at a time, at a stride that's right for you. Someone who has strong right-brain tendencies, for example, may develop his or her magickal aptitude more slowly and logically. Left-brainers, being driven by instinct and intuition, might make spiritual strides more quickly. The learning pattern we develop comes from our basic nature and needs to be honored. How fast you learn magick has no bearing on how *good* you'll eventually be. After all,

Auntie Trish's Fourth Rule of Magick

You have no limits in magick other than those you create.

Along the same lines, and as your guide to making magick easy, I also have to tell you that sometimes the road to powerful, life-changing magick isn't always "easy"!

Auntie Trish's Fifth Rule of Magick

Most worthwhile things in life have obstacles that have to be overcome and require real effort on our part; magick is no exception.

This rule keeps us honest. In this case the obstacles are usually those we put in the road ourselves: disbelief, insecurity, lack of focus, or impatience. Apply faith, two willing hands, a strong will, persistence, and a loving heart to this equation, however, and you will eventually experience success!

Through faith all things become possible. If you can't believe that the spark called magick exists within you, the world, and the universe, then you won't be able to kindle any figurative fires. Set aside the tendency to question everything long enough to just *be*. Breathe deeply and look at the world with a child's eyes in that moment. See the magick in how the grass grows, how the stars shine, in the warm smile of a stranger, and especially in yourself. Aha! Now you're getting there. Don't stop!

Two good hands and a keen mind are the greatest gifts the creator (the god/dess) gave us. They allow us to reach out for help, accept help, think about our choices, discern what's best for us, and then act accordingly. And, as the saying goes, "A mind is a terrible thing to waste." Contrary to what you may have heard, magickal methods don't arbitrarily set aside rational processes. Instead, you will learn to work *with* those processes and then reach beyond them into the world/not-world where the magickal tapestry begins.

Willpower drives energy through this tapestry and toward the goal. To understand this, think for a moment of how much mental force an obstinate child puts into her words and actions to get what she wants. The will of the magick user has similar potential in an adult, sensible context. It puts a focus and force behind whatever energy you create.

Bearing this and the fact that humans have free will in mind, each person who works magick remains wholly responsible for whatever happens as a result, because it is his or her will that steers the power created. This is why so many books on magick, including this one, issue caution.

Auntie Trish's Sixth Rule of Magick

**Be careful what you wish for and about how and why
you use the gift of magick.**

Magick has the power to curse and cure equally. It is the human will (read: *your will*) that ultimately decides which.

Persistence supports your magick through tangible and spiritual efforts that continue until you see some results. Finally, love binds all these things together. Love creates a functional unit through which our magick flows for the greatest good, even when we can't see the bigger picture.

Is Magick Harmful?

Absolutely not. I won't go into a long-winded explanation of how and why witchcraft and other related belief systems got such a bad rap. Suffice it to say that whenever a new religion is born, the practitioners of that faith often try to replace prevalent, popular practices by demonizing them, which of course aids conversion. So, over time, paganism and other magick traditions went underground, especially during the witch hunts. People turned to quietly practicing their faith at home and handing down those traditions through oral history. In the meantime, the "other guys" continued to disavow magickal beliefs as silly, superstitious, or downright sinful.

I am happy to report that magick is none of these things. Think of magickal energy as an electrical current. Magick is just as neutral as that. The only thing that changes the way electricity gets used is what we plug into it. Similarly, the only thing that makes magickal energy into something positive or negative is the will and intention of the practitioner.

Unfortunately, due to free will and human diversity, there can be "bad" magick users, or those who step over the line between good and bad during times of duress. That's simply the way of things, and I don't see it changing anytime soon unless humankind can overcome all its deadly sins all at once! Consequently, the reason for my giving you rules and guidelines in this chapter is to keep you on the right spiritual track. There is a threefold law in magick that says what we get out of magick is going to be three times what we give. So anytime people use magick for ill gain, they're really only hurting themselves. Remember:

Auntie Trish's Seventh Rule of Magick

Magick is a tool, and we are the ones who control
how we choose to use it.

What Are the Principles
of Folk Magick?

The wonders of the human mind are only now slowly starting to be understood and appreciated, and I suspect we're seeing but the tip of the proverbial iceberg. Einstein understood this untapped, unseen potential when he said, "It is not a long step from thinking of matter as an electronic ghost to thinking of it as an objectified image of thought." What we think, what we believe, what we willfully project through imagery is very important to how magick works and to understanding folk magick's principles.

Consider for a moment the type of circumstances gloomy people seem to draw to themselves versus those that positive, proactive people attract. This is the principle of like attracting like, which is at the heart of understanding how magickal energy works. People who think negatively about themselves and believe they deserve little in life usually get just that. People who think positively and believe they deserve the best that life and their own two hands can offer usually get far better results. The main difference here is easily seen in the way people think, talk, behave, and tackle daily circumstances.

The like-attracting-like principle holds true for magick on many other levels beyond the obvious one—the need to believe in what we're doing and trust that it will manifest in the best possible way. See, folk magick bases its methods on symbolism, sympathy, and imitation. Beginning with *symbolism*, folk magicians believe that a symbol is just as powerful as what it represents. This *belief* changes the way they *think* about that object and how they *treat* it. Note, however, that the folk magician's chosen symbols *must* have personal meaning for the whole process to work. Without personal meaning, the symbol becomes like a foreign language that one cannot use effectively.

For example, one spiritual healer might choose an amber crystal to entrap disease in much the same way amber entrapped bits of plant matter when it was forming. Another healer who has no idea what that particular stone is or represents couldn't use that tool as effectively as the first, because the personal meaning—the spiritual connection—isn't there. Like a plug and socket, without one the other has no power! Zolar, an occult writer of some infamy, understood this when he said, "Symbols are the product of ideas, so in their turn, ideas are the symbols of thought."

Sympathy means that objects and people have the capacity to affect one another through their connection, whether that connection is literal or figurative. For example, yellow plants were often used as part of ancient cures for jaundice because of the color's sympathy with the sickness. In another case, the blade of a weapon that caused a wound would be treated in the same way as the wound itself (with salve). Still another example is that of burying the afterbirth of a child beneath a healthy tree, so the child grows as strong and healthy as that tree. Again, anyone choosing this particular approach would first have to *trust* in its validity and understand the key principles of *action following thought* and *like affecting like*.

Finally, *imitation* was among the most popular forms of early folk magick, because it provided a visual affirmation of the magick's success. For example, when shamans wanted crops to grow high, they would jump high to show them what to do (e.g., "*willful projection*"). When they wanted a successful hunting expedition, it would be painted as an already achieved *reality* on the cave wall. Both these examples illustrate symbolism, faith, and action working together to help energy find its path to the goal.

▲▲▲

SEVEN KEY PRINCIPLES OF FOLK MAGICK

1. Like attracts or begets like.
2. Will guides and energizes magick, but also makes us responsible for the results.
3. Action follows thought, which therefore aids with magickal manifestation.
4. Symbols are just as powerful as what they represent in the sacred space.
5. Objects and people can affect each other over vast distances through the laws of sympathy.
6. Imitation stresses and illustrates willful projection.
7. Magick must have meaning; it will not work without it.

▼▼▼

Does Folk Magick Have a Religious Element?

Not necessarily. All folk magicians accept the fact that the energy of life exists all around us. Nonetheless, not everyone chooses to worship that energy or its creator, and not everyone accepts an ethical code that would denote a "religion" in their practices. In effect, magick is a method and a philosophy—a means to an end and a way of thinking differently. So someone with an established belief system could conceivably add a magickal dimension to it by adapting the words and methods magick teaches suitably to that faith.

If you are someone without a particular religious preference, I suspect that over time you will find yourself adding morals, standards, or doctrines to your magick practice without even realizing it. This is a natural expression of your inner vision and the process of deciding exactly how to use magickal tools in your life.

At some juncture, you may also find yourself choosing to follow a particular facet of the Divine to guide and strengthen the energy you create. This facet might be called the god, the goddess, the Sacred, Spirit, Athena, Isis, Thoth, Odin, or hundreds of other culturally diverse names. Which designation depends a lot on your image of the Powers that be.

I count myself among this group, often indicating that power by the term "god/dess" (to denote both male and female). Why? Because I get to a point in my studies and research where there are no concrete answers—only the spark of magick. That little spark ignites a whole world of wonder that I believe started with a vast power that I cannot begin to describe or fully understand.

Wistfully, I cannot help but also think of the ancient Romans who invoked a specific god or goddess during rituals and then prayed to any "unnamed or unknown deities" to assist with prevalent needs. In keeping with this idea, it certainly can't hurt to release our magick into the guiding hands of a greater power—figuratively covering all our bases. This way, the resulting energy is more likely to flow in tune with universal law and in keeping with what's truly best, instead of just what we *think* is "good" or "right."

Auntie Trish's Eighth Rule of Magick

**What we think is best and what's really good for us
are often two very different things.**

You will have to decide for yourself if you're comfortable with or inspired by the idea of working with the Divine in your magickal arts. It's not a necessity, but it does open the door to amazing energy and endless possibilities if you trust and believe.

Does Folk Magick Have a Psychic Element?

I always laugh when my friends tell me what a royal pain it is to have a psychic witch for a friend. They can't get anything past me, or at least not very often. Be that as it may, working with magick doesn't automatically mean that you'll start seeing the future or showing signs of other psychic abilities. Honestly, not all psychics are witches or magicians, and not all magicians are psychic. There is, however, a strong link between the two, and one definitely can affect the other.

Those who have already discovered some type of psychic ability in themselves might find the study of magick a little easier. Why? Because they've already accepted the fact that not everything in this world has a pat, cookie-cutter explanation. They've also accepted the concept that the human mind has the capacity for great wonders when released from conventional expectations. Beyond this, individuals in this category have learned to listen to gut instincts and the small voice of Spirit within— two abilities that every folk magician values.

In looking at how magick might affect psychism, remember that magickal methods stretch the human mind into uncharted territory, into realities that go beyond the physical and tangible. Since understanding and using this process is a function of the intuitive self, developing your magick skill might result in increased psychic awareness quite naturally, and you should allow for that possibility. Nonetheless, the operative term here is *might*.

Exactly why some individuals never have the psychic dimension accessible to them, other people experience random psychic occurrences, and still others exhibit an amazing psychic propensity is something about which I can only conjecture. I suspect the answer lies in how persons' natural, genetically encoded aptitudes combine with the various environmental influences in their lives. This would explain why dramatic events often elicit a sudden onset of psychic talent. Whatever the actual cause, don't berate yourself if psychism doesn't evolve as quickly or impressively as your magick skill. It's a nice aid, but:

Auntie Trish's Ninth Rule of Magick

You don't have to be a psychic to be a skilled magician.

Say What?
Defining Our Terms

Like any group of people, those who work with magick have a specialized vocabulary to differentiate various kinds of magick and the procedures or items used to produce a specific effect or object. To make your reading easier, I've provided a Glossary at the end of this book. Refer to this section anytime you come across an unfamiliar term or one whose meaning seems different in the given context from what you'd normally expect. In reading this, however, bear in mind:

Auntie Trish's Tenth Rule of Magick

Don't get too hung up on jargon.

In magick, talking the talk isn't half as important as walking the walk. Yes, you'll need to understand it when reading metaphysical books and articles and in communicating with other magick practitioners, but generally you won't want to wield your mystical vocabulary with individuals who aren't involved in similar studies. Why? Because average folks, some of whom don't even realize magick exists outside of fairy tales, are likely to misunderstand or misconstrue magick terminology. It tends to make people fearful or put them on the defensive. Let's face it, two thousand years of bad press is pretty tough to overcome.

With these people, the way you live your life is far more meaningful than words or trappings. So when your conservative Aunt Maude comes over, you don't necessarily have to start spouting all your newfound knowledge and trendy magickal words. In fact, the topic might not come up at all! That doesn't mean you have to hide in the broom closet; it just means being sensitive and insightful in the way you communicate about your magick interests and studies.

Can I Create My Own Spells and Other Magickal Methods?

Yes, and I highly recommend trying it once you know a little more about putting together the various parts of a specific magickal procedure effectively (Chapter 2 will help with this). I know a lot of people reading this will feel awkward and nervous about creating a spell or ritual from scratch. To allay your natural concerns, first return to Rule 1. Being your own priest or priestess means that you know yourself well enough to put together the most meaningful magickal symbols to make any spell, ritual, or other procedures successful and fulfilling. That doesn't mean you can't refer to the examples left by earlier practitioners as well as modern writers as a guide!

Along the same lines, remember that someone somewhere had to create the first spell, and a whole lot of spells and rituals thereafter. In fact, people in very diverse cultural settings all had to face a moment when they took creativity in hand and found a way to build magickal energy for the first time. You can bet the cave people weren't born having grimoires handy, let alone a skilled cunning person in their midst! With this in mind:

Auntie Trish's Eleventh Rule of Magick

Personally devised magick is a birthright.

The only difference today is that we don't have to go it alone. We have historical and modern texts to guide us, along with people in the magick community. So when you're not sure, consult a trusted author or fellow practitioner for advice on a way to create the right procedure for the situation at hand. As the old saying goes, the only "stupid" questions are those that remain unasked.

How Important Is Timing Really?

Some of the spells and rituals in this book, and many others, suggest a specific time frame for enacting the process. This comes from very ancient beliefs that trust in the moon, the stars, the planets, and other celestial/symbolic dimensions to give form and greater potency to the magick created. In an ideal world, it certainly would help to have auspicious timing on our side, along with all the perfect components and other beneficial environmental factors. Unfortunately, most people's lives aren't ideal!

The folk magician recognizes the undeniable truth that people have jobs, kids, and numerous other things that fill each day. Sometimes, as much as we might not wish it, spirituality takes a back seat to all this commotion. So we can't always manage to work our magick at the best times. In fact, we might often find ourselves blending magick with the daily routine or squeezing a spell in before morning coffee! This was true for folk magicians in the past too, so relax.

In and of itself timing won't make or break your magick. In fact, if you think about time in different terms—as a human creation—you might come to the conclusion I did many years ago. The universe probably doesn't care what time we say it is! It's a different time depending on where you are in the world, so it's really all relative! Since magick is said to work outside of time, I follow Rule 12 with a gleeful heart:

Auntie Trish's Twelfth Rule of Magick

Anytime is the right time for magick.

In other words, if you believe that timing is important to your work, then make it part of your magick. Since you trust that timing *helps*, this trust sets up a positive mind-set, which yields more positive results. If timing isn't important to you, however, or if you just can't focus on it with your schedule, then add timing as an extra dimension to your magick when you can and don't worry about it otherwise. I provide some specific ideas about timing in Chapter 2.

What Should I Expect from Magick?

Magick rarely yields instantaneous results and sometimes what we get isn't what we expected at all. Now, I know that's probably not what you wanted to hear, but it's the truth. See, a lot of different factors can affect your results. Say, for example, the phone rings in the middle of a spell. That distraction can shift your focus to another matter altogether and cause what manifests from the magick to change from the original intention to a different outcome following the change in your thoughts!

I tell my students to expect nothing and hope for everything from their magick. This isn't a lack of faith; it's being realistic (now, there's a word I bet you didn't expect to see in a book about magick). By expecting nothing, you don't foresee achieving a goal or meeting a need simply by casting a spell or two. Instead, you stay involved and make concrete efforts to try and accomplish that goal in nonmagickal ways. Meanwhile, if the magick is working properly, its energy supports your tangible efforts. If not, the positive outlook generated from your hopefulness will fill in a lot of gaps!

Even after fourteen plus years of practicing Wicca as foundational to my beliefs, I find myself amazed by the sense of humor and quirky timing that magick seems to exhibit when it manifests. In fact, I always warn my students that if the universe can find a way to make us laugh, it will. I personally believe that "god" is the originator of Murphy's Law. These bits of comedy relief sneak into our magick lives in unexpected ways.

To cite a personal example, I was at a gathering one time where everyone was standing around a beautiful ritual fire. There were no chairs or tables, and I had my staff in one hand and a goblet in the other. Outdoor gatherings often bother my back, and I needed to stretch, so I just lifted up my arms with objects in hand and did so. Just at that precise moment a pocket of air burst in the fire, making it *appear* as if I had caused the resulting flurry of sparks. It was very dramatic. A guy next to me simply remarked, "Not bad!" To this day I love to share this story because it reminds me, and everyone listening, of Rule 13:

Auntie Trish's Thirteenth Rule of Magick

Humor is good soul food and one of the most powerful natural forms of magick available to us at all times.

Are There Any Other Rules I Should Follow?

Magick isn't like a lot of other belief systems that have one sacred book to refer to when ethical questions arise. That leaves the job of determining what's right and best up to us. On the other hand, during my travels I have met with hundreds of people in the magick community who all had similar advice about working positive magick. Their advice is shared here for your consideration:

- *Always work with nature, not against it.* That doesn't mean shunning technology. It just means staying mindful of the earth in the way you compose your spells, rituals, and so on. For example, if you're going to bury something as part of a spell, make sure it's biodegradable!
- *Avoid participating in any procedure that makes no sense to you or that you object to for some reason.* Either adapt the process or find another one that's more personally significant, and never go against personal taboos. If you're in a group setting, you can either decline to join in or simply close your energy off from the magick circle, so you are neither helping nor hindering the work.
- *Accept that magick will manifest in its own time and way, even if your timetable or "ideal" is different.* Energy follows the path of least resistance, making for some interesting outcomes. For example, someone casting a prosperity spell might be given an arduous task at work

that highlights aptitude over several weeks, then later get a raise for those efforts. Or the person might get offered a second job that improves prosperity!

Another good example occurs in relationship magick. We don't want to manipulate other people's free will, so we simply ask the universe for a suitable mate. Now, the type of person who is best for us and the one we envision as the romantic ideal are *invariably* different! I've watched it happen again and again. There is good news, however. If you can get past your "ideal" long enough to see the gift when the universe presents it, it almost always works out wonderfully.

- *If you can do it yourself, without magick, by all means do so!* You might be surprised to discover that a lot of pagans and witches I meet work very few spells and rituals on a regular basis. Instead, they live their beliefs, adding in magickal procedures both when circumstances seem insurmountable and when they need a spiritual buoy. This strategy has a lot to do with the sense of self-responsibility that goes with all magickal practices. We're responsible for our lives and the living of them. Magick is an aid to that process, not a crutch.

- *Let your magickal intentions drive tangible actions.* In other words, don't cast a spell for a new job, then sit at home waiting for it to come to your door. Magick requires honest effort on our part to manifest beneficially. So in this case, redo your resume, read the want ads, network, and pound pavement. Each effort then becomes an open door through which the universe lets your magickal energy flow toward the best possible results.

- *Unless it's an emergency, avoid working magick when you're angry, sick, tired, or very harried.* All of these things will detract from your ability to focus. Besides, you don't want any of that negative energy seeping into your magickal effort.

- *Have fun!* Playfulness and pleasure are incredibly helpful in magick. Playfulness encourages experimentation, so that you find the best way to weave your magick. Pleasure helps you appreciate the wonders of magick, especially when it manifests—which brings me to my last point.

- *Be thankful.* I can't tell you how many times people see the results of their magick and forget to be thankful for it. Stop for two seconds and count your blessings. Thank the Powers, and pat yourself on the back for a job well done. A heart that's full of gratitude is also one that is always ready to give and receive blessings!

Review: Auntie Trish's Rules of Positive Magick

1. Be your own priest/ess.
2. Magick doesn't have to be flashy to be effective.
3. Know yourself.
4. You have no limits other than those you give yourself.
5. Worthwhile things take time, magick included.
6. Be careful with your wishes and your gift.
7. Magick is only a tool, and you control how you choose to use it.
8. What we think is best and what's good for us aren't always the same thing.
9. You don't have to be psychic to be an effective magick user.
10. Don't get too hung up on jargon.
11. Personally devised magick is a birthright.
12. Anytime is the right time for magick.
13. Humor is good soul food and one of the most powerful forms of magick.

CHAPTER 2

Getting Started

If I have ever made any valuable discoveries,
it has been owing more to patient attention
than any other talent.
SIR ISAAC NEWTON

Well, we've got to start somewhere! I must confess that it's difficult to decide exactly where to begin when everything from entire cultures to the world's mythologies has been touched by magick's spark. Thankfully, even with such an abundance of information from which to choose, a lot of the world's folk magick features common denominators—fundamental strategies that appear again and again, no matter the setting.

The purpose of this chapter is, therefore, to familiarize you with some of these common denominators. Additionally, we'll review some of the factors that make magickal efforts more successful and ascertainable (at least from a personal perspective). After all, we cannot prove magick works with 100 percent certainty. And many people will describe the results achieved from magick as "just a coincidence." For those practicing this art, however, it's beautiful symmetry! Faith combined with honest effort, the right symbols, and the best personal attitude makes all the difference.

Helpful Tactics

As you might expect from the information I've given you already, not all folk magicians approach magick the same way. They might not even use the same method twice because of the spontaneous, environmentally inspired nature of the art. So don't feel you have to use each of the approaches I'm giving you here for every magickal procedure you enact. In fact, one well-chosen act often proves more beneficial in folk magick than trying to cram too much in the magickal pot.

How do you choose which approach is best? Usually by trial and error. Yeah, I know, you probably wanted a more concrete answer. But since I am not you, I cannot choose for you. Try each system and see which ones help you focus your mind and will. Also consider which ones make sense for your specific situation. Let me cite a personal example. I wanted to cast a spell to halt gossip at my office. I found a spell that suggested chanting at a given point in the procedure. To me, however, the idea of verbalization made no sense. Thinking back to the laws of sympathy and like attracting like, I felt silent visualization had greater symbolic value for silencing those wagging tongues, so that's what I did (and yes, it did seem to help)!

See, this is where knowing yourself and being your own priest/ess is so important. Although I can't say how the spell would have manifested if I used the original, I can say it felt much better during the casting process. This confident, comfortable demeanor can make all the difference in the world in the results.

AMBIANCE

No folk magician would tell you that you *have* to have a special work space or perfect conditions for magick. The whole world is a workroom available to be explored and used as circumstances and needs dictate, and the pace of our lives rarely makes for perfect conditions. Even so, urgent situations might inspire a desire for additional environmental support systems that will bolster magickal methods. Why does this work? Because what's going on around you—what you hear, see, smell, and so on during the magick—changes how you feel, improves the sense of something magickal happening, and therefore can increase the ratio of success you experience exponentially.

So how do you create a special ambiance for magick? Well, begin with yourself. Make sure you're in the right head space. In other words, don't act out of anger or desperation. Working magick from either of those mental perspectives yields erratic results, if any at all. So calm down first and try to stay focused, no matter how chaotic the circumstances.

Next, look at your surroundings. Is it the best place you could choose for the magick you want to create? For example, if you're doing a wish spell that calls for casting herbs or flower petals to the wind, getting outside would certainly help (or minimally having ready access to a window). Also, is there any chance you might be interrupted here? Can you turn off the phone, put a note on your door, and get some privacy? If so, go for it!

Other environmental touches include picking out some incense that somehow reflects your goal, putting on soothing music, adding symbolic decorations, and lighting a few candles. For example, if you were working on healing a relationship, you might use rose incense, romantic music, decorate with hearts and flowers, and light pink or red candles for love! If you wish, also take a warm bath beforehand to relax and put on a special outfit afterward that makes you feel really "witchy"! In other words, do everything in your power to make even a bathroom feel mystical, and the resulting magick will flow more powerfully, naturally, and comfortably.

BREATH

Have you ever noticed how you feel light-headed when you run and don't breath correctly? When you breath properly (from the diaphragm), however, this doesn't happen. You might get winded, but you never lose your center of gravity. This has a lot of bearing on magick, where staying in focus and being centered are essential to success. So even though you've been breathing since day one, part of your magick training includes a brief lesson on quality breathing.

MAGICKAL BREATH

To practice proper breathing, lie flat on the floor. Put one hand on your stomach just below your lungs. Now take a deep breath. If your chest lifts up, you're breathing wrong. Fill your diaphragm from the bottom up so your hand gets lifted just as you finish taking in the breath.

Next, try to do this in such a way that the exhalation of one breath leads into the inhalation of the next without any real gap. This takes a little practice, but you'll find it helpful to meditation and as a great coping mechanism when life gets crazy. Do this a couple of times a day, perhaps while in bed, until you feel adept.

Application: The next time you're feeling angry, scattered, airheaded, or off balance, stop and breathe! Take three all-connected breaths and see how you feel afterward. The sense of connection and focus you feel at this point is exactly what you want to take into your magick.

Breathing is also a great aid to magick in that it keeps us on an even emotional keel. As we inhale, we take in life-giving oxygen. As we exhale, old, useless hot air is released. Along with that release, a lot of tension and other negative energies get borne away. Blood pressure evens out, and therefore we calm down. So taking three to ten deep breaths before enacting any magickal procedure is a good practice to make part of your routine, especially if you feel harried or upset.

MEDITATION 101

Not every folk magician meditates, but meditation is a method that appears in many mystical traditions (like Buddhism) and one that a great number of modern magick practitioners use successfully. I think you'll find it a helpful technique, so at least give it a try. See, meditation will help you relax. From a purely pragmatic standpoint, this could become a very important gift to yourself, especially if your stress levels are high.

Even medical science agrees that this kind of "down time" improves overall well-being, the ability to cope, and the body's capacity to fight sickness.

From a metaphysical standpoint, something very interesting happens when our tensions fade. Think of anxiety as a giant clog in the artery of magick. Once you remove that obstacle, magick flows smoothly and effortlessly. So go with the flow!

Second, meditation teaches us to slow down, disconnect from the material, turn inward, and focus our thoughts on one thing. In magick, the ability to shut out the outside world and think only of the goal is vital. Without this mechanism we cannot effectively direct our will and the energy created.

A good meditative technique to use prior to your magickal methods follows here as an example. For those of you who want a more detailed guide, I highly recommend *Meditation Made Easy* by Lorin Roche, Ph.D. This book is very reader-friendly and one of the most practical meditation resources you'll ever own.

Pre-Magick Meditation in Seven Steps

1. Get comfortable. Sit where your back is straight and supported and where you can stay in that position for fifteen to thirty minutes without shifting a lot. Constant movement during meditation decreases its value for some people. No one ever said you had to look like a guru to be one!

2. Take a moment and read over the spell, ritual, divination method, or other spiritual information you're planning to use as part of the magick. This will keep the symbols and procedures fresh in your mind.

3. Take three all-connected breaths as described above.

4. Close your eyes and think about the material you just read. Does everything flow for you? Do the symbols make sense? Do you like the words and actions? If the answer to any of these questions is no, you need to determine what you can do to change the approach so it becomes wholly yours.

5. You may find yourself getting distracted by the events of the day or things that have weighed heavily on your mind. Don't try to fight this. It's quite natural. Sort through those things so you can clear them away, then go back to thinking about the magickal methods/information at hand.

6. Once you've settled on the approach you want to use, continue breathing in the all-connected manner described earlier. Slow your breath down slightly. There's no need to hurry now. Put aside your expectations and the things you have to do later. Just try to sit, breath, and be. If you find you have trouble with this step, try adding some quiet music to the background, stretching, or changing into more comfortable clothing, and then starting again from Step 1.

7. At some point you'll feel a distinct shift. The ideas and methods that were revolving around in your head move down into your heart and center of gravity. This is where they need to be before starting your magickal routine. Think of this as a mental-physical alchemical process through which you accept the magick you want to create into yourself so you can manifest it without later. By the way, each person reaches this point at his or her own pace, so don't judge the success of the meditation by how long it takes.

For those of you who find meditation daunting, there are some other things you can try. Add chanting (sacred sounds), burn incense, find a dark and restful meditation area, or take a premeditation bath to decrease stress in your body and mind. Almost everyone needs to practice this art for a while before seeing impressive results, but even small improvements are very worthwhile. Just stopping once in a while to really breathe can be a meditation if you allow it. Try it right now! Stop what you're doing and breathe deeply three times, connecting one breath to the next. Afterward, make notes of how you feel in a personal magickal journal.

YOUR MAGICKAL JOURNAL

A magickal journal is very similar to a diary or a spiritual journal except that you'll be keeping your intimate thoughts about magick and spirituality in the book instead of daily events or other spiritual matters. I recommend that all my students keep one because, over time, it shows you in your own words how you've grown and changed.

The physical book doesn't have to be fancy. Use a bound diary available at gift shops, a three-ring binder, a spiral-bound notebook, or your computer! Date each entry, and then write about your Path and the way it's developing. What have you learned? What do you want to learn? Where do you see yourself in a year? Write it all down.

Review your journal every couple of months. I think you'll find the results very enlightening.

PROJECTION/DIRECTION

Magick won't do much good unless you move the energy toward your goal! To understand this, think of what happens with a charged battery. The energy is all there, ready and waiting to go, but until you actually put the battery into something and flip the switch, it remains dormant. Projection is the mechanism through which you'll turn the magickal "switch" so everything heads in the right direction.

Folk magicians project in lots of ways. Some imitate or pantomime their goal as if it were already accomplished, thereby showing the energy exactly what to do. Others might direct the end of a wand to the area in which they want the energy to go, like taking a pointer to the universal chalkboard. Still others might bury a symbol in the earth, so the associated energy grows by natural design!

FOLLOW THE YELLOW BRICK ROAD?

One of my favorite examples of projection comes from a personal experience. I was on an airplane in very rough weather, literally riding the outer edges of a tornado. Needless to say, I was scared and wanted to cast a spell for safety. Being on a plane left me with very few options that wouldn't make other passengers antsy. So I reached inside myself, began to meditate, and used a thought-powered phrase from an old movie as a projecting mechanism. As I visualized the plane landing safely, I kept repeating "There's no place like home" inside my mind until the rough ride was over. Sounds silly, I know. Even so, it made me feel better, and it left me with a very practical lesson I have applied again and again, namely, that jingles, aphorisms, and other familiar phrases make excellent projective tools if the symbols are right. Because we know these phrases so well, we don't have to think about them and can use the extra mental "space" for focusing on our magick and its goals!

All of these approaches and many others have merit. You'll have to determine which one makes sense for you. Very visual people generally have no problem imagining the final resting place for their magickal energy in great detail, so they can use visualization as a guiding force. Those who don't visualize well will have to be a little more creative. Whatever method you decide upon, carve out a path for your magickal energy, so that it goes as directly as possible from you to the goal.

VISUALIZATION

Visualization has numerous uses in magick, not the least of which is based on the phrase "Seeing is believing." When we create a positive scenario in our mind, it supports the magick created in several ways. First, because we're seeing things with spiritual eyes, it boosts faith and confidence. No matter the outcome of your magick, these two things are bound to improve your circumstances simply through their effect on attitude and actions.

Second, purposeful imagining can help with projection and direction of the energy produced. For example, try "seeing" your magick as a dart and your "goal" as a target. Got the image firmly in your mind? Okay, now release the dart to hit the mental bull's-eye. Keep your goal in mind the whole time the dart's flying. By so doing, you're guiding the power you've created along its way.

Third, visualizations can be as diverse and detailed as your imagination will allow. Consequently, there's no limit to the ways in which you can apply this skill! In particular, you can use simple visualizations to charge your magick tools and components.

CHARGING AN OBJECT THROUGH VISUALIZATION

1. Hold the object in your strong hand (the one you write with) or hold both hands palm down over the item.

2. Close your eyes and begin to imagine a radiant white-silver light pouring down from above you into the area at the top of your head (the crown chakra, which represents our link to Spirit). You might start to feel warm or tingly or hear a slight humming at this point, which means you're doing it right.

3. Let the energy flow freely from the top of your head down to your heart, then out through your arms and hands. As you envision this, keep a strong sense of the final application for the item in your mind. And hey, if your energy is a little low, direct some of that white-light energy into your bloodstream to fill every cell of your being!

4. Continue until you feel that you and the object are saturated with the white-light energy. I can't tell you exactly how to know this, but some individuals start getting itchy palms or sense heat bouncing back to them as if it's hitting an already stuffed space. These are the types of indications to pay attention to.

By the way, components and other magickal tools can be recharged. If you use an item regularly (like an amulet you carry with you), it will probably need an energy boost from time to time. When exactly? Anytime you notice that the item starts feeling as lifeless and flat as two-day-old ginger ale—or, more blatantly, anytime it doesn't seem to be working right! At this point, bolster the energy matrix of the item using this method or one of those suggested in the Glossary. If you wish, also ask for the blessing of your god/dess during this time.

Another function of visualization is that of helping us to internalize what we're learning. Our lives are moving at warp speed, leaving little time to truly integrate everything that happens to us. This seems especially true with spiritual matters, because our society doesn't always emphasize that human dimension. But you can change that by combining meditation and visualization.

The best way to illustrate how this works is to look at a specific scenario. Say, for example, you're trying to understand the symbolism of a tarot card. In this case, begin meditating and then bring the image of that card into your mind. Next, enlarge it and look at every little detail. What do those details represent to you? Finally, look at the image as a whole composition in which each part adds to meaning. By the time you're done with this kind of meditation/visualization, you'll have a much better comprehension of that tarot card, how it applies to your life, and how to interpret it in any reading!

SACRED SPACE

Among witches and many other practitioners of magick, you'll hear the words "sacred space" often. Some people feel it's very important to set up a protected sphere of energy around any area in which magick is about to occur. Other people don't bother with this step, especially if they're working with very simple magicks. I'm somewhere between these two groups.

For very important matters, complicated procedures, or any magick in which you're trying to get rid of a negative spiritual influence, I think a formalized sacred space is a good idea (call it metaphysical insurance).

The ritualistic nature of creating sacred space helps ensure that you're in the right frame of mind for magick. Additionally, a well-designed sacred space keeps any unwanted energies out and your magick firmly within until you're ready to project it.

Finally, sacred space has an ambiance all its own. Within this sphere there's a connection with Spirit, a sense of being part of all time and all space at once, and a distinct hush that makes whatever happens there really special. That's why you hear many practitioners use the phrase "out of space, out of time" when talking about sacred space. The sphere marks the line between world and not-world, where your magickal tapestry begins to take shape.

Here's how to make one yourself:

Creating Sacred Space in Ten Steps

1. Clean up the area in which you're going to work. I've yet to see a messy church. Your apartment, back yard, house, or room is about to become a church, so treat it accordingly. No, you don't have to redecorate; just make things neat, so the externals aren't distracting and project the image you would want to show to an honored guest.

2. Decide which part of this area will act as the central point and figure out where the four directional points lie. If you wish, decorate these four points with symbolic tokens like feathers or bells for east (air), a candle or incense for south (fire), a glass of water or seashell for west (water), and a stone or seeds for north (earth). These little tokens help welcome the elemental energies (read: nature spirits) you're going to be invoking when creating sacred space.

3. Make sure you have everything you need at the center point of the circle before starting. Once the sacred space is created, you'll want to stay inside until you're done with your magick.

4. Stand in the middle of the area. Shake out your hands, stretch a bit, and take three deep, cleansing breaths to get yourself centered. Now visualize the same white light as before pouring down into your body. Once you feel all warm and tingly, walk to the eastern point of the area and hold out your arms as if to welcome an old

friend. Say something like, "Welcome powers of the east and air. Fill my words with magick." Envision this spot in the room being filled with light pouring out of your hands.

5. Move to the south (clockwise), continuing the visualization so the light spreads to that spot and say something like, "Welcome powers of the south and fire. Ignite my heart with magick."

6. Move to the west, continuing the visualization so the light now covers three-quarters of the room and say something like, "Welcome powers of the west and water. Flow into this sacred space with magick."

7. Move finally to the north. Now your mind's eye should see the whole area covered in a silvery-white glow, all around, above and below. Say something like, "Welcome powers of the north and earth. Give my magick rich soils in which to grow."

8. Go to the center of the space and do whatever work you have at hand (for example, a spell, the rest of a ritual, or a meditation). Also take a little time to pray if you can. Let the magick settle in your mind and heart too!

9. When you're done, say farewell to the powers you called upon in the invocation, reversing the process and moving counterclockwise. Use whatever words feel comfortable to you.

10. Make notes about the procedure in your magick journal. What felt good? What did you sense right after the magick sphere went into place? What parts do you want to use or adapt in the future?

Since our life's needs don't always surrender to pragmatics or even what we might wish to do under ideal circumstances, the simplified nature of folk traditions comes as a relief. Though it is always helpful to create a sacred space when working this kind of hearth-and-home magick, it may not be *necessary*. Truth be told, I often do without. Instead, I use one of two quicker approaches that get the job done even when my kids are being uncooperative.

The first approach is visualizing yourself in a protective, white-light bubble so that you're less likely to experience outside interference. If you wish, also pray to your vision of the god/dess to oversee your efforts. This technique is especially useful when you have to work magick in a very public place. Without it, the odd intermingling of energy can really set things askew.

The light bubble is spiritually generic—it will work for everyone, no matter their Path. It's based on my personal belief that sacredness is engendered as much by attitude as by actions and words. Therefore, if you start treating yourself as a sacred space, you can work magick anytime, anywhere, without more formalized routines. In the words of Buddha, "Wherever you live is your temple if you treat it like one."

The second alternative is to pick out four symbolic objects for earth (north), air (east), fire (south), and water (west). What you choose doesn't matter as long as the symbolic connection is obvious to you, but I suggest you keep them small for easy storage. For example, try a crystal or potted plant for earth, a feather or air freshener for air, a candle or lighter for fire, and a seashell or sand for water. When you have a few free minutes, whisper a suitable invocation like those given previously into each object three times to charge it with elemental energy. After this, repeat the elemental name into the object as well (for example, if you've chosen a crystal for earth, whisper the word "earth" into it three times).

When you're done, wrap these objects in a white cloth or put them in a special box until needed. Then the next time you need to set up sacred space quickly, bring out the tokens and put them as close as possible to their directional correspondences wherever you're planning to work. As you set out each one, repeat its elemental name to activate the energy. When you put the objects away, do so in reverse order to disengage the sphere.

Spellcraft Secrets

Actually, what I'm about to share with you aren't really secrets. The title was just to grab your attention. Now that I have it, there are things you need to understand about my version of magick to realize the greatest amount of success when using Part Two of this book.

Note that when I use the word *spell* here, it's for brevity. I'm actually including related forms of magick such as amulet creation, charms, and even mini-rituals. They're all intertwined, and what works well in one area very often works well in another.

SUCCESSFUL SPELL CONSTRUCTS

Fruitful spellcraft depends on many things, including your environment, your frame of mind, and the meaningfulness of the magickal method you've chosen. The most important factor to success, however, is following a tried-and-true construct. One such pattern is seen, with minor variations, over and over again throughout the world's magick traditions.

This spellcraft construct has ten steps, given here for reference:

Spell Casting 101

1. *Know what you want.* Flesh out the details of your desired goal. To help with this step, follow the five steps given in "Details Count" below.
2. *Decide which magickal process you want to use in obtaining that goal.* Again, bear in mind that the process should symbolize your desire somehow. If you want love to grow, for example, you could perhaps use a spell that included rich soil and seeds (figuratively planting the emotion). If you want your garden to grow, you might choose a mini-ritual in which a jumping dance is performed around the garden like those done by farmers of old (warning: wait until your neighbors are asleep!).
3. *Choose suitable tools and components.* Gather them together in one place so you don't have to hunt for an item in the middle of your work (you can wait until an astrologically auspicious time for this step if desired).
4. *Create sacred space before you begin,* if you wish.
5. *Express your need/desire literally or symbolically* through your words, tools, components, and/or actions. For example, you might construct a spell to improve self-love that included speaking the phrase

"I love you" three times while looking in a mirror, followed by a self-hug (wrap your arms around yourself). Here the tool/component is a mirror, reflecting the self in truth. Your words reaffirm the goal and help internalize it in body, mind, and spirit (which is why it's repeated three times). The hug is a physical confirmation of that energy.

6. *Build energy to support that goal* through things like chants, incantations, meditations, imitation, song, or dance. The more senses you can get involved in this step the better the results will be.

7. *Keep your mind on the goal throughout the procedure.* Also add visualization if you find it helps you focus.

8. *Detach the energy from yourself and project it outward.* The energy won't do much good if it's still tethered to you or the sacred space. Visualize it being disconnected or cut it away from yourself by a loud noise and/or fast movements like slicing your hands up and out toward the direction in which you want the energy to move.

9. *Release the sacred space* if one was created.

10. *Ground yourself.* Sit down, get your breathing back to normal, and perhaps eat something crunchy. Magick takes a lot of personal energy, and you might find yourself light-headed or jumpy afterward if you don't do this step.

You won't see each of these steps detailed in the applications portion of Part Two due to space constraints, but please keep them in mind when you work. I think you'll find them quite helpful. Also, make a mental note that once you're done with the magickal method, there's no rule that says you can't repeat it to support the energy. If it makes you feel more confident to regularly reenact a spell or ritual until the magick manifests, definitely do it. It certainly won't hurt, and the benefits of the faith that this engenders shouldn't be underestimated.

DETAILS COUNT

Although folk magick is simple, the details still count. Every part of your magick process needs to make sense considering the needs and goals at hand. Somewhere along the way your magickal process needs to answer these very important questions:

1. For whom or for what is the magick intended?
2. What type of energy do you want to create?
3. Where does the energy need to lodge itself to do the most good?
4. When do you want the magick to manifest?
5. Why are you doing this (i.e., what's your true motivation)?

The first point here is perhaps the most important, and I can cite two examples to illustrate why. In one case a woman wanted a friend's help during a fertility spell she created for herself. Unfortunately the woman forgot to specify the "who" part of the magick, and the friend got pregnant instead (at an inopportune time, I might add). In another case a person cast a love spell, detailing all the characteristics she wanted in a companion. Well, she got a companion—a dog who fit the description perfectly! This last illustration is also the poster child for Rule 13 (the universe has a sense of humor and uses it as a teacher)!

Next, detailing the type of energy tells the universe the correct pattern for power. For example, there are many types of abundance. Do you want financial abundance or an abundant garden? The matrix for each of these is vastly different, since one deals with the material world and the other deals with nature.

The third point may have been answered in the first question, but the person, place, or thing for which magick is intended to work and where the energy lodges itself are *not* always the same thing. To give you a good illustration, say you're casting a spell to help a friend get through a difficult professional situation. Here the spell is intended to help your friend, but the energy might be better directed to the office and/or any perceived sources of difficulty.

The "when" part is pretty obvious. Some things can wait, other things cannot (or so we think). If the magick is open-ended and it won't matter exactly when the energy starts working on your behalf, you can skip this part. But I think you'll usually want to put some time frame into the equation.

Finally, the "why" is important from two standpoints. Returning to Rule 8, we don't always know what's best in any given situation. By sharing the "why" with the Powers that be and releasing our magick so it flows for "the greatest good," we may be able to avoid that pitfall. Second, honestly recognizing your *true* motives for any magickal procedure will keep you from overdrawing the karmic bank account through regular withdrawals. Manipulation and/or harmful intentions drain those resources quickly.

TOOLS OF THE TRADE

In reading the section that follows on components, it might be difficult to determine which items qualify as magickal tools and which are components. To help make this differentiation in your mind, remember that a tool is something that extends the person beyond normal limits. Just as a hammer gives a carpenter greater ability to drive in a nail than a hand might, a wand allows a magician to better "drive home" the magick to its mark. For a diviner, a tarot deck, rune set, or crystal ball is a tool. For a witch, an athame (sacred knife) is a tool.

The word *component*, on the other hand, implies something that's placed with other items as one part of a greater whole. In our example, the components of a carpenter's work might be wood, glue, and nails. For the magician's work, trying to list every possible component is impossible. Why? Because folk magicians use the components they relate to most strongly (which of course differ from person to person) from an endless array of choices. The whole world is filled with natural and human-made components that the magician can make use of, ranging from meteorites to rainwater to television sets!

Don't let this abundance worry you. The only real tool you need for folk magick is you. Everything else is icing on the mystical cake you're creating. Honestly, I suspect that the god/dess isn't impressed by our clever use of symbolism. Symbols are simply human conventions aimed at transforming *our* thoughts, which in turn transform the energy associated with them. Eventually the folk magician hopes to develop the mind, will, and sense of self-reliance enough to get past the symbols altogether, and simply *think* and *be* the magick! Now wouldn't that be neat?!

CHOOSING YOUR COMPONENTS AND TOOLS

The second most important decision you'll make in magick is what to use to create the energy (the first one was to undertake a magickal procedure at all). I mentioned in the introduction that components and tools are the basic ingredients of your magickal recipes. Anyone who has ever baked a cake knows that if you don't put the recipe together correctly, the cake will fall, burn, or taste awful. Folk magick is quite similar. So the question now becomes: What constitutes "correctly" following a magickal recipe?

Well, the first step is having the ingredients you need or viable substitutes handy. Part Two of this book contains a comprehensive component listing. As you look though it, you'll see that there's a whole world of power right under our noses, but having so many choices doesn't help matters! Returning to the illustration of baking a cake, you might know you want it to be chocolate when all is said and done, but what *kind* of chocolate: white, dark, German, milk? With the cake the decision usually boils down to personal taste or what's in the fridge; with magick it boils down to what symbolism and correspondence best suits the circumstances and very often what's available in the magickal pantry.

So to help you get started, here's what I recommend:

1. Choose tools, symbols, components, or props that immediately come to mind considering the theme of your magick. If you think of apples as having to do with health, for example, then an apple is one potential component in any magick for well-being.

   If there are several potential choices, go with quality ingredients over quantity. Although it's not necessary to go over budget in purchasing magickal components, magickal energy does respond proportionately to quality-based ingredients (like organic herbs instead of those that have been chemically treated). This is why you see old spells often calling for very costly components such as diamond dust.

2. Go to the themes and correspondences given in this and other reputable sources (a suggested reading list is provided at the end of the book). See if any of the components or tools listed make sense to you and can augment your planned procedure. Returning to the

42

example of health, we find that nutmeg is an herb traditionally used in healing preparations. So perhaps you could add this traditional symbol to your own chosen one and blend apple juice with a bit of nutmeg, energize it, and then drink the potion to accept that energy into yourself! Alternatively, you could use dried apple peel and nutmeg as a health-improving incense to change your aura and the atmosphere of your home.

3. Try to choose handy components that can physically undergo the change you're trying to make metaphysically. To illustrate, say you want to get rid of a nasty habit. Well, then you'd want to find a symbol of that habit and make it visually disappear during the procedure by, for example, burying it, burning it, or flushing it down the toilet. This way, the sensual impact of the magick confirms your desire to not only the universe, but your own subconscious and spirit. More examples of this can be found in the next section, "By Earth, Air, Fire, and Water."

4. When you don't have the components or tools you'd prefer, it's time to start looking at what you *do* have. Go to the thematic correspondences given at the end of this book and see which of those you have on hand. If you have more than one, pick out only those that you feel best about. Remember: meaningfulness is the key to magick.

BY EARTH, AIR, FIRE, AND WATER

In Part Two of this book you'll quickly begin to notice some themes in the way components get used once they're gathered. Specifically, the elements of earth, air, fire, and water come into play in very creative ways. For example:

- A seed might be planted in soil to help magick grow or to symbolically ground a problem.
- An object could be buried in soil for a period of time to absorb earth-related energies (growth, maturity, stability, foundations, fertility, etc.).

- Flower petals might be tossed to the winds to release a wish.
- The magician might stand with his or her back to a specific directional wind to propel the magick forward: a southerly wind to carry love and passion (e.g., warm it up), a westerly wind for healing and the intuitive nature, a northerly wind for development, and an easterly wind for positive beginnings.
- Herbs might be burned on a ritual fire to release their energies and send the practitioner's prayers to heaven.
- The flame of a candle might be allowed to burn away a symbol in the wax in order to "burn away" a problem (fire represents illumination, energy, power, the conscious mind, and destruction).
- A feather might be floated on moving water to transport the magician's desire out to the world.
- Charged water might be sprinkled around a home as part of a blessing (water represents the emotional nature, our intuitive/feminine self, wellness, and creativity).

You'll want to refer back to these examples when making or adapting your own magickal methods. Why would folk magicians want to mingle these kinds of approaches with their components so frequently? Because to us, nature is a very powerful ally and teacher. We use the world's symbolism as a way of keeping ourselves in touch with the earth and honoring its role in our spiritual development.

Additionally, most folk magicians regard nature as the most perfect representative of the Divine. In each grain of sand and wildflower the patterns of creation exist, along with a universe of energy. When we begin to truly understand these patterns and energies, our magick grows by leaps and bounds.

EXTRA DIMENSIONS

In the next chapter I'm going to be discussing some specific types of magick that folk magicians use regularly. Around this core, some people like to add other tactics to give their magick a more sensual dimension. If you're one such person, here are some ideas you can play with when time permits. I'm mentioning them here because they can also be used in combination with the other methods discussed in this chapter:

- *Costumes/robes:* If clothes make the person, what kind of magician do you want to be? If, for example, you're feeling very witchy, you might wear a black robe. Or if you're trying to get in touch with the lunar/water nature within (which is more intuitive), you might want to wear a very fluid robe in silver and blue tones. Or if you're doing a spring ritual celebrating the earth's awakening, you might want to don a mask covered with flower petals.
- *Chanting:* Though we see it more often as part of meditation, chanting has the capacity to help raise energy simply through volume or speed. This seems especially true in groups where a chant that represents the goal naturally rises like a cresting wave, then slows after the magick is released. Here's an example I like to use for increasing the energy in my work space:

> *Raise the Wind and Earth,*
> *Raise the Water and Fire*
> *Raise the power ever higher.*

To try this yourself, start saying it over and over again, beginning in a whisper. Let your voice rise naturally as you feel the distinct hum of magick in the air. When you release whatever magick you've created, slow the chant down again until silence surrounds.

By the way, other verbal expressions like prayers and songs can be just as effective if you're more comfortable with them. As you speak and sing in the sacred space, your words have the power of willful intent behind them. This changes the vibrations around you to mirror your goals and therefore improves the results of the effort. This is also why so many spells include incantations as part of the process.

- *Dance:* Dancing around a ritual fire is something you can see at almost every outdoor magick gathering. This dates back to the time when humankind was organized into tribal units and the fire represented the central point of the community. Dance naturally expresses our joy in magick and helps build energy through movement. Better still, most magick dances don't require Fred Astaire's dexterity! They're simple stepping or jumping patterns that anyone can follow, or you can make up your own inspired form of movement! As with chanting, dances rise to a pinnacle when energy peaks, then slow to a standstill afterward.

- *Magickal Work Space:* Not everyone has the resources to set aside one room or one place for regular magickal workings. But if you do, I recommend it. Over time that spot or room becomes saturated with your energy and resonates with magick that will boost any effort's power level.

- *Timing:* In Chapter 1, I spoke briefly about timing as an adjunct to folk magick. Truthfully, the study of auspicious times to work magick can be quite an undertaking, ranging from a list of moon signs, star positions, and monthly attributes to the hour of the day! In an effort to stay true to this book's title, I want to give you three simple timing hints here that you can add as desired to your chosen methods. If you want more detailed or complex ideas about timing, I suggest referring to a good astrological calendar or almanac.

▲▲▲

TIMING TIPS

1. Day or Night: Working during daylight hours accents the conscious mind, anything that needs illumination, leadership abilities, strength, energy, and vitality. Evening hours accent the creative, spiritual, instinctive, maternal self.

2. By Moon Phase: A dark moon is considered a time for rest. The only type of magick done during this phase traditionally is banishing. When the moon begins to wax, it represents slow, steady growth within you, a relationship, or any situation. A full moon symbolizes things coming to maturity or fullness and is an excellent time for almost any kind of magick. Finally, the waning moon

accents decrease (like weight loss) or turning unwanted energies away from yourself.

3. Dawn, Noon, Dusk, or Midnight: These points in the day evoke strong imagery for our conscious and subconscious mind, so they naturally help your magick. Dawn represents a new beginning, renewed hope, and leaving the past behind. Noon represents fire energies—purification, casting a light on any shadows, reason, authority issues, and so forth. Dusk represents closure, introspection, and restful energies. Finally, midnight is, of course, the Witching Hour, when the veil between the worlds grows thin and magick is afoot!

- *You:* It constantly amazes me how many of my students forget the tool they always have with them—their own body! Your finger becomes a wand to direct energy flows, your feet can stamp out unwanted energies, and other physical positionings can accent or symbolize your goal. For example, if you're doing the old folk spell that calls for putting a small piece of lead in your shoe to curtail flights of fancy, you might want to sit on the ground or floor to stress that contact with earth too.

This brings me back to an important reminder: magick is inside you every moment of every day just waiting for expression. It needs no tools or components other than those provided to you by nature: two good hands and a heart full of expectation.

CHAPTER 3

Folk Magick Fundamentals

*Trust your natural responses and
everything will fall into place.*
LAO-TZU

Now that you know the main tactics folk magicians use, the next step is applying those tactics to specific types of magick. But which ones? After all, the world's mystical traditions offer a lot of variety from which to choose.

To make magick easy, I've assembled simple instructions for executing specific categories of magick in this chapter. Each of these constructs is common to folk traditions, and I feel you'll have little trouble, if any, learning them. The extra benefit to using these particular magickal methods is that the components for each are readily found in and around the home.

This chapter also provides some suggestions on using and adapting the fundamentals to Part Two of this book, "The Components." Note that all the constructs explored in this chapter appear throughout the component listings under applications with suitable examples, so you'll have plenty of illustrative material to use in personalizing things to better meet your needs, goals, and vision.

It's a Kind of Magick

I vividly remember the first bit of folk magick I ever tried. It combined the tactic of physical action with number symbolism, knots, and candles. Basically, I was instructed by my friend, a Cabbalist, to describe an item I'd lost on a piece of paper and fold that paper seven times (the number of completion). Next, the paper was to be tied with string using seven knots, leaving enough loose string so the bundle could be placed across the table from me. In the center of the table was a lit candle.

Next, I concentrated on my desire to find that item. Slowly I pulled on the string so that visually the object of my desire neared. When it reached my hand, the paper and string were ignited by the candle and burned together to release the energy of the magick. Not long thereafter I found the item in question. A coincidence? I don't think so.

I share this example with you here for two reasons. First, I must confess that until I actually *tried* the approach, it seemed kind of silly or too simple to work. I just couldn't understand how string and paper could turn into a kind of magick. At the outset I felt awkward, clumsy, and unsure, as if walking for the first time. And in a sense I was—as least astrally!

Once the effort was under way, however, my feelings changed. As I began to really focus, I could sense a shift in the air and tingling in my senses. It *felt* magickal and very "homey." It was also an incredible relief to take a positive step and see concrete results when regular recourses had failed—it was empowering and quite addictive!

Second, this example shows how the traditional forms and components for folk magick can mix and mingle with one another quite well. There's nothing that says you can't blend two or more constructs together, just as you might blend two or more components! That's one of the great beauties of folk magick: it's very flexible according to the mood and the muse!

I should mention that the methods reviewed here are also listed separately in the Components section of the book. At first this might seem confusing, and truthfully what separates a component from a magickal mode isn't always easy to delineate. For our purposes, a *construct* is a magickal mode in which the item (a candle, a poppet, etc.) is the central focus for creating or directing the energy desired. A magickal *component*, however, is secondary to the procedure. It adds symbolic value and improves sensual input, but may not be *necessary* to completing the spell successfully.

For example, in the candle magick spell detailed in the next section, you will see that a candle is the central construct. Rose oil is a component. The spell could still be done without the rose oil. Without the candle, however, another procedure would have to be considered.

CANDLE MAGICK

I suspect candles were used in folk magick simply because they were so handy. Until the invention of electricity, candles were the main form of lighting other than natural light! I will be covering the history and folklore behind candles in more detail in the Components section. As a magickal method, however, candles have to be looked at a little differently.

When using a candle as a construct, the color of the candle, its aroma, anything carved in its surface, its shape, and how long it burns are all considerations. Each of these factors somehow represents your goal. For example, red is a color we associate with love, as is the scent of a rose, the image of a heart, and the number two for partnership. Putting this all together, your candle magick for love might then follow this outline:

CANDLE MAGICK LOVE SPELL

- Get a red candle.
- Find or make rose-scented oil and dab it on the candle's surface (inspires the sense of smell akin to aromatherapy).
- Carve the image of a heart purposefully on the candle before it's lit or choose a candle shaped like a heart (stimulates the visual sense).

- Allow the candle to burn for two hours (sympathy, since we think of love as a partnership between two people). Possibly drip a little of the wax on a love letter to your intended, symbolically sealing it with a "kiss."
- Save the candle remnants to repeat the spell until the wax is totally spent, thereby releasing all the energy you've put into it (finishing the candle also subconsciously reinforces the idea of the spell being completed).

Use this basic pattern for any type of candle magick you want to perform. Simply change the colors, aromas, symbols, and actions to match your goal.

As mentioned previously, you need not have each element illustrated here for the candle magick to work. From a symbolic perspective, simply lighting the candle represents your desire for the magick to begin. So if all you have is a white candle, use it! White is a good generic color for any kind of magickal purpose. You can then carve a symbol of your desire in the wax with your fingernail or a toothpick. Light the candle, keeping your mind on the goal, then let the candle naturally burn out or burn it for a symbolic number of minutes or hours.

By the way, for those of you who live in apartments with strict codes regarding open-flame candles, modern technology offers a wonderful solution: electric candles! The little ones they sell at Yule (Christmas) are great because you can use different colored bulbs to represent your goal. In this case, plugging in the candle or turning its switch (if battery operated) is the equivalent of the lighting process.

COLOR MAGICK

Color magick is based on the idea that different hues affect the way we feel and act, even if we don't consciously realize it. Modern psychology has substantiated this belief, giving our folk magick a little more foundation upon which to build.

For color to be a magickal construct, it has to be the central thing through which you're focusing your energy. So one of the most potent forms of color magick also happens to be the easiest to add to your daily routine: that of choosing specifically colored clothing to wear—colors that symbolize the energy you want to generate in and around your life! The symbolism here is pretty potent when combined with the tactic of physically putting on that energy (by getting dressed).

A second way to make color a construct is to choose all the components of a spell according to their color rather than any other symbolic value. The main advantage here is that no matter what the component might mean in another spell, when color is being used as a mode, the component is simply a representative of its color's symbolic value. This has the extra benefit of giving you a lot of flexibility. Even when you don't necessarily have the item preferred for a spell, you'll likely have something of the right color to use as a substitute!

For the purpose of using color constructs, here's a brief peek at what each color represents metaphysically. For more details, especially regarding various tints of any one color, go to the Components section. The symbolism remains the same:

COLOR CORRESPONDENCES IN BRIEF

- *Red:* Energy, power, love, vitality, passion, zeal.
- *Orange:* Hospitality, warmth, manifestation, friendship, harvesting what you sow.
- *Yellow/Gold:* Sun and fire magick, strength, courage, intellect, and other masculine attributes.
- *Green:* Growth, healing, prosperity, vitality, fertility.
- *Blue:* Peace, hope, happiness, faith, devotion.
- *Purple:* Spirituality, leadership, higher learning, authority, magickal mastery.
- *Brown:* Grounding, foundations, stability, enrichment.
- *Black:* Rest, change, banishing, binding.
- *White/Silver:* Moon and water magick, intuition, creativity, and other feminine attributes.

As with the other constructs here, you can combine colors together so they better represent your goal. For example, blend orange with red in your wardrobe to encourage a loving, warm reception when you visit an old friend. Or wear blue and purple regularly when you're trying to inspire inner peace.

GREEN MAGICK

Green magick is a subclass of the herbal arts, of which you'll see tons of examples throughout the Components section. Germinating seeds, full-grown plants, trees, bushes, and various other plant parts were common constructs in folk magick, because they were so handy to come by. During the thousands of years that our society was mainly agrarian, finding a petal, a seed, or other plant part wasn't difficult! Thankfully we still have access to the natural world.

An excellent example of green magick begins with a germinating seed, seedling, or a cutting that represents your desire (like one from a rose bush for love). Name that young plant after your goal. Each time you water and tend it, whisper your desire into the plant. Visualize your goal slowly becoming a reality. By the time the plant flowers (matures), you should begin to see the magick manifesting! Throughout this process, the young plant is always the focus for the energy.

In a second example, plant two blossoming plants (floral bushes are a good choice) next to each other. As they grow, mingle their branches together so they intertwine. As this occurs, name the two plants after any area of life (or any two people) where partnership, cooperation, mutual effort, and other similar energies are needed. The plants' growing together encourages that situation to blossom into something long-lasting and unified, like the plants.

Green magick also includes the psychic art of divination. Here the plant matter might be tied into a pendulum, burned on a fire, or tossed on water or its growth observed to learn the answer to a question. In shamanism specifically, the spirit of the plant was invoked during the divination process to help answer the query, but this additional dimension isn't seen much in folk traditions. For the folk practitioner it was (and is) enough to know that creation and creator are one. Creation expresses the creator and bears that magickal imprint for us to see, if we but learn to *look!*

In these three examples, it's always best to choose a flower or herb with the correct metaphysical correspondence to your need or question, even as our forebears did. This boosts the overall power created. Why? Think of the energy that the seed or seedling uses to grow. That energy bears a metaphysical imprint—the pattern of its correspondences. So as the seed grows, the pattern also grows outward toward manifestation!

To know what kind of plant to use for flower or seed magick of your own devising, simply turn to the themes and correspondences given in the Appendix and look up your goal. If the central theme of your magick isn't there, look up synonyms and related topics. For example, you could use any of the flowering components listed for devotion, love, peace, fidelity, and harmony as part of a flower spell aimed at improving a relationship. Even better, plant one seed from each list in a window box near your hearth (the heart of a home) or where you and your partner spend a lot of time. This way, all the qualities that strengthen relationships will likewise develop in and around your home!

FOOD AND BEVERAGE MAGICK

I am a dyed-in-the-wool, wooden spoon—wielding, pot-toting kitchen witch. If there is any way I can make magick consumable, I do! Part of this has to do with a love affair I have with my pantry: I really enjoy cooking. The positive energy created from my exuberance seems to make everything taste better and function better magickally. Also, the symbolism of eating and drinking as a way of internalizing energy is very potent to me. What better way to transmit a pattern into your aura than through your digestive system, which nourishes your body every day?

For food magick to work well as a construct, you first have to stop thinking about your kitchen as just another room in the house. With pantry enchantments, the kitchen becomes a sacred space and whatever you're cooking becomes the vehicle through which energy will be transmitted. And since you have to eat anyway, why not make every meal magickal?! It makes me tempted to get a chef's hat that reads: Witch in the Kitchen—Beware!

As with candle magick, there are certain key considerations. These include the ingredients chosen (if there's a choice), how you prepare the food or beverage, what you do while the edible cooks, and even how you serve it. Let's put these considerations into an example of making a side dish for prosperity. Here's the basic process:

FOOD MAGICK FOR PROSPERITY

- Choose spinach, which is both green and aligned with prosperous energy, as the key ingredient.
- Stir clockwise as the spinach warms to attract positive energy.
- Visualize money floating into your home or recite an incantation that expresses your need.
- Eat the spinach while working on your checkbook, and perhaps pour a little of the juice into rich soil so money grows.

As before, you don't necessarily have to include each of these steps. Nonetheless, the more dimensions you give the magick, the more multi-dimensional your results will be.

I have included a lot of edible components in Part Two of this book to get you started. Please know, however, that how you feel about a particular food or beverage is far more important than the historical-cultural associations I've given. If, for example, your family has a tradition of making a specific kind of a cake on your birthday, you probably associate that flavor with joy, blessings, and continuance. So if you're going through a "blue" period, make that cake to lift your spirits! It doesn't matter if the ingredients have nothing to do with happiness metaphysically—the personal meaning remains the key to making the magick happen.

I've seen people try to put together magickal recipes out of ingredients they wouldn't normally eat. This really defeats the purpose. If you struggle to get something down your throat, and squinch up your face in a resounding "yuck," all the magick in the world won't help you internalize that item's energy. The negativity generated by your dislike pretty well cancels any good it might have done. So a good rule to follow in kitchen witchery is: cook what you love, knowing that love itself is powerful magick.

KNOT MAGICK

Knot magick probably originated in seafaring communities where fishermen tied a little magick into each knot to secure a good catch. And why "knot"? The symbolism of capturing energy within a stronghold is so potent that it's still among the most popular constructs in folk magick.

For the knot magick construct you need nothing more than a piece of string, yarn, or rope, a length of cloth, a scarf, or anything else that can easily be bound in some manner. As you bind each knot, you secure energy inside it through visualization, projection, verbalization, or other tactics of your own choosing. Frequently the number of knots you make is symbolic of the goal, but in this case numbers would be an optional component. Counting spells also often appear in knot magick, the total count representing the goal and helping to build the energy (one knot is tied during each line of the incantation).

Here are some of the interesting ways in which you can adapt knot magick so it includes other components:

- Choose a scarf or tie of a particular color, like green for health, and then bind magick for well-being securely within. Wear it anytime you feel a case of the sniffles or flu coming on (color is the component here). Change the color to suit your goals, then the knotted scarf turns into portable power!
- Dab a symbolic aromatic (a component) on the knot before binding it. Then when you need to release the energy, the air will be filled with the right vibrations to help manifestation.
- Bind something into the knot to represent the goal. For example, old wind knots often included a feather (a component that symbol-

izes air). Note that wind knots can be used to stop winds or bring them, but old folk tradition says you should never do more than two at a time. Three is considered an interference with nature's order and a sign of greed.

- Wait to make your knots during an auspicious time (the component), like tying love knots during a full moon so love grows full.
- For very personal magick, braid your hair (the component). This is a simplified type of knot magick that keeps the associated energy with you wherever you go. Unbind it when you no longer have that need, or when you want to release that energy to do its work. To this, you could add ribbons of a suitable color (a component) tied at each braid or some aromatic hair oil (a component) that matches your goal.
- You may wish to bury or burn knots for banishing or protection from something afterward (earth/fire tactic) to keep that energy away from yourself.
- To add a visual element, find a specific type of knot that somehow represents the goal. For example, a square knot might symbolize foundations (the square being representative of the four corners of creation), and a slip knot might be an excellent choice when you want a problem to disappear!

Bear in mind that some magickal knots should never be undone, like those used to bind negativity. So make sure to use something you won't necessarily need again or something you don't mind leaving knotted. Other magickal knots can be undone whenever you have a need for the energy you've placed there. So when you make this kind of knot, consider making a string of them or an extra separate one so you have it handy for future use (just remember to label it with the intended use when you store it away).

MOON MAGICK

In some instances you'll find the moon used as an influential component in magick (like waiting until a waxing moon to cast a spell for increased finances). In others, the moon is the key to the entire process, which then qualifies it as a construct. Perhaps the best example of the latter comes to us from farming communities as recently as the 1920s. Many farmers depended on the moon's phases in sowing, weeding, and reaping crops. They waited until the moon waxed to sow above-ground crops and waned for reaping, and when the moon was dark they weeded the field, trusting in the moon's magickal energy to help the natural order of things along.

Beyond this, many old folk spells invoke the moon in an incantation asking the moon to influence the question or desire at hand. Alternatively, some spells invoke the moon's influence by requesting that manifestation come by "the next moon." These too qualify as a construct, since the moon becomes the focus through which energy flows.

Since our society has changed much in the last century, I expect that you won't be looking to the moon as a component in timing your magick too often. Even so, I wanted to present the construct option for your consideration.

NUMBER MAGICK

Determining whether a number is being used as a magickal construct or component can be difficult. Generally, a number can only be considered a construct if it appears again and again in any magickal procedure's instructions. For example, in ancient healing arts a cunning person might choose a specific number of components for a potion, work on a special date during a special hour, and repeat his or her incantations a specific number of times. The numbers seven and three are the ones we see most often in folk remedies, representing completion and the triune nature of humankind (body, mind, spirit). In either case, the number's symbolism is the key to opening the energy flow.

Another example exists in what I call counting spells. Here the spell is designed with an incantation that includes a numerical count. For example, an incantation might say:

On the count of one the spell's begun.
On the count of two, let the magick ring true.
On the count of three, the magick is me.

This example shows that the incantation is a vehicle for building a cone of power.

Should you wish to use numbers similarly, a brief review of symbolism follows here; greater detail is given in the Components section of this book:

NUMBER CORRESPONDENCES IN BRIEF

1 represents Singularity, Unity, the Source (God Aspect), Self, and Wholeness.

2 represents Duality, Partnership, and Balance.

3 represents Triune Nature, Symmetry, and Centering.

4 represents Earth, Ambition, Finances, Victory, and Foundations.

5 represents Intuition, Flexibility, and Alertness.

6 represents Protection, Completion, and Faithfulness.

7 represents the Goddess Aspect, the Moon, Perspective, and Fulfillment.

8 represents Leadership, Change, and Energy.

9 represents Assistance and Principles.

10 represents Logic, Wisdom, and Judgment.

You can certainly combine numbers in magickal modes as with other forms. For example, you might choose twelve components to help improve personal fortitude. To this symbolism you could add working at noon (the hour of twelve) and an incantation that's repeated four times to emphasize putting down roots and holding one's ground. Again, each step here emphasizes numerical symbolism over any other part of the magick as the key to generating and projecting energy.

POPPET MAGICK

Poppets are small figurines made out of cloth, wax, wood, herbs, and/or other symbolic components. When using poppets as constructs, you need to consider three things: the process of making the poppet, its component parts and overall appearance, and what gets done with it afterward. Every component in the poppet is chosen for its symbolic value, as is its completed shape, and the poppet itself becomes the focus for energy during and after the creation process.

Some people reading this description might mistakenly equate poppets with Voodoo dolls stuck with pins. Although the two techniques are definitely related, folk magicians and the Voudon use poppets for positive magickal ends too, including healing, love, and prosperity. Here's one example for prosperity (more illustrations are given in the Components section):

PROSPERITY POPPET

1. Get a piece of fabric from the individual for whom the magick is intended. This fabric should come from an old shirt or other garment worn often so it bears that person's energy signature. (Note: If you create a poppet for someone else, please ask permission first or the magick borders on being manipulative.)

2. Cut this into the rough image of a person (two thicknesses, if sewing).

3. Sew the image together so you can stuff it with herbs representing prosperity like alfalfa sprouts, tulip petals, and oak leaves (this reflects internalizing the energy for prosperity so the person can manifest it externally).

4. If sewing isn't your strong suit, use the flat image decorated with fabric markers so it bears some physical resemblance to the person and put the poppet, symbolic of the individual, in a bed of herbs so it is surrounded with that energy.

A few other hints will help you use poppet magick more effectively. First, remember that poppets can represent anything, including animals and vehicles. So if you want to protect your car, you might create a car poppet and put it inside a reflective box (to reflect away problems). Or stuff it with cloves (for banishing bad spirits), wrap it in a white cloth (the color of safety), and tuck it in your glove compartment!

Second, poppets can be any size. You could, for example, make a poppet pillow to bring sweet dreams and prophetic visions while you sleep. This is an excellent project for kids too; it gives them a sense of control over a seemingly uncontrollable experience (namely, nightmares).

Third, remember the elemental tactic when working with poppets. Say, for example, that you want to get rid of a negative personal habit like smoking. Make a poppet of yourself, stuff it with your last pack of cigarettes, and burn the poppet to "burn away" that habit! After this, make a second poppet of yourself and draw the image of clogged lungs on its surface with water-soluble marker. Then wash the poppet in flowing water to help the natural healing process along. Really, the options here are limitless.

POTION MAGICK

Potions are one of the most time-honored constructs of witches everywhere, and they combine very nicely with kitchen witchery (see Food and Beverage Magick). Nearly all old books of magickal instructions include a hearty sampling of potions for all occasions. The whys of this are fairly easy to discern: the ingredients needed for potions weren't complex, and they could be prepared at the hearth with little trouble. Additionally, other than agricultural mixes, most potions were made for consumption, thereby transporting the magick to where it was most needed: inside the person.

Ancient potions were created from a variety of mediums including water, milk, wine, beer, and mead. The alcoholic substances were often preferred over water and milk, because they had a lower chance of bearing disease. Today, when most folks don't have to worry about the quality of drinking water, this may seem odd—but consider what tainted substances might do to magickal energy, no matter how well contrived!

In designing your own potions, you have many options. A potion can be made from two ingredients or hundreds. The ingredients need to maintain a congruity with regard to the potion's symbolic value, and they also have to play nicely with each other in the witch's cauldron! Why? Because in potion creation, the whole becomes more than the sum of its parts. The whole is the construct that carries the energy. With this in mind, here are my personal recommendations for making potions successfully:

- In measuring your ingredients, bear in mind the energy pattern each represents. Do you want each of these energies in equal proportion? Do you need more of one than another? Allot each component accordingly.
- As with food magick, potions meant for consumption need to be palatable, so watch your proportions and don't ruin the flavor.
- Consider blending the ingredients for your potions in the same order they would follow in the manifestation of your goal. For example, a love potion might start with a base of warm milk (for emotional warmth). To this add a tiny sliver of lemon peel first (for friendship), a dash of rosewater second (to inspire romance), and a bit of vanilla last (to round out the relationship with love). This mixture is put together in the same way that most long-lasting relationships develop, creating the right pattern for success.

Remember that not all potions have to be consumed to be effective. Some might be created, for example, to help heal the earth—and these would rightfully be poured into the earth's soil. If you do make a potion that isn't edible due to the ingredients, just make sure to label it properly (inside the bottle and out; to do the former, put a crystal or something in the bottle to remind yourself that the potion isn't potable). This will avoid any mix-ups.

STONE MAGICK

Crystals, metals, minerals, and amalgams have been part of magick forever. A stone (this word is being used very broadly here) becomes a construct anytime it bears or transmits energy. This is most easily seen in amulets and charms, respectively. (There are lots of examples of both throughout the Components section—look under the specific stone in which you're interested.)

There are three distinct advantages to working with stones as a construct in magick: durability, variety, and assimilative ability. Beginning with durability, when you transport energy in a stone, you don't have to worry much about the stone breaking. It also won't be hurt if something spills on it accidentally! Additionally, if you want the magick to last a very long time, you can't ask for greater longevity than that of a stone!

As for variety, nature has been very generous with her gifts to us, and the New Age market has made those gifts very accessible. We can buy everything from tiny tumbled rocks to huge crystal clusters at nature stores, gem and mineral shows, and many gift shops. So you can use stone constructs for everything from personal magick to making stone structures that energize large areas of land! This second option is wonderful for people who have big yards where energized stone circles become a sacred site in which magick can be rendered regularly.

Finally, many stones exhibit a natural ability to hold energy. The best-known example is the quartz crystal, which is used to power watches. Other stones glow in specific kinds of light, alluding to energy transfers—again, some wonderful symbolism with which to work.

Here are some hints on mingling stone constructs with other magickal components:

- Wrap the energized stone in a natural cloth (a protective component) of a suitable color (a sympathetic component) that represents the goal.
- Bury the stone to release its energy into the land, or toss it in water to transport the energy through that elemental medium (earth and water tactics).
- Get stones that have small holes (natural or human-made) so that you can string them in patterns (building the right energy), bead them into a representation of the goal (visual cue/component), or put them on a gold or silver necklace (the precious metal can augment energy if chosen for its symbolic value).

- Add the stone to a power pouch that has other supportive components within. These usually get carried or placed in a specific location where the energy will do the most good.
- Press a sympathetic stone into the wax of a candle and let the candle burn down to the stone to release the energy (note: this might be considered the blending of two constructs, depending on your viewpoint).
- Meditate (a tactic) with an energized stone on one of your chakras (this might be considered a component) to open and augment the flow of energy. For example, put a moonstone for insight over the area of your third eye (the middle of your forehead) to improve psychic ability. Afterward you might use the surface of that stone for scrying (careful scrutiny of an item/object while in a meditative state and watching for prophetic visions).

WISH MAGICK

This is what I usually call wishcraft. It's something we all know from our childhood—wishing on stars, wishing on birthday candles, wishing on coins tossed in a fountain, and so forth. Though the base component that carries the wish varies, it is ultimately the wish itself that patterns the magick you create.

I love using wish magick as a construct because it's familiar and user-friendly. No one's afraid of making wishes. No one thinks of it as "supernatural" or full of hocus-pocus. Consequently, of all folk magick modes, wishcraft is likely the one nearly everyone can use effectively with the least practice.

The only requirement is that you truly believe your wish is possible and worthy of notice by the universe. Without belief, wishing becomes an exercise in futility.

Wishcraft works because it expresses our will through a traditional medium, often one that's been passed down through the family or one shared by a trusted friend. I still remember my mother as she "coached" me through youthful wishes: those recited when a friend said the same word at the same time as I did, those whispered into the winds of dawn, those etched into winter ice layers on my window. Each of these child-hood moments has found its way back into my life now as a magickal expression driven by warm memories, love, and a hopeful heart. There's no reason you can't use wishcraft similarly.

Here are some examples of wishcraft, each of which uses a different component to carry the energy once the wish is made:

- Tossing a wreath, headpiece, or other flammable token into a ritual fire (especially at Beltane [May Day]) while making a wish.
- Carrying an agate stone to help fulfill a wish (this is said to work best for men).
- Inscribing a candle with a wish and letting the candle burn completely out.
- Putting a wish into a bottle and floating it out to sea (today we might wish to substitute something more biodegradable for the bottle).
- Wishing on a falling star (or repeating your wish three times before it goes out of sight).
- Wishing on auspicious days (like your birthday).
- Wishing right after you see the first robin of spring.

As you can imagine from reading this short sampling, the number of items used as wishcraft components is pretty amazing. I personally found over three hundred in different cultural settings! This tells me that wishing is a key to unlocking a lot of our magickal potential as humans, not to mention the child within each of us who dares to dream.

WORD MAGICK

The last construct we're going to explore here is the art of word magick, which is based on the knowledge that words have power. Just think of how people react when you compliment them or when you yell. The reactions aren't just facial; there's a ripple effect that's pronounced throughout an individual's aura. With word magick, you'll be using this ripple effect to change your own aura or the vibrations in larger areas (the only limit being how far your voice can carry).

In recent years a version of word magick has come into the public eye in the form of affirmations. An affirmation is the planned repetition of a key phrase or phrases that reflect what you're working toward. This exercise accomplishes several things. First, it refocuses your attention on something good that you want to develop in yourself or a specific goal. Second, since affirmations are always shaped positively, your overall thought patterns are more positive. Third, the verbalization releases supportive energy to the area around you and into your aura. Consequently, affirmations are perfectly useful as a kind of word magick just as they stand.

We can certainly return to traditional verbal charms for word magick or to chanting and other sacred forms of expression through which we can detail our wills. But to be honest, I've found another modern commercial technique works even better: jingles! Take any one of those annoying jingles that you can't get out of your head and change the words so it mirrors your desire. Repeat it a couple of times initially to get the energy rolling and again every time it comes to mind. Each repetition sustains the spell, and trust me when I say you'll have no trouble remembering the darn thing.

This construct has three very important advantages. First, you always have your words (or thoughts if you can't say something out loud). Second, word magick is by far the most flexible construct for adapting to different tactics and components. Finally, word magick isn't proprietary, meaning that though the words carry the magick, they don't overshadow the symbolism you're creating with components and tactics.

Gauging Magickal Results

When all is said and done, it really doesn't matter what approach you take to folk magick as long as it works and it stays within the bounds of the responsible use of power. But with all the naysayers in the world, how do you gauge the results of your magick? How do you know that what you're seeing is a result of willfully and carefully guiding energy to its mark, especially if it's not exactly what you asked for?

This part of the equation takes us back to our expectations. We need to remain open to the idea that magick might not manifest exactly according to plan. We also have to trust in both the universe and ourselves. In the final equation everything really does boil down to the unseen, unquantifiable element of faith that tingles inside us each time magick blossoms into reality.

For some readers that tingle simply won't be enough, which is why I highly recommend keeping a magickal journal. Each time you enact a magickal procedure, detail it in the journal. Date the entry. Then watch the world around you and every aspect therein. Each time something happens that makes you stop and wonder if it's part of the magickal pattern you created, make a note of it. Continue in this way until the magick manifests. I'm willing to bet you'll see some truly miraculous twists and turns in there—things that some might call coincidence, but we know better. We call it magick.

Creating a Personal Spellbook

Witches call a personal or group spellbook a Book of Shadows. Why Shadows? Because magick lives in a realm that is just beyond light, just short of darkness, just outside of here, and just inside of now. It's shadowy and elusive if you don't know how to look within with the eyes of spirit. But by this point in your studies, you should have no problem with seeing magick and magickal potential and in translating that into a viable, successful, and fulfilling format that suits your life and reality.

By keeping the records I've recommended in the last section, you'll begin to see some really wonderful results from various attempts. The best of these magickal recipes are the ones that you'll want to keep in your personal spellbook so you can refer to them again and again. To help you with this process before moving into the Components, I'd like to provide you with some ideas on putting this collection together.

FIVE STEPS FOR SPELLBOOK CREATION

1. Look through your journal and pick out the processes that were the most effective and personally fulfilling.
2. Separate these into themes (love, health, peace, prosperity, luck, divination, etc.).
3. Group the spells of similar themes together and transfer them into a more permanent collection (perhaps a blank bound book, or create a cyber spellbook on your computer system).
4. Leave plenty of space after these entries so you can keep adding to the book. Also make sure you have space in which you can add new themes or types of magick.
5. Consider noting personal insights about particular kinds of magick as they seem pertinent.

You can get as fancy with this process as you wish (and as your schedule allows). For example, some people make their own paper and scented inks. Other people simply use three-ring binders for their spellbooks so they can update and change things without ripping out pages. It's really up to you.

I strongly advocate being conscientious about maintaining the book once it's started, though. I believe that while you experiment, create, adapt, and make notes of successful procedures in this grimoire, you cannot help but grow as a spiritual being. You will also be developing your own folk magick tradition in the process and saving that tradition in a format in which you can treasure it and use it for many years to come!

PART TWO

The
COMPONENTS

Slip in a doodle, an idea wrapped in steam
some ink tars the feathers that tickle my dreams
here, conjured in fancy a whim waits to sneak through
tops of strong pantry kettles, tonight's dinner: spell stew!

THE LORESINGER

Introduction

Cooking requires that we be fully present. . . . It keeps bringing us back to what is happening in the moment and continually calls our attention to what we are doing.
BETTINA VITELL, *A TASTE OF HEAVEN AND EARTH*

Throughout the first three chapters of this book I've repeatedly compared magickal methods to culinary efforts. In reading the above insightful quote it's easy to understand why. Magick is soulful cooking. It is the blending of inspiration and will with simple, everyday items to create something spectacular—something that motivates us mentally and feeds us spiritually.

As spiritual chefs, we can't just randomly start tossing things into our cauldrons, however. Instead, we have to remain aware of what we have to work with in selecting our mystical recipes, then carefully choose, measure, and balance the ingredients as we put them together. This section will help make the decision process easier as well as give you some hands-on examples to try.

In putting this component list together I considered several things. The first was convenience. For magick to be easy, its ingredients need to be accessible, and I believe you'll have little trouble finding most items listed here. For the frugal witch, I've also offered some instructions on where to find or make certain items at more reasonable prices.

The second consideration was flexibility. This list can easily be applied to a wide variety of magickal processes, including using the items as:

Divination tools/focals: For scrying you can pick out a crystal whose attributes match your question. For example, you can observe the surface of a rose quartz to answer a question about love. Or you could try watching the flame of a pink candle anointed with rose oil. For pendulum work, tie fresh greenery (again, from a plant whose theme matches your question) with a string; returning to the love example, a tiny rose briar might be a good choice. Items like rice, tumbled stones, and beans can be made into drawn or cast divination systems. Really, the options are pretty open-ended.

Keys for dream interpretation: Most people who work regularly with magick discover that many of its symbols begin appearing in dreams. These dreams often teach us more about our spiritual path and our abilities and provide insights for coping with daily reality. So when any of the components here show up in your nightly visions, consider what lessons or information they may be trying to impart. For example, seeing an amethyst crystal in your dreams might indicate the need to better control your personal energy or focus on communication skills.

Ingredients for incense: Wood powder, herbs, flowers, and spices are best, but you can also add crystals or other small symbolic tokens to the container to augment the associated energies.

Meditation/visualization focus: Aromatics, candles, music, and the like are often used as meditation aids. Beyond this, some of the items listed here make good imagery in a visualization, for example, seeing a rose open up in your mind's eye when you want to open yourself to love.

Magickally augmented foods and beverages: Add components to foods and beverages to internalize energy, to ground yourself after a spell or ritual, or to use as thematic edibles to highlight a celebration.

Offerings for the Divine: If you've chosen to follow a specific vision of the Divine in your magick, there may be times you want to set out an offering by way of thankfulness or to inspire divine assistance. In this case, the chosen offering should be something the god or goddess holds as sacred, something that represents your desire, and/or something that's not necessarily easy for you to give up. The first approach requires that you know what pleases your deity (i.e., do some research). The second approach symbolically conveys your need or goal through the gift. The third approach recognizes that sometimes we must give to receive.

Components for mystical oils: Use mystical oils for anointing, to mark an object as yours, to empower yourself or any spell component, or to aromatically change the vibrations of an area. Oils can be made from both crystals and plant parts, but choose a base oil with a long shelf life for best results. If an oil ever gets cloudy, toss it out. Once it "turns," the magickal power disperses.

Constituents for potions: Use potions for internalization of energies, to soak in to change your auric vibrations, or to pour out in libation in a ritual setting.

Elements for power pouches: A power pouch is like a fetish in that you put small tokens inside that represent your needs and goals and then carry the pouch with you. Nearly any small component is suited to this task. Just don't use too many—you don't want the power pouch to be too big.

Recipe options for spellcraft: Probably the most popular application, all of the items in this section can be considered in designing your own spells (amulets, charms, and the like are included in this category). To decide which ones are best, look at the list of themes and correspondences, see which ingredients you have handy, and then decide if you want to use all, or just a few, of these components. Remember, spells don't have to be overly complicated to work well; they just have to be meaningful.

If you're using this section to find substitutes for items in prefabricated spells that you don't have or don't like, you can follow the same process. There are only two precautions. Maintain a congruity of meaning and, just as in cooking, don't tinker with the recipe too much! As the old saying goes, "If it ain't broke, don't fix it!"

Ritual symbols/tools: In creating sacred space, get inventive and use elementally suitable components at the four corners of your circle to augment the power. Elemental associations are given for each component in this section. Also, a lot of these things make wonderful decorations for a ritual when they're thoughtfully chosen and arranged. Beyond this, some items can become magick tools once prepared and blessed, such as a small tree branch that you carefully sand and decorate as a wand.

The third consideration in assembling Part Two was that of providing a variety of quality components balanced with common sense. Although I believe that magick will respond to the excellence of the components you choose, I don't think this decision should overextend your pocketbook. It would be wonderful, for example, to use a diamond as part of a love spell, but that's not feasible for most folks. Consequently, I didn't include diamonds in this listing. Instead, I'd recommend a good-quality quartz as a viable substitute. Why? Well, it *looks* like a diamond and has the right energy matrix to help you achieve the same goal!

As you can see from this example, we have the ability to safeguard the insights and practices of our ancestors, while mindfully adapting those practices to today's reality. By so doing, we begin weaving a whole new body of magick that blends the best of tradition with a vision of the future—a future in which magick will not only be easy, but will again be regarded as a natural aptitude available equally to all.

CHAPTER 4

Traditional Components

AGATE

THEMES: Dreams, Communication, Fear, Gardening, Health, Money, Peace, Protection, Victory, Wishcraft.

CORRESPONDENCES: Since the seasonal and elemental correspondences for this stone vary with its color, this category might be considered under Spirit stones. Blue lace agate, for example, is aligned with the season of spring and the element of water, while moss agate is aligned with earth. Use your instincts in choosing an agate specifically for its elemental correspondences.

HISTORY AND FOLKLORE: The myths of many cultures include descriptions of astral cities whose walls, roads, or towers are formed from agate, alluding to its protective nature. In Exodus, the breastplate of the Hebrew high priest's garment included agate among its adorning stones. Cornelius Agrippa, a well-known occultist of the late fifteenth century, advocated wearing an agate ring on Wednesday to augment magickal works of "science." Talismanic texts of the 1500s say that agates grant women's desires and fulfill men's wishes, and an old poem says that those born under the sign of Gemini would do well to wear this stone for health, courage, and wealth. Finally, folk remedies in Europe recommended steeping an agate in consumable liquid and drinking this to cure disease, or wearing an agate to remain immune to venomous bites.

SAMPLE APPLICATIONS: If you find yourself having trouble communicating effectively, agate is a great stone to choose for a charm or power pouch. Carrying black and white agates in particular is said to make a person more agreeable, temperate, persuasive, and bold. The extra benefit here is that this stone also protects you from storms and inspires good dreams (put it under your pillow for this purpose).

Agates that have a white ring pattern are called "eye agates." These are powerful amulets against the evil eye. Carry one anytime you feel you're under a magickal attack to turn the negativity away. Alternatively, bless and energize a brown agate, which brings victory.

For magickal gardeners or anyone seeking improved prosperity, the moss agate is a great companion. It will help you develop the proverbial green thumb with plants or money! For workaholics, a banded agate decreases stress and the blue lace agate inspires inner peace. Finally, if you have a special wish, toss an agate of a color symbolizing your desire into a well or any source of running water to start that energy flowing.

ALFALFA

THEMES: Money, Providence.

CORRESPONDENCES: Earth.

HISTORY AND FOLKLORE: Alfalfa has been known to Chinese medicine for thousands of years as a remedy and an overall tonic to improve vitality. Perhaps the best-known bit of folklore about alfalfa is that any home in which this plant grows or is preserved will never want for food.

SAMPLE APPLICATIONS: Many magick books recommend using dried alfalfa in incense, scattering it around the perimeter of the house, or carrying a sprig in your wallet, purse, or checkbook to promote financial increase and protect yourself from money problems. Another excellent application for alfalfa is adding the sprouts to your diet regularly to encourage sensible application of your resources, which is perhaps the best money magick of all!

ALMOND

THEMES: Divination, Health, Spellcraft, Wisdom.

CORRESPONDENCES: Air, Artemis, East, the God Aspect, Hecate, Zeus.

HISTORY AND FOLKLORE: Greek legends allude to the almond tree as a symbol of devotion and faithfulness. This is interesting considering biblical translations call almond trees "watchful." Aaron's rod was also purportedly made of almond wood.

Phrygian cosmology indicates that an almond tree was the father of life and the universe akin to the world tree of other legends, and in Islamic tradition it represents heavenly hope. Folk remedies recommend eating five almonds as a cure for fevers and intoxication. Alternatively, eating them is said to encourage wisdom.

SAMPLE APPLICATIONS: In some magick traditions a wand of almond wood is favored for casting spells or as a symbolic representation for the eastern quarter of the magick circle. In either case, it might be best decorated with feathers and an "air" stone like pumice or mottled jasper. Alternatively, an unadorned branch naturally shaped like a capital Y is favored in Tuscany for a divining rod.

In a ritual setting, almonds make a suitable offering for Zeus, Hecate, and Artemis. They are also an excellent edible for any marriage or hand-fasting rites (handfasting is a magickal version of marriage that may or may not be legally binding), which is why marzipan and candied almonds are still favored at receptions to this day. Almond wood mixed with dried almond flowers makes a nice blend for devotional incense to honor the masculine aspect of the Divine or to augment that energy in yourself.

In oil form, almond provides an excellent base for anointing blends, especially those intended to open psychic senses or those for improving love of any kind, including love of self. Simply warm one cup of oil with one tablespoonful of an appropriate herb. Stir clockwise to encourage positive energy, then strain and store in a dark container. Use as needed.

ALOE

THEMES: Beauty, Blessing, Healing, Longevity, Luck, Peace, Protection.

CORRESPONDENCES: Moon, Venus, Water.

HISTORY AND FOLKLORE: The aloe plant comes to us by way of Africa. According to popular lore, Cleopatra attributed her great beauty to the wonders of this plant's juices. Egyptians believed it conferred longevity on those who used it regularly, and even today the pilgrims to Muhammad's shrine hang aloe there as a prayer to bring blessings home with them. Planted on a grave site, aloe affords a spirit peace.

The Romans used aloe for healing, and people in the Middle Ages favored it as a magickal component for fumigating evil spirits out of an area. Grown in the home, aloe extends protective energies all around, inspiring luck and warding off accidents.

SAMPLE APPLICATIONS: From a pragmatic viewpoint, since aloe is a healing gel, consider making it part of your healing garden and any magick work for well-being. And since aloe combats the effects of being burned, it might also be used symbolically by applying it to one's temples or heart chakra after an emotional "burning."

Keep an aloe plant in your home for safety and peace to all who dwell there. Perhaps place an amethyst and moss agate in the soil to accent those energies and help the plant grow into fullness alongside the love in your home. Finally, aloe makes a suitable offering to, or decoration for, the Roman goddess Venus because of her beauty. If used for this purpose, dab a bit of gel on yourself before going into social situations to bring out your personal comeliness.

ALLSPICE

THEMES: Creativity, Luck, Playfulness.

CORRESPONDENCES: Fire, Uranus.

HISTORY AND FOLKLORE: Magickally, allspice has been favored as an ingredient in incense or oils meant to attract better fortune.

SAMPLE APPLICATIONS: As an herb under the dominion of Uranus, allspice releases the inner child who dares to dream. It kindles a sense of living presently, of truly enjoying each moment. So if you find yourself with a bad case of the blues or feeling very listless, add this spice to your magickal foods, beverages, incense, or other preparations to change those vibrations.

Additionally, allspice can improve your creativity. For artists who are experiencing blockages or need fresh inspiration, this is an excellent choice. Take three allspice berries and place them in a cloth beneath your pillow saying, "I place these berries three by three, bring inspiration back to me!" Keep a tape recorder or paper by your bed that night so you can record any nudges that come through your dreams. The next day, keep the berries in your pocket as a creativity charm.

ALTAR

THEMES: Fellowship, Offering, Unity, Worship.

CORRESPONDENCES: Spirit.

HISTORY AND FOLKLORE: The dictionary defines an altar as a high place, a region in which the Sacred Powers meet and commune with humankind. Traditional altars were made out of stone, wood, precious metals, gems, and other materials as available. On them, the tools of one's religion and various symbolic items were laid out for ritual use.

In some settings, the altar was the central focus, akin to a ritual fire, around which people would gather. There each person was equally important before the Divine. There each person could express his or her thankfulness for blessings, leave suitable offerings and prayers, and then enjoy fellowship with others of a like mind.

SAMPLE APPLICATIONS: Modern magicians may or may not have an altar, depending on whether or not they've decided to invite the Divine into their magick practices. If you have, then suitable images or symbols of that divine aspect should be placed on the altar along with other necessary items for your practice. Alternatively, an altar can also be a sacred spot where you honor the powers of all creation, a place where you keep your ritual tools in between uses so they stay protected and energized, and a location in which to place tokens that represent various magickal goals that support your ongoing efforts. This place need not be fancy to be functional. Mine is the top of my magick library's bookshelf, for example. What's most important is that any altar you devise somehow reflects your Path. To this foundation any number of additional touches are nice, such as seasonal additions to honor the earth's cycles.

AMBER

THEMES: Anti-magick, Beauty, Courage, Fertility, Healing, Spellcraft, Strength, Success.

CORRESPONDENCES: Fire, the Goddess Aspect, Sun.

HISTORY AND FOLKLORE: Amber is one of the two oldest stones used by humankind, second only to the pearl. A tremendous amber trade flourished as early as 2000 B.C.E., likely encouraged by the associated folklore that credited the stone with healing powers. This association remained constant throughout history, appearing in practices as diverse as ancient Muslim customs and the superstitions of early nineteenth century Europe!

The Chinese say this stone houses a tiger's soul, which gives it talismanic associations with courage and strength. Italians carry amber to protect themselves from witchcraft. In other traditions the warmth of this stone is believed to be a spirit that gains power from sunlight. Alternatively, this warmth is credited to the goddess, who gives life to all things and therefore "activates" any magick to which the stone is added. Dog owners sometimes use amber to quiet overly energetic dogs.

SAMPLE APPLICATIONS: Many magicians throughout the eras have felt that amber is more effective when carved into a specific image that represents your goal, specifically an animal image. If you desire courage, for example, carry an amber carving of a tiger. Should you wish to conceive, carrying an amber carved in the shape of a rabbit would be fitting!

As an amulet of health, the amber is unequaled. Keep a blessed, energized piece around your home and rub it against your body when you feel the sniffles coming on. This creates natural static (which releases the stone's power) and puts the stone in direct contact with the sickness's "spirit" to trap it within.

Shamans and witches alike enjoy using this stone to boost the power of a spell. Its fiery nature increases energy and encourages success. As an attraction (versus projection) stone, carrying an amber brings what we most need into our lives, including spiritual lessons. So be prepared!

AMETHYST

THEMES: Anti-magick, Beauty, Conscious Mind, Control, Dreams, Faithfulness, Love, Meditation, Peace, Psychism, Safety, Weather Magick.

CORRESPONDENCES: Bacchus, Diana, Water.

HISTORY AND FOLKLORE: The word *amethyst* comes from a Greek term meaning "nonintoxicating" because of the long-held belief that the stone would keep someone from drunkenness. Drinking from a cup fashioned from amethyst improves self-control, intellect, meditative focus, and business acumen. According to Hebrew tradition, amethyst was one of the stones of the high priest's breastplate and encouraged faithfulness, visions, and dreams.

An amethyst plunged purposefully into a body of water brings a fertilizing rainstorm, one carried into battle protects the bearer from the enemy, and one rubbed on the face accents inner and outer beauty. A ring of amethyst shaped like Cupid was said to have been worn by St. Valentine, giving it some associations with love.

SAMPLE APPLICATIONS: If you have an amethyst ring, shamanic tradition says wearing it on the third finger of your left hand will protect you in any undertaking. This is especially true for anyone born in February.

Carried as part of a medicine bundle, an amethyst turns away unwanted spellcraft aimed in your direction. It also helps with any matter in which temperance is necessary.

Amethyst beads make an excellent addition to dream catchers, and a heart-shaped amethyst crystal is a fitting decoration on a love altar, where you want emotion tempered with sound judgment. Hang a crystal in your car for safe travel, put one on your third eye (the middle of your forehead) as you meditate for tranquillity and psychism, or take a handful of tiny tumbled stones and toss them into flowing water to bring a light rainfall where one is needed.

ANT

THEMES: Community, Fertility, Organization, Tenacity, Wisdom.

CORRESPONDENCES: Earth, Spring (except flying ants, which are Earth/Air, and fire ants, which are Fire/Sun/Summer).

HISTORY AND FOLKLORE: The ant's industrious and sagacious nature is characterized in Aesop's fable of the ant and the grasshopper. In it, ants toil all summer storing up food while grasshoppers simply sing and dance and then have nothing to eat come winter. The Book of Proverbs exhorts us to study the ants in order to learn wisdom.

Some myths include the ant's hill as part of the creation story, giving the soil and the ants some associations with fertility. Among the Chinese the ant represents order and virtue, in Hindu stories it symbolizes the changeableness and transience in our existence, and in Native American tradition it is an icon of patience and the value of planning.

SAMPLE APPLICATIONS: We know from studying ants that they work in cooperative, well-ordered communities in which each member has a place and a duty to perform. This makes them an excellent animal spirit to call upon in any matter that requires mutual effort and good structure. To accomplish this, visualize yourself outside a door that leads into the soil. Here you'll find a colony of ants, one of which will approach you and share its insights. Alternatively, carry the image of an ant with you anytime you want to foster patience or wisdom.

If you dream of ants, it represents prosperity coming to you or the need to apply yourself to improve present circumstances, especially in a social situation. When ants appear on your doorstep, it is said they bear a message of guidance from the gods, so consider what the universe has been trying to tell you lately.

APPLE

THEMES: Death (spirits), Fertility, Health, Knowledge, Longevity, Love, Luck, Wishcraft.

CORRESPONDENCES: Aphrodite, Diana, Freyja, Gaia, Hera, Loki, Odin, Venus, Water, Zeus.

HISTORY AND FOLKLORE: In many of the world's myths a man offers a woman an apple (or vice versa), the acceptance of which indicates a new depth to their relationship. This makes the apple both a love food and one of fertility. In the biblical rendition of this tale, the apple takes on a secondary association with knowledge, for which some price is paid. In Teutonic tradition the gods and goddesses receive apples to renew their youth, giving it additional associations with longevity, and it's also a food in the land of the dead.

Until recent times, farmers gave offerings of cider to the apple trees during Yule to ensure a good crop the coming year, and the drinking of wassail (a spiced apple beverage) ensures good health for everyone. Perhaps such customs and myths explain why folk remedies recommend that a sick person tie a string to an apple tree, attach the illness, and leave it there. Similarly, warts rubbed nine times by an apple, which is then sliced in nine pieces and buried, is said to alleviate the problem.

SAMPLE APPLICATIONS: A fun activity seen during Halloween is bobbing for apples, which not only brings luck, but allows you to literally "bite into" good health (and you need not wait until Halloween to try it!). Alternatively, slice an apple in half and carve your wish into it (make it one suitable to the apple's energy). Bury this in rich soil to start the manifestation process.

Carrying apple seeds inspires fertility, both literally and figuratively, burning apple seeds makes a great component for love divination, and leaving apples or apple seeds at the graves of beloved friends and family members brings their spirits joy and peace. Dried apple peel is a good additive for love, health, and luck incense or sachets, and a bit of apple wood makes a good charm to improve personal longevity or increase the longevity of any special project.

ARROW

THEMES: Anti-magick, Divination, Elements, Guidance, Luck, Pathworking, Protection.

CORRESPONDENCES: Element varies with direction (think of a compass); Artemis, Helios, Ishtar, Kama, Usil.

HISTORY AND FOLKLORE: The use of the arrow dates back to Paleolithic times, which is why it has remained a strong symbol in many settings, not just magickal ones. The myths of the world are filled with magick arrows that reveal secret things (Germany), divine arrows that destroy an enemy (Madras), directional arrows that guide (Japan), summoning arrows that draw a helpful spirit (China), and arrows that transport the bearer to other realms (Arabia). Ancient people specifically used arrows in religious ordeals, as protective amulets, as good luck charms, as offerings to hunting gods and goddesses, and for divination.

SAMPLE APPLICATIONS: Arrowheads or arrow-shaped pendants make an excellent choice for an amuletic base, especially for anti-magick charms and to protect the bearer from sickness. To key this token to yourself, rub some oil from your skin on it and dab it with personally preferred cologne or perfume. When you need a little extra luck, touch the token as you might a touchstone.

In a ritual setting, four arrows pointing outward can symbolize the four elements and the corners of creation. Arrows can be used in path-working exercises, offering the person specific choices in the direction he or she takes. Alternatively, an arrow makes a good wand that guides magick to its target. Finally, an arrow in your dreams often indicates a message. See where the arrow lands for more insights.

ASH

THEMES: Creativity, Justice, Luck, Protection, Safety, Strength.

CORRESPONDENCES: Fire, the God Aspect, Odin, Poseidon, Sun.

HISTORY AND FOLKLORE: The ash tree often figures heavily in ancient cosmologies as the world tree whose roots feed the universe and whose branches become the stars. Norse mythology uses ash as part of the creation story to fashion the first man. Because of this importance, ash trees were often the site of various judicial undertakings.

The Celts felt a spear fashioned from ash was a great asset to personal strength and it acted as a protective amulet, and any piece of ash carried was considered a protection against drowning in Greece. Beyond this, an ash leaf when plucked and carried brings luck and protects the traveler while abroad.

SAMPLE APPLICATIONS: In a ritual setting, a wand of ash is a good tool for casting the magick circle, and it can also represent the god aspect in this form. If paired with alder wood, it represents the union of god and goddess (similar to the pairing of chalice and athame).

Another old bit of popular lore says snakes won't cross ash leaves or wood. If we accept this protective power in a figurative sense, it becomes an effective tool for safeguarding your home. In this case, put some ash leaves under the rug in your entryway or bury some wood near the threshold to keep any human "snakes" neatly outside!

Finally, some people believe ash was effective in protecting one from werewolf attacks. So consider carrying a piece with you to keep those emotional wolves out of your life!

BANANA

THEMES: Courage, Fertility, Luck, Protection.

CORRESPONDENCES: The God Aspect, Maia, Water.

HISTORY AND FOLKLORE: Since ancient times bananas have adorned altars to the gods in India, where they also appear on the marriage altar, likely to promote fertility and invoke blessings. Hawaiians use banana peels to protect themselves from negative energy, in Polynesian tradition the banana represents courage and valor, and in the southern United States growing bananas near your home promotes luck.

In Bantu tradition the afterbirth of a child is buried under a banana tree so the child will have luck and grow strong. This is not surprising since in this and other Oceanic traditions (New Guinean, Polynesian, etc.), the banana replaces the ash as the world tree.

SAMPLE APPLICATIONS: Anytime you want to improve rapport between a man and a woman (especially in bed), try making a magickal banana cream pie! Banana accents the masculine half and fertility, and the cream is the goddess/feminine aspect. Eat playfully!

Dried bananas (available in supermarket bulk food departments) make a good charm for bravery, making positive changes, or improving good fortune. These can also be powdered for adding to your incense (but I prefer a banana-scented oil). Finally, bananas appearing in your dreams may indicate the need to reconnect with the god aspect in yourself, or a potentially hazardous situation of which to be aware (the peel).

BARLEY

THEMES: Banishing, Blessing, Jealousy, Love.

CORRESPONDENCES: Cronus, Demeter, Earth, Indra.

HISTORY AND FOLKLORE: As a staple food for early communities and an ingredient in brewing since 2800 B.C.E., barley is found in many early rituals. Hebrews included it on the altar as an offering for jealousy, and in India the grain is sacred to Indra and often used during rites-of-passage events (birth, death, weddings) to promote love and blessings. Meanwhile, Europeans thought the last sheaf of barley in a field concealed dwarves, and that nine grains of barley applied to a sty and buried would alleviate the malady.

SAMPLE APPLICATIONS: Sprinkle barley around the sacred circle in late summer or early fall to honor the harvest, disperse evil, and promote blessings to all who gather within. Keep a sheaf of barley in your kitchen so your food is always filled with loving intentions. And when you find the green-eyed monster getting the best of you, add barley to your diet (perhaps in bread or multigrain cereal) to banish that negative tendency.

BASIL

THEMES: Death, Fertility, Grounding, Happiness, Love, Luck, Peace, Protection.

CORRESPONDENCES: Fire, Lakshmi, Vishnu.

HISTORY AND FOLKLORE: In Italy basil represents true love, and pots of basil are often exchanged by lovers. In India, the herb is grown in nearly every Hindu temple as a plant sacred to both Vishnu and Lakshmi, who are protective, beneficent figures especially to those desiring children. Those who seek fertility often obtain a sprig of basil from the temple and keep it in the bed or drink it in a tea.

Persians and Egyptians grew basil in cemeteries, intimating something about the herb brought peace to the dead. In Moldavia basil is given to gypsy-hearted souls to keep them a little more firmly rooted. Finally, smelling basil is said to generate happiness, and when it is received as a gift, it promotes luck.

SAMPLE APPLICATIONS: Grow a pot of basil in your home to promote peace, love, and joy. If you can put the pot in a southerly window where the aroma will be carried on warm winds, all the better. Perhaps hang a suitable crystal over the plant (amethyst is a good choice), so the herb receives the benefit of sympathetic energy and grows toward that goal!

People who always have their head in the clouds should put a basil leaf in their shoe for grounding. Foods with basil are good after-ritual choices to help reestablish our earthly connections. For Summerland rites or conception spells, burn basil in the sacred space.

BAY

THEMES: Divination, Love, Protection, Success, Weather Magick, Wishcraft.

CORRESPONDENCES: Apollo, Eros, Fides, Fire, Sun, Zeus.

HISTORY AND FOLKLORE: Bay was part of the ancient divination rituals at Delphi, and it also appeared regularly in Greece as a decorative head wreath in any celebration that honored success and achievement. Any home that had bay within would certainly be safe from thunderstorms, since the herb pleased Apollo. Meanwhile, Romans often offered this herb to Fides, a goddess who would grant devotion and great honors to those who pleased her. Today bay is considered a love herb, and one that helps manifest wishcraft.

SAMPLE APPLICATIONS: Wreaths of bay can be hung in your kitchen to add victorious energies to your foods or worn at rituals that commemorate specific achievements in a person's life. Bay branches and leaves are a perfect offering for Apollo (and for invoking any of his attributes, which are pretty diverse). Break up a dried leaf and burn it just before you do any type of divination, or use the leaf itself as the focus of your fortune-telling efforts. If the leaf pops and burns brightly as you pose a question, the answer is yes!

Write a wish on a fresh bay leaf and keep it in a box. When the leaf dries, burn it to manifest the magick. Or bury the leaf to help the energy grow. This seems especially effective for wishes pertaining to love.

Finally, some ancient magicians felt that bay is magickally coupled with marigolds, meaning each herb strengthens the other's properties (both having very strong ties to the sun). Keep this in mind in designing your magickal recipes.

BEANS

THEMES: Banishing, Death, Divination, Learning, Luck, Potential, Psychism, Spirits.

CORRESPONDENCES: Air, the God Aspect (the bean), the Goddess Aspect (the white flower).

HISTORY AND FOLKLORE: Ancient Aryans considered beans a food of the dead, as did the Romans. The ancient Greek oracles included beans as part of divinatory procedures, specifically for drawing lots. Meanwhile, across the world the Japanese tossed beans on their threshold to chase away negative spirits and encourage luck. (It's interesting that Romans had a similar custom that called for throwing black beans behind oneself to cast off ill fortune and any restless familial spirits.)

In folklore beans are the instrument of important life lessons, like seeing the value and potential in small things (notably: in "Jack and the Beanstalk").

SAMPLE APPLICATIONS: During summer rites, a growing bean plant in blossom can effectively represent the union between male and female, god and goddess on your altar. Eat beans anytime you want to open yourself to new possibilities, especially psychic insights about the future, or to receive messages from spirits.

If a problem or bad habit is plaguing you, name seven beans after that situation/difficulty (for example, if you've been depressed, name the beans "gloom" or something similar). Then once a day over seven days throw one bean away behind you and don't look back, saying "Away from me, all negativity. Behind me to stay. I begin anew today!"

BEAR

THEMES: Astral Realm, Courage, Leadership, Power, Protection, Reincarnation, Spirituality, Tenacity.

CORRESPONDENCES: Artemis, Callisto, Diana, Earth, Thor, Zeus.

HISTORY AND FOLKLORE: Many shamanic traditions consider bear hair a potent amulet for power and courage and to ward off disease. In the world's folktales the bear is often characterized as a guardian and helpmate to those who seek spiritual insights or to travel the astral realm safely. Additionally, because of the bear's hibernation cycle, it has often been associated with death and rebirth.

In Native American traditions the bear represents unmatched strength, leadership, and tenacity. On the medicine wheel, those born between August 22 and September 22 are under the bear spirit's influence and will find themselves to be paced, watchful, and somewhat unobtrusive unless called to action. Finally, in dream imagery, a running bear portends joy and fighting a bear implies you will soon face oppression.

SAMPLE APPLICATIONS: If you are planning to undertake any shamanic journey, the image of a bear is a very fitting one to place in the northern quarter of your sacred space as a protector and guide. When you feel the need for more "backbone" or wish to develop administrative skills, carry an image of a bear with you (you can often find stone carvings at nature shops, or you can draw an outline of the constellation Ursa Major, the Great Bear, or Ursa Minor, the Little Bear).

BEE

THEMES: Community, Cooperation, Creativity, Fertility, Messages, Money, Omens, Organization, Persistence, Zeal.

CORRESPONDENCES: Air, Aphrodite, Demeter, Fire (stinger), Indra, Kama, Krishna, Ra, Zeus.

HISTORY AND FOLKLORE: Egyptians claim that bees were created from Ra's tears, while in Greece a bee could house the spirit of one of Aphrodite's faithful priestesses. Ancient pagans also associated bees with spirits, but more as an emblem of the soul's immutable nature.

The Qu'ran says bees are faithful, intelligent, and wise, while Christianity characterizes them as cooperative and orderly. In many other settings bees conveyed messages between the worlds, which may be why Europeans observed the behavior of bees as an omen of things to come.

SAMPLE APPLICATIONS: We still hear the phrase "busy as a bee" in conversations today, indicating that the bee's symbolism has remained fairly constant in human awareness. This makes the image of a bee a very good charm for modern magick users, especially those facing heavy workloads requiring fortitude and enthusiasm. You can still often find such an image in jewelry departments as an addition to a charm bracelet! Alternatively, if you have a special request or message you want to send, try whispering it to a bee (carefully) as part of your magickal methods. (Note: We will be covering the uses of honey separately from its makers later in this section.)

BEER

THEMES: Dreams, Law, Offering, Purification.

CORRESPONDENCES: Fire (alcohol), Hathor, Isis, Odin, Ra, Water (liquid).

HISTORY AND FOLKLORE: As early as 2800 B.C.E. a variety of beer was appearing on Egyptian altars (not to mention those of Greece, Rome, and Germany) as a sacred beverage that honored and pleased several gods and goddesses. Considering this, it's not surprising that Egyptians also felt dreaming of beer was a positive omen, and to avoid bad dreams, they simply rubbed their faces with beer before going to bed. Meanwhile, in Norse regions the beer hall was one of the few places where legal transactions could take place, and in Europe beer was being used in purgatives and remedies because it was safer than drinking water.

SAMPLE APPLICATIONS: In modern magick beer is sometimes part of a ritual cup for libations or sharing around the circle. For the latter purpose, the beer is often made with special ingredients (specifically herbs) that accent the meaning of the gathering. To do this yourself, you need only steep a significant herb in the beer beforehand, so the energy and flavor are both incorporated.

If you suffer from nightmares, you might want to try a creative adaptation of the Egyptian cure. Dip the fingertips of your strong hand in a bit of beer (a good quality is suggested). Dab this counterclockwise on your face three times, especially your forehead, for banishing and say, "Darkest dreams away from me, I purge myself of negativity."

BELL

THEMES: Fertility, Focus, Power, Prayer, Prophecy, Protection, Weather Magick.

CORRESPONDENCES: The Goddess Aspect (some correspondences may change with the base metal used, silver-toned being lunar).

HISTORY AND FOLKLORE: Bells have always been regarded as protective. The Hebrew high priests wore bells in their skirts, horsemen put bells on tackles, and bells toll in churches—all frightening away any spirits or evil lingering nearby. Folktale motifs also tell of "belling the cat"— which becomes an early warning system for forthcoming troubles.

Some cultures considered bells a symbol of fertility (probably due to the womb shape), Siberian shamans used them as prophetic tools and power boosters for incantations, the ancient Chinese rang bells to conjure rain (while Europeans rang them to stave off thunderstorms), and many religious traditions use them to honor the gods in prayer or worship. Note too that in the East prayer bowls (which are basically bells without clappers) and gongs (oversized bells) are both used as meditative tools to focus the mind and soul into symmetry and center the will.

SAMPLE APPLICATIONS: A survey of modern magick traditions shows bells being used predominantly for two functions. The first is to signal and direct the beginning of magick (such as in a spell where the last part of the incantation says, "With the ringing of this bell . . ."). The second is as protective amulets, such as bell wind chimes hung in windows or single bells hung in a car.

BERYL

THEMES: Communication, Congeniality, Divination, Law, Learning, Love, Motivation, Protection.

CORRESPONDENCES: Moon.

HISTORY AND FOLKLORE: Historically beryl (a green-colored stone in the emerald family) was used to protect the bearer against foes, especially in legal situations. Carrying it also averts thievery, improves intelligence, motivates, and makes a person more likable in social settings. In the Middle Ages, beryl was one of the stones favored for scrying, especially when shaped in a sphere. Finally, in Germany married couples exchanged beryl to rekindle love, while others carried it to improve overall communications.

SAMPLE APPLICATIONS: Beryl is a great addition to power pouches and other amuletic creations if you need a little extra incentive. For those who find themselves feeling awkward in social settings, energize and bless a piece. Carry it regularly so that your words, actions, and the interpretation of them all flow harmoniously.

BIRCH

THEMES: Anti-magick, Cycles, Protection.

CORRESPONDENCES: The Goddess Aspect, Spring, Thor, Water.

HISTORY AND FOLKLORE: The ancients used birchwood as an effective amulet against lightning, the evil eye, and injury. In Rome, branches of birch preceded leaders in order to clear the way, a symbolic protective measure. In Norse mythology, the birch is sacred to Thor and symbolizes spring's return, and by extension rebirth (cycles). Europeans used birch branches to "beat the bounds"—an annual observance that chased away evil spirits and safeguarded the region from witchcraft. In modern magick, a birch in blossom represents the goddess.

SAMPLE APPLICATIONS: Consider using a birch rod as a ritual broom handle (you can probably replace the handle of any broom you get at the supermarket with it). With your birch broom you can sweep the sacred space clean of unwanted energy. Decorate it with some fresh white flowers and you have a beautiful symbol of both god and goddess (the rod represents the masculine, the flowers and wood the feminine).

Ground birchwood is a good base for protective incense (I use an old pencil sharpener and finely sliced pieces to get a good consistency), and it also can be sprinkled around your residence in this form to protect it from weather damage and the occupants or visitors from accidental injuries.

BLACK

THEMES: Banishing, Death, Grounding, Rest.

CORRESPONDENCES: Earth, Saturn.

HISTORY AND FOLKLORE: We all know the old tales of black cats being witches' familiars, but why black? As the color of night, a time during which our ancestors felt vulnerable, black began to be associated with evil. Since this is the color we see when we close our eyes, it also gained associations with sleep and death, which is why some cultures mark graves with black stones. Finally, in modern magick practitioners use the color black to help with banishing or grounding spells and rituals.

SAMPLE APPLICATIONS: There used to be a time when anyone called a witch would be depicted in a black cone-shaped hat and black robe, because of the superstitions and misunderstandings surrounding our arts. Thankfully, the modern witch knows better—we wear pretty much any color we want. That doesn't mean black has lost its symbolic value, however.

To get rid of excess negativity, carry a black object with you for twenty-four hours and then toss that item as far away from you as you can (make it biodegradable, please). In some mystical traditions it's customary to wear black robes during winter rituals to honor the darkness and then switch to white robes in the spring to welcome the sun. Add black into your wardrobe anytime you need to keep your feet firmly planted in reality.

BLOOD

THEMES: Courage, Energy, Healing, Oaths, Offering, Power, Strength, and many more.

CORRESPONDENCES: Fire.

HISTORY AND FOLKLORE: The ancients felt that people's souls were tied to their blood, making it a very powerful magickal tool. For a while this belief resulted in blood sacrifices to the gods when great needs arose. Later, blood was believed to bear all the best attributes of the person or creature from which it came. So those wishing for courage or strength might dab themselves with the blood of a bear. Oaths or peace treaties sealed with blood were considered immutable.

SAMPLE APPLICATIONS: The concept of blood sacrifice has thankfully long gone the way of history. Magick practitioners today recognize the potent symbolism in blood, but often recommend using a viable substitute due to health considerations and common sense. Any red item, especially red liquid (tomato juice, pomegranate juice), can be used. Remember in magick the symbol is as powerful as what it represents as long as you maintain congruity of meaning in your substitution. Another alternative is saliva, discussed later in this section.

Should you happen to scratch yourself or get caught on a pin, you might want to save a few drops of blood to dab on your magickal tools or around your sacred space or to add to other spell components. The first action marks the items/area with the most personal energy signature you have; the second boosts magickal power. Under no circumstances should you try to undertake a blood oath or other rites where blood mingling occurs, however. The risks today are too great. Again, find a suitable alternative to the blood, proceed with the right attitude, and you'll do just fine.

BLOODSTONE

THEMES: Communication, Fear, Opportunity, Peace, Prophecy, Spellcraft, Strength, Success, Truth, Weather Magick.

CORRESPONDENCES: Aries, Fire.

HISTORY AND FOLKLORE: Bloodstone is one of a couple of crystals that are said to turn dull or shatter when their owner is in danger or going to die, which makes it a prophetic amulet. Egyptian soldiers sometimes carried bloodstone for strength, courage, or victory and to protect themselves from bleeding wounds (due to the red tint). Among many ancient people it was carried to banish discord, inspire honesty, improve communication skills, create opportunities, and invoke rain.

SAMPLE APPLICATIONS: Some modern magicians like to use bloodstone as a support system for spells. It improves the overall results of any magickal effort. Beyond this, having bloodstone as part of a power pouch is certainly apt, considering it inspires vitality and insightfulness. If you'd like to try using bloodstone to invoke rain when it's *really* needed, gather a handful of tiny tumbled stones and toss them in an open body of water saying, "Rain to me, heavens be free!" Note that I issue caution on playing with weather patterns too much out of respect for Mother Nature. Listen to nature's voice for guidance in this matter.

BLUE

THEMES: Dreams, Health, Joy, Meditation, Peace, Truth, Wisdom.

CORRESPONDENCES: Water, Venus.

HISTORY AND FOLKLORE: Considered the color of wisdom and honesty in many esoteric traditions, blue's day is Friday, its planet is Venus, and it corresponds numerically to six. In druidical custom, blue was a sacred color, a knotted blue ribbon being given to their bards (individuals who not only entertained but guarded oral histories).

Among Scottish people blue is considered a healing color, and in the 1600s it wasn't uncommon to see people in northern Europe wearing a blue scarf to keep colds away. Similarly, in Asia, wearing or carrying blue items protects the bearer from the evil eye.

SAMPLE APPLICATIONS: Use blue accents in your bedroom or meditation room to inspire spiritual dreams and improve your reflective abilities, or add it to your wardrobe when you need a little extra happiness.

Write your charms for peace or happiness on blue paper to improve the sympathetic energies. For example, you might write the phrase "let the blue calm of the sea bring peace to me" on the paper. Carry this with you regularly until the energy saturates your aura.

Burn a blue candle anointed with olive oil as a focus for magic directed toward wise decision making. To improve the results here, carve an X in the wax about midway down (to represent the crossroads). Let the candle burn down so that the X is melted away.

BOOK

THEMES: Divination, Knowledge, Magick, Spellcraft, Wisdom.

CORRESPONDENCES: Earth/Air.

HISTORY AND FOLKLORE: The ancient words "as it is written" ring loudly in our ears even today. For hundreds of years the written word was regarded as a kind of magick all its own because very few people could read or write. Some languages, like ancient Hebrew, had mystical meaning when written in specific manners. Books like the Bible were long used for a kind of divination known as bibliomancy, and many witches still maintain grimoires or Books of Shadows (tomes of magick suited to their Path).

SAMPLE APPLICATIONS: To try bibliomancy yourself, take a book whose contents you admire. Close your eyes and think of a question. Bring as much dimension to that question as possible by visualizing the details. When you feel your palms getting warm or itchy, open the book and put your finger randomly on a passage to see what message lies there. Beyond this, for any magick practitioner I recommend reading as a pastime over TV any day. It broadens horizons inside and out!

BOTTLE (JAR)

THEMES: Elementals, Energy, Protection, Wishcraft.

CORRESPONDENCES: Vary by shape, but usually the Goddess Aspect.

HISTORY AND FOLKLORE: Stories of finding a genie or imp in a bottle appear repeatedly in folklore, including tales from Arabia, Finland, and the Philippines. The custom of stuffing wishes in a bottle and setting it out in the ocean is also well known. These two examples show that bottles have a strong affinity with wishcraft and elemental beings. Beyond this, bottles "hold" things, so why not energy? This may be why they were chosen as protective items (such as the witch bottle described below).

SAMPLE APPLICATIONS: To make a witch bottle for yourself, take any glass jar and begin filling it with unsavory, sharp, reflective items like mirror pieces, old nails, and so on. When it's filled halfway, put the cover on the bottle tightly and visualize the rest of the jar being permeated with white, sparkling light. Bury this near your residence saying, "All evil spirits depart, only blessings impart. Keep negativity away, forever to stay." The bottle will continue radiating protective energy for as long as it's left undisturbed.

Another fun project is making a family wish bottle, which is kept in a central location. On special occasions like New Year's, birthdays, and the like, people can put in wishes. Once a year (May 1, Beltane, is a good time), read the wishes out loud, then burn the paper within to release those prayers to the four winds and the Divine.

BOX

THEMES: Protection.

CORRESPONDENCES: Earth.

HISTORY AND FOLKLORE: All kinds of boxes appear in magickal stories from those that can curse, such as Pandora's box, to those that help by capturing a prankster like the Coyote of Native American tradition. In nearly all instances, however, the box is a safety zone that energy cannot leave or enter without being willfully directed.

SAMPLE APPLICATIONS: Many modern magick practitioners use specially designed boxes to house their ritual tools, spell components, and divinatory items. The variety is hard to detail here, but most have a natural white cloth lining and some type of decorative top bearing magickal sigils. The purpose of such a container is to keep unwanted hands or paws away from the items and to safeguard the items from random energy that might hinder free-flowing magick. For your box, consider choosing the base material for its symbolic associations and then decorate it yourself, so the final package bears your energy imprint.

BRASS

THEMES: Healing, Money, Prophecy.

CORRESPONDENCES: Fire, Sun.

HISTORY AND FOLKLORE: In medieval times oracular heads of brass were said to have been made by magicians in Portugal. When gold has been impossible to obtain for magickal purposes, brass has long been considered a suitable substitute. Beyond this, the most popular folk remedy still seen today is the use of brass jewelry to allay aches and pains.

SAMPLE APPLICATIONS: Since brass is considered a health-producer, cooking with brass-bottomed pans in your kitchen might not be a bad idea for kitchen witches. When you wash these, use a gentle soap and rub clockwise so positive energy remains in the metal. Also, try meditating with a piece of brass on your third eye to open prophetic abilities.

BREAD

THEMES: Blessing, Friendship, Kinship, Longevity, Luck, Miracles, Offering, Prosperity, Travel, Weather Magick.

CORRESPONDENCES: Ceres, Demeter, Earth, Indra, Ishtar, Osiris.

HISTORY AND FOLKLORE: This staff of life is considered sacred by many peoples and a suitable offering for the Divine. When the last sheaf of wheat from a field is made into bread, it confers long life to whoever eats it. In Spain, when a storm is coming, bread is put on a windowsill to prevent weather damage. Throughout Europe, throwing away bread is akin to tossing out one's good fortune with the garbage. Similarly, bread should always be broken rather than cut to keep from cutting off blessings. Russians exchange bread as a symbol of friendship, and Gypsies carry bread for safe travels and to promote luck.

SAMPLE APPLICATIONS: When you desire friendship or love or need a "miracle," release dry bread crumbs to the birds and let them carry your desires on their wings. To bring longevity to a situation or pet project, carve an image of it in a piece of bread with a toothpick, then toast it (warmth activates energy), and eat it (to internalize the magick). Carry dry bread (like crackers) anytime you travel for safety and improved good fortune.

BROWN

THEMES: Fairies, Grounding, Spirituality.

CORRESPONDENCES: Earth.

HISTORY AND FOLKLORE: The ancient fairies known as brownies, gnomes, and dwarves were often depicted as wearing robes of this color, which alluded to their connection with the earth. During the Middle Ages monks wore brown to represent their retreat from worldly (temporal) things.

SAMPLE APPLICATIONS: Brown is the color of earth's soils, so metaphysically this color can be substituted into any spell that calls for dirt.

Consider making yourself a monk-styled brown ritual robe for any magical activities where you want to be wholly focused on spiritual matters. Add dark brown into your wardrobe whenever you need to keep one foot on the ground, or use brown-colored foods to internalize this energy (meat in particular has that effect).

Also, some witches I know burn a brown candle as one way of clearing away "muddy" situations.

BUTTERFLY

THEMES: Freedom, Happiness, Love, Luck, Reincarnation.

CORRESPONDENCES: Air, Eos, Horae, Spring.

HISTORY AND FOLKLORE: In Greece it was believed that souls became butterflies between incarnations, and the spirits of the seasons (the

Horae) were portrayed with butterfly wings. Chinese lovers exchange jade butterflies to symbolize two souls joyfully united. In much of Europe, being kind to these creatures brings luck.

SAMPLE APPLICATIONS: When you feel constrained by circumstances, dress in light, diaphanous, and colorful clothing and do a mimelike dance of a butterfly in flight (if you have nosy neighbors, make sure you have some privacy). Let this creature's gentle spirit lift the burdens you bear. Carry a carving of a butterfly (choose a suitable stone) to inspire love, good fortune, or happiness. Meditate on the stages of a butterfly to better comprehend the mysteries of reincarnation.

CABBAGE

THEMES: Comprehension, Fertility, Love.

CORRESPONDENCES: Moon, Water.

HISTORY AND FOLKLORE: The old wives' tale of children coming from the cabbage patch gives this vegetable some fleeting associations with fertility. Folklore tells us that when two people plant cabbage together, their relationship will flourish, which may be why English custom dictated the use of cabbage stalks in love divination. Finally, the ancient Greeks believed that eating cabbage could cure confusion or insanity.

SAMPLE APPLICATIONS: Add magickally prepared cabbage to love or fertility foods or those dishes aimed at improving your understanding of a situation (particularly a relationship). If you happen to know where some cabbage is growing, go out with a loved one, holding hands, and randomly pick a stalk. Taste the heart. If it is sweet your love will remain true.

CANDLE (WAX)

THEMES: Divination, Focus, South, Spirits.

CORRESPONDENCES: Fire, the God Aspect (the wax body), the Goddess Aspect (the flame), Spirit.

HISTORY AND FOLKLORE: Candles have been used in religious settings for thousands of years to symbolize the presence of Spirit and its warm light. They're featured heavily in global pyromantic techniques (divination by fire), in which the candle flame is observed while a question is posed. A candle flame's behavior and the way the wax melts can indicate the presence of spirits (a blue flame or a spiral sheet of wax down one side), and dreaming of a vibrant candle portends the receipt of an important letter.

SAMPLE APPLICATIONS: The mystical, warm glow of a candle makes it perfect for creating a magickal ambiance. Most people find that the gentle nature of the light improves spiritual focus, and the candle itself can become a construct for spellcraft (see Chapter 3). To see if it will help you, close your shades and put a candle (any color) on a table. Sit down, shake out any tensions, take a deep breath, and light the candle. Observe the flame, not overly intensely, just as part of the entire scene before you. Keep breathing slowly, in an all-connected manner. Do you notice that the edge of the flame becomes blurry and melts into the rest of the room? This is the first step toward learning how to enter a trance!

CARNELIAN

THEMES: Blessing, Communication, Courage, Health, Jealousy, Luck, Peace.

CORRESPONDENCES: Fire, Isis, Muhammad, Sun.

HISTORY AND FOLKLORE: Egyptians called the carnelian the blood of Isis and used it regularly as part of burial rites to still restless spirits. Muslims say that anyone who wears this stone will receive both peace and blessings. Arabic and Australian folk traditions recommend the stone as a health amulet and a charm for courage, Germans used it as a good luck talisman (especially combined with onyx), Spaniards regarded carnelian as having the power of effective speech, and in the Orient it was donned to prevent jealousy and envy.

SAMPLE APPLICATIONS: Carry a sun-charged carnelian with you when you feel nervous or unsettled. To generate more luck for those who live in your home, wrap a piece with copper wire a personally fortunate number of times around the stone. Then hang it somewhere in your home where it will regularly catch the sunlight on its surface and then reflect that energy into your home. This charm can be improved by putting a mirror behind the carnelian.

CARROT

THEMES: Clarity, Passion, Vision.

CORRESPONDENCES: Autumn, Fire, the God Aspect.

HISTORY AND FOLKLORE: The best-known bit of lore about carrots is that they aid eyesight, but this can be extended to spiritual vision too. Beyond this, the carrot is a natural phallic symbol, which is why it was eaten to increase passion.

SAMPLE APPLICATIONS: The orange color of carrots makes them a nice accent for the autumn harvest altar, especially as a symbol of the fertile god's providence and productivity. Add carrots to your diet anytime you need to see things more clearly or when you want to bring real passion into any endeavor. To energize the carrots beforehand, carve a pentagram on them (or a symbol of your endeavor), then cook (heat equals power), and eat (internalization).

CAT

THEMES: Longevity, Luck, Magick, Money, Protection, Wishcraft.

CORRESPONDENCES: Bast, Diana, Freyja, Hecate, Moon.

HISTORY AND FOLKLORE: The Egyptians deified cats, specifically in the form of the cat-faced goddess Bast, who presided over joyful expressions. They believed carrying the image of a cat would protect the bearer from all misfortune. Similarly, the Chinese painted lanterns with cat faces for safety in the home. In Greece we find Hecate, the patroness of witches, sometimes turning into a cat, which may be why the cat became the most infamous of all familiars of witches.

In Arabia, cats can be genies in disguise, and if you find a cat's whisker you can burn it and make a wish! Malaysians use cat whiskers in spells for luck and money, and the Japanese keep images of the Beckoning Cat (with one paw up) anywhere they wish to encourage fortune. These beliefs may have inspired some of the later superstitions about stray cats bringing money with them. Finally, we all know that cats have nine lives, which makes them a symbol of longevity.

SAMPLE APPLICATIONS: Follow the Egyptian custom of carrying the image of a cat (perhaps a picture of your pet) with you whenever you feel overexposed or in danger. Alternatively, to keep your home safe and filled with luck or prosperity, paint the image of a cat on one of your lampshades (change the color of the cat to suit your specific goal). Each time you turn the lamp on, you activate the cat magick! Or carve an image into a candle and burn the candle when the need arises.

If you own a cat, watch for it to shed claws or whiskers. The claw sheaths can be used as part of rituals and spells, especially those to honor a cat familiar or totem. Burn the whiskers on a sacred fire for wishcraft. Note, however, these parts must be *found,* not taken from the creature, for the magick to work.

CATNIP

THEMES: Fertility, Happiness, Insight, Love, Playfulness.

CORRESPONDENCES: Bast, Water.

HISTORY AND FOLKLORE: Carrying catnip or drinking it in a tea is an old bit of cunning magick for conception. As an herb sacred to Bast, it is an excellent choice for promoting upbeat attitudes. As beloved of cats, the herb grants insight (we once thought cats could see in the dark) and a playful demeanor. Beyond this, since catnip is under the influence of Venus, it is useful in love magick, especially if mixed with rose petals.

SAMPLE APPLICATIONS: If you have chosen Bast as a patroness or have a cat totem, familiar, or spirit guide, it is wise to keep fresh catnip around as an ingredient for your incense or as a suitable offering. Some magick practitioners like to leave a sprig of catnip in their Book of Shadows, so the herb's energy saturates the pages with intuitive comprehension. Sprinkle a little catnip under your rug to lift a bad case of winter blues (but be forewarned that any cats nearby will want to play there!). Drink a cup of catnip tea to promote self-love and a greater sense of playfulness (add a little honey for taste and emotional sweetness).

CAT'S EYE

THEMES: Anti-magick, Concealment, Happiness, Offering, Prosperity, Protection.

CORRESPONDENCES: Earth, Moon (the sheen).

HISTORY AND FOLKLORE: Because of the eerie resemblance of this stone to a cat's eye, the ancients used it to ward off the evil eye based on the law of sympathy, which says like affects like. Assyrians credited this crystal with the power of invisibility (specifically to one's enemy), the Ceylonese used it as an anti-magick amulet, and both the Chinese and Indian peoples esteem cat's eye as a stone that promotes joy and prosperity. It is considered a suitable crystal to offer to any Hindu god or goddess.

SAMPLE APPLICATIONS: Anytime you're feeling overexposed or rather depressed in a particular setting, place four of these stones at four points around yourself (like the four corners of a desk). They will create a shield of concealment that deters those who would work against you and radiates happier vibrations all around. Also, carry tiny tumbled cat's eye stones in your wallet or checkbook to keep money where it belongs and foster more of it.

CEDAR

THEMES: Money, Prophecy, Prosperity, Protection, Purification.

CORRESPONDENCES: Fire, Odin, Sun.

HISTORY AND FOLKLORE: The Hindus used burning cedar as part of prophetic rituals, while the Native Americans often added it to the fires for purifying in sweat-lodge rituals. Common folk tradition says that carrying a sliver of cedar promotes financial gain, while having cedar in the home prevents lightning strikes.

SAMPLE APPLICATIONS: Magickally, cedar is paired with amethyst, so a cedar box is an excellent choice for storing your amethyst crystals, or one decorated with an amethyst makes a suitable housing for magickal tools or components. Try dabbing a bit of cedar-scented oil on your temples anytime you're trying an exercise to improve prophetic abilities. Since cedar is readily available at the store as a moth inhibitor, keep some with your clothing to generate vibrations for prosperity and personal protection from "bugs."

CELERY

THEMES: Clarity, Divination, Focus, Insight, Passion.

CORRESPONDENCES: Fire (if applied for the conscious mind or passion), Water (for divination or instinctive matters).

HISTORY AND FOLKLORE: Cooking with celery seed brings mental keenness and possibly an improvement in divinatory abilities. Celery stalks are thought to be an aphrodisiac.

SAMPLE APPLICATIONS: The beauty of working with celery is it is edible, has very portable parts (the seed), and is readily available at the supermarket in both seed and vegetable forms! Sprinkle some seed in your shoes in the morning for alertness. Toss a little into your magickal incense before trying any divinatory system, or eat celery as part of a special meal prepared for a significant other to warm things up a bit!

CHALICE

THEMES: Abundance, Fate, Fertility, Forgiveness, Hospitality, Love, Oaths, Unity.

CORRESPONDENCES: Bacchus (the wine god), the Goddess Aspect, Water.

HISTORY AND FOLKLORE: Because of its shape, the chalice, or cup, was an ancient symbol of femininity and the womb, giving it strong associations with fertility and abundance. The chalice plays an important role in Christian stories, symbolizing forgiveness and acceptance of one's fate. In Switzerland, among Gypsies, and in pagan circles it's quite common to see a couple drinking from one cup to link their destinies, seal their pledge, and represent ongoing unity. Similarly the ancient Germans had a Minne chalice that was poured out in remembrance of a departed loved one or as part of betrothal rites. Modern Wiccans and pagans still use cups passed around the ritual circle to energize the spirit of harmony and show welcome to guests.

SAMPLE APPLICATIONS: Around the world, chalices holding sacred beverages adorn altars to gods and goddesses; as such they continue to be regarded as an effective ritual tool for the modern magician. Here they can represent the goddess or water element and hold libations or shared beverages. Anytime you want to inspire greater coherence in your family, prepare a special beverage and serve it clockwise around the dining-room table from one cup. Drinking from the cup represents each person's willingness to put hand and heart into making that magick happen.

CHAMOMILE

THEMES: Energy, Gardening, Stress, Success.

CORRESPONDENCES: The God Aspect (solar gods especially), Summer, Sun.

HISTORY AND FOLKLORE: The ancient Egyptians dedicated chamomile to the sun god likely due to its use in treating fevers. It is said that plants will thrive in any garden where chamomile grows or is strewn into the soil, and carrying chamomile in your pocket promotes success. Aromatherapists use chamomile to decrease stress; conversely, the Victorian language of flowers calls chamomile energetic.

SAMPLE APPLICATIONS: For midsummer rituals this is a magickal herb par excellence! Use a sprinkling to mark the perimeter of the sacred space and toss some into the ritual fires. This invokes and honors the sun god. Get some chamomile tea bags at the supermarket, charge them in sunlight for a while, then steep them in tea to calm jittery nerves. Alternatively, you can focus on the solar, energetic nature of the herb to give yourself or any magickal components an energy boost when needed.

CHERRY

THEMES: Healing, Learning, Love, Luck, Passion.

CORRESPONDENCES: Water.

HISTORY AND FOLKLORE: Cherries and cherry trees appear repeatedly in folk remedies associated with health. The Romans favored cherries as an aphrodisiac, while in Japan it is the fruit of love. Some ancient grimoires recommend cherry juice as a suitable substitute for blood in spellcraft, cherry blossoms represent learning, and dreaming of cherries foretells that improved luck is on its way.

SAMPLE APPLICATIONS: Adding a little cherry juice or fresh berries to your diet when you're ailing certainly won't hurt anything—they're rich in vitamins. As you nibble or drink, think warm, loving thoughts toward yourself and let the fruit do its work. Add cherry pits to sachets or power pouches designed for love or good fortune.

CHESTNUT

THEMES: Congeniality, Courage, Health, Love, Spirits.

CORRESPONDENCES: Fire.

HISTORY AND FOLKLORE: It was common in Germany to carry a chestnut in one's back pocket as an amulet against backaches. In Tuscany, chestnuts are regarded as suitable foods for, and offerings to, ancestral spirits to keep them happy. In other areas people consumed chestnuts to improve male virility or to banish social awkwardness.

SAMPLE APPLICATIONS: I cannot help but wonder if our fall tradition of roasting chestnuts began with superstitions about ghosts (namely, keeping them away!). Even if that's not the case, it's certainly an effective way to warm up the chestnut's energy and internalize it. I would also recommend carrying a chestnut as an antighost charm or part of a power pouch to help maintain and improve health.

CHRYSANTHEMUM

THEMES: Fairies, Gardening, Happiness, Longevity, Power, Purity, Spirits.

CORRESPONDENCES: Fire, Sun.

HISTORY AND FOLKLORE: The Chinese regard the chrysanthemum as the flower of immortality, while the Japanese call it the "golden flower" and consider it a blossom of purity, filled with supernatural power. European superstitions tell us that growing chrysanthemums in your garden keeps ghosts away, but attracts the fairy folk. Chrysanthemums in a bouquet represent the ability to stay cheerful even under difficult circumstances.

SAMPLE APPLICATIONS: Chrysanthemum flowers are edible, especially as part of a salad designed to encourage happiness or increase magickal power. If eating flowers isn't your cup of tea, steep the petals for tea instead! The resulting tincture can be dabbed on the windows and doors of your home to safeguard it from ghostly guests. If you want the fairies to help you with your garden, plant chrysanthemums all around the perimeter.

CINNAMON

THEMES: Death, Energy, Love, Passion, Psychism, Purification.

CORRESPONDENCES: Fire, Sun, Venus.

HISTORY AND FOLKLORE: Egyptians used cinnamon as part of embalming procedures. In Hebrew and Chinese tradition, cinnamon was one of the anointing oils and purifying incenses for the temples. The Chinese customs seemed to mirror some of the Egyptians' as well, in that cinnamon was a food for the dead that granted eternal life. Romans used it as a passion enhancer. As an aromatic, cinnamon is said to stimulate energy, appetite, and psychic awareness.

SAMPLE APPLICATIONS: Because of its energetic attitude and the dominion of Venus, modern practitioners often use cinnamon in love spells and potions (it appears in this function in the Middle Ages too). Additionally, because of the implied preservative nature (eternal life), this is an excellent herb to extend the "shelf life" of charged amulets and other magickal tools.

CIRCLE

THEMES: Cycles, Elements (all), Equality, Magick, Reincarnation.

CORRESPONDENCES: Spirit.

HISTORY AND FOLKLORE: In the first century A.D. one name for a magician was "circle drawer." King Arthur's meeting place was a round table to give all participants an equal voice and promote unity, and the Celts often sat in circles during meals for similar reasons. Following suit, witches still meet in circles and sing a song that says, "We are a circle, within a circle, with no beginning and never ending."

SAMPLE APPLICATIONS: Circular objects like marbles and small balls make wonderful components in spellcraft, especially where you want to invoke the attention of all elemental beings, honor the earth, or focus on the cycles in your life. When you sense partiality or prejudice in a situation, use a drawn circle with your name in the middle as an amulet, or put your name and the names of all parties involved around the edge of it.

CLOVER

THEMES: Anti-magick, Love, Luck, Fairies, Psychism.

CORRESPONDENCES: Air, Spring.

HISTORY AND FOLKLORE: In farming lore, clovers in a field represent rich soil. Carrying a two-leaf clover attracts love, a three-leaf clover protects the bearer against witchcraft, and a four-leaf clover brings luck, improves psychism, and allows the bearer to see fairies.

SAMPLE APPLICATIONS: Exchange blossoming clover as part of hand-fasting or marriage rituals to inspire ever deepening love. Do not dispose of them, but carefully press them in your remembrance album to keep love safe. Dried clover flower is a good ingredient to add to luck incense or any spellcraft designed to heighten your psychic awareness. Put clover in your shoes before taking a nature walk and you might just catch a glimpse of the wee folk!

COAL

THEMES: Congeniality, Divination, Luck, Money.

CORRESPONDENCES: Earth.

HISTORY AND FOLKLORE: The magickal use of charcoal was far more pre-dominant back when it was a heating fuel. During the Middle Ages, highly polished canal coal was used to fashion divinatory mirrors and scrying balls. In English tradition, finding a piece of coal portended good fortune or financial improvements, and people often carried a piece for luck especially in matters where congeniality was required from authority figures.

SAMPLE APPLICATIONS: Untreated hard coal is not easy to find these days (most have had chemicals added to improve burning). If you want a piece, I'd suggest trying a rock and mineral show or calling the geology department of any nearby college for assistance. Lapidaries in your region may be able to help too. Once you obtain some, it can be pow-dered and applied to the surface of a scrying mirror or kept whole and used as a charm to attract luck and money.

COFFEE

THEMES: Conscious Mind, Energy, Hospitality.

CORRESPONDENCES: Fire.

HISTORY AND FOLKLORE: There is evidence that the Aztec and Incan people both revered coffee and used it in their observances. Written history shows coffee appearing in the religious observances of the whirling dervishes in A.D. 1000. Here and in much of Arabic society, coffee was a sacred beverage shared with guests in a circle as a sign of hospitality, something that continues even in Westerners' homes today!

SAMPLE APPLICATIONS: Considering how much many of us value our morning cup of coffee, it may well be that this constitutes a magickal ritual to which we only need add some willpower and purpose. Stir clockwise to draw in positive energy, so you'll be alert and aware all day, or to encourage an ambiance of welcome wherever you go. Stir counter-clockwise to throw off negativity. Add other flavorings (spices, flavored creamers, etc.) that symbolically represent your goal or add milk to balance the conscious mind with lunar/goddess-centered thoughts.

COINS

THEMES: Choices, Divination, Luck, Money, Safety, Travel, Wishcraft.

CORRESPONDENCES: Earth, Moon (silver coins), Sun (gold coins).

HISTORY AND FOLKLORE: Many ancient peoples, including the Egyptians, buried their dead with coins so they could pay their way in the afterlife. Romans got a little more creative and used coins for lot divination, a system we still see today with minor changes such as "flipping a coin." In the tarot, coins represent temporal matters (work, money, etc.). Burying a silver or gold one beneath your doorway is supposed to bring money into the home, as does turning a pocketed coin by the new moon. A coin attached to any vehicle is said to keep it safe no matter how inclement the weather. Finding a coin with your birth year on it brings luck.

SAMPLE APPLICATIONS: Anytime you have a difficult decision to make, bless and energize a special coin (perhaps one that was fashioned in the same country as your magickal Path; for example, if you like the Celtic folk magick you might want to get a Scottish or Irish coin) and carry it with you. Each time you think of the choice you have to make, touch the coin to give yourself focus. Alternatively, keep a small-change jar in your house specifically for wish magick. Toss a coin into any public fountain with your wish. This purportedly appeases the indwelling water spirits, who will react kindly to the gesture and help manifest your desire.

COPPER

THEMES: Focus, Health, Protection, Spirits.

CORRESPONDENCES: Aphrodite, Astarte, Fire, Sun, Water (less common).

HISTORY AND FOLKLORE: In earlier times, copper was one of the metals considered suitable for fashioning ritual tools. Babylonians said it was sacred to their fire god, and many other shamanic traditions placed it under the sun's dominion due to its color. The only exception was among lake-dwelling Native Americans who felt it was given by a water god. In the Middle Ages, it was common to wear copper to ward off evil spirits, while today it is worn to augment healing or focus energy flows.

SAMPLE APPLICATIONS: Some practitioners like to use a copper wand to guide energy, since it's a natural conductor. Also, whenever you want to keep magickal energy with you, tuck a small piece of copper in your pocket so the conductive power is directed inward (note: hardware stores sell copper wire, which is small and bendable and can be fashioned into a symbol of your desire). Or buy a length of wire long enough to lay around the perimeter of your living space (beneath the earth) to ground negativity and keep wandering spirits away.

CORAL

THEMES: Anti-magick, Clarity, Conscious Mind, Dreams, Fertility, Health, Longevity, Luck, Peace, Sleep.

CORRESPONDENCES: The Goddess Aspect, Water (except for fire coral).

HISTORY AND FOLKLORE: In China and among the Hindus coral is one natural formation thought suitable for decorating sacred sculptures. Arab tradition says it grants longevity as long as it remains unbroken, Persians and Greeks alike hung it in fruit trees to increase yields, and Oceanic civilizations attributed it to the mother goddess. In many of these regions wearing coral acts as an anti-magick charm, and one that hones the conscious mind for fighting against things like fascination (charm). Albertus Magnus (1200–1280) seemed to agree when he recommended it for wisdom and to cure madness.

SAMPLE APPLICATIONS: Hanging or displaying a piece of coral in one's home quiets discord, and if attached specifically to the bed, it keeps nightmares away and inspires a restful night's sleep. Rubbed against an afflicted part of the body, coral helps balance the auric field and wash away negativity like the waves from which it comes. For best results, return the coral to flowing water after it's been used magickally for this purpose.

Coral is still often carried by dancers for luck, so if you want to step lively, give it a try! Alternatively, carry or wear coral when casting spells that are designed to augment mental clarity.

CORN

THEMES: Abundance, Blessing, Cycles, Luck, Providence.

CORRESPONDENCES: Autumn, Demeter, Fides, Fire, Mithra, Saturn, Spirit.

HISTORY AND FOLKLORE: Corn was so important to the New World ancients that they often personified it as a god or goddess, for example, the Corn Maiden. In numerous settings as diverse as ancient Russia and Victorian America, the last sheaf of corn was often carefully harvested and kept from one year to the next to ensure continued abundance, providence, and blessings to the land and its people. While in the home, this sheaf brings improved luck.

SAMPLE APPLICATIONS: You can often hear a song at modern magick gatherings that includes the verse, "Corn and grain, all that falls shall rise again." This, in simple form, shows how corn's planting and harvesting cycle is a microcosm of the cycles in all things, which affect us so deeply. Scatter corn around the perimeter of the sacred space during harvest rites or when you have a pressing need that can be answered by nature's bounty. It's also easy to internalize corn's energy by eating it steamed or baked into bread. For extra sweet blessings drizzle honey on the bread.

COSTUME

THEMES: Communion, Dance, Divination, Elementals, Focus, Glamoury, Insight, Spirits.

CORRESPONDENCES: Vary by costume; Spirit.

HISTORY AND FOLKLORE: In tribal settings, in particular, masks and costumes served very important ritual functions. First, they helped practitioners separate themselves from the temporal world and commune with a specific spirit (the one symbolized by the costume). Second, for participants it transformed the wearer from a familiar face to the image of a god, goddess, spirit, or deva (elemental spirit) being venerated. This helped focus the attention of everyone gathered on the purpose of the rite.

The number of societies in which costumes and masks appear are amazingly diverse, from Oceanic groups to Native Americans. In many of these settings we find costumes combined with sacred dancing that's intended to concentrate the awareness of the dancer on divination or communion with helpful spirits, particularly to discern the cure for a sickness or the solution to a pressing community problem like drought.

SAMPLE APPLICATIONS: Clothes change the way you feel and behave. In a ritual setting this can create enough of a transition that it helps you reach higher meditative states and better direct the magick created. Simply choose a costume that honors the powers you're calling on or somehow represents the purpose for your efforts. As you don the clothing, likewise "put on" the cloak of magick in your attitude and demeanor.

Glamoury—the art of shifting auric energies for specific external effects—in particular benefits from the use of costumes, often made from everyday clothing. The idea behind glamoury is to accent specific positives: leadership qualities, beauty, charisma, and so on. We do this by shifting our auric fields so they vibrate on the same keynote as the quality we want to magnify. One easy way to do this is by dressing the part so the visual impact is as strong as the atmosphere you're producing aurically.

CROSS

THEMES: Astral Realm, Balance, Banishing, Choices, Death, Elements, Fertility, Focus, Goals, Protection, Weather Magick.

CORRESPONDENCES: Air (eastern arm), Earth (northern arm), Fire (southern arm), Frey, Hecate, Indra, Spirit (center), Water (western arm).

HISTORY AND FOLKLORE: Nearly four hundred different varieties of cross motifs appear around the world, some on altars, others on art, others in processionals, and still others in the legends of the gods themselves. Crosses mark important locations, and they draw our attention to a central point (focus and balance). They became the foundation for weather vanes and were often used magickally for calling the winds.

In India, Buddhist tradition tells us that the cross represents the sacred fires of creation, making it both male and female. For Hindus, it is sacred to Indra and often used to encourage fertility. Mexican sorcerers (and others) use the cross to represent the four corners of creation. Northern Europeans attribute an equidistant cross emblem to the god Frey, while Greek tradition personifies Hecate as the goddess of crossroads (the meeting place between this world and the next). To this day we use the phrase "at a crossroad" to symbolize decisions, and the cross is still considered a protective amulet.

SAMPLE APPLICATIONS: I personally like using crosses for goal-oriented magick because they allow us to "mark" the target and help with focusing on that target. In this case putting a symbol of your goal in the center of an equidistant cross works well in conjunction with an incantation. Alternatively, crossing something out is a common symbol for banishing in our culture, so we can use it to "cross out" energies we don't want. Mindfully carving equilateral crosses or drawing them on an object invokes the protective energies of the elements on that object. When you have a difficult choice to make, visualize yourself at a crossroad marked with those choices. Look down each avenue to better understand where each will take you, then move toward the one that's most positive and life-affirming.

CROW (RAVEN)

THEMES: Change, Clarity, Communication, Faithfulness, Law, Love, Messages, Perspective, Prophecy, Shapeshifting.

CORRESPONDENCES: Air, Apollo, Athena, Odin.

HISTORY AND FOLKLORE: Egyptians considered the crow a symbol of a happy marriage. In Greek tradition, this bird was sacred to both Apollo and Athena, which may be why it appeared as part of augury. The Japanese mirrored this custom, considering the crow a messenger for the Divine, while the Celts attributed crows to Odin as messengers. Medieval bestiaries say crows are soothsayers and also represent love and loyalty because of their highly devoted parenting. In Native American myths, crows protect sacred laws, and they symbolize transformation (shapeshifting) and prophecy.

SAMPLE APPLICATIONS: Crows are very watchful creatures. By learning from them we can begin to see things in our life with greater clarity (the bird's-eye view, if you will), and our spiritual vision will also broaden. Carry crow images or a found crow feather (taking one is considered spiritually "rude") to augment any of its attributes in your life. Alternatively, go to a place where crows fly and reach out to that spiritual essence. Fly on the crow's wings and gain perspective for the past, present, or future.

DAISY

THEMES: Divination, Happiness, Purity, Wishcraft, Youthfulness.

CORRESPONDENCES: Fire, Summer, Sun, Thor, Zeus.

HISTORY AND FOLKLORE: This simple edible flower gets its name from a combination of two words—"day's eye"—because it turns its face to follow the sun's movement through the sky (which also gives it associations with the sun and fire). In a similar vein, the ancients often associated daisies with thunder (storm) gods and may have offered them as invocatory blossoms.

Victorian custom had it that once seven daisies gather beneath your footsteps, summer has officially arrived. It is perhaps for this reason that it became a traditional midsummer decoration. In the language of flowers, the daisy represents youth's innocence and purity, while dreaming of a field of daisies portends joy.

SAMPLE APPLICATIONS: Because of the folk name Moon Daisy, some practitioners use this flower as a water/lunar symbol or component. Even so, it seems more customary to put it under the sun's dominion, which is how I've categorized it. Use daisies to decorate spring and summer altars to honor the sun. Keep fresh bouquets in the house during storm months to keep the thunder gods happy. Wear a daisy to better understand your inner child and let him or her out to play once in a while. Put daisies under your pillow to dream about loves present, past, or future.

DANCE

THEMES: Communion, Community, Friendship, Insight, Kinship, Manifestation, Power, Prophecy, Spirits, Vision, Worship.

CORRESPONDENCES: Vary by intention.

HISTORY AND FOLKLORE: The expressive nature of dancing found its way into hundreds of ancient rituals including those for courtship, friendship, cooperation, crop growth/abundance, successful hunting expeditions, spirit communion (animal and otherwise), healing, divination (ecstatic dance), and victory. In his 1920 study of sacred dancing, W. O. E. Osterly attributes this amazing diversity and prevalence to emotional expression and the desire to use the resulting energy to alter one's perceptions and way of interpreting the world or the cosmos. In the words of a New Guinean shaman, "Dancing makes spirits rejoice."

SAMPLE APPLICATIONS: The movements of a magickal dance symbolize our inner intentions manifested outwardly. Each motion unites body and spirit to generate energy that supports our goals. Sacred dances need not take any form other than what you feel inspired to do. As an old African saying goes, "If you can walk, you can dance." Simply let some suitable music or drumming vibrate through you and move you. Sacred dancing eventually reaches a pinnacle at which you either perform your spell/divination, release the power created toward the goal, release the energy to the Sacred Power being venerated, or open yourself to receiving information from the spirits via communion. After this, the dance slows so you gently return to normal awareness. Clockwise dances raise positive power. Counterclockwise ones decrease or banish specific types of energy.

DANDELION

THEMES: Anti-magick, Divination, Fairies, Happiness, Health, Psychism, Spirits, Wishcraft.

CORRESPONDENCES: Air (leaves or head gone to seed), Fire (the golden blossom), Hecate.

HISTORY AND FOLKLORE: Rural American folklore says that dandelions foretell the weather. If they remain closed, it will rain. Blowing on the head of a dandelion gone to seed is also a form of divination, often done to determine how many children people will have or when they will marry. European beliefs instruct us to gather dandelions on Mid-summer's Day and rub them on our skin for health and protection from magick. Seeing blossoming dandelions in a dream foretells of joyful friendships and/or other relationships.

SAMPLE APPLICATIONS: Dandelions represent oracles in the language of flowers, making them an excellent addition to psychic diets (the leaves make excellent salads and the flower heads make a lovely wine). The dried head of a dandelion is often used today as a way of asking the sylphs (air spirits) for assistance in manifesting a specific wish. Voice the wish just prior to blowing on the top of the seeds and releasing them to the winds.

DICE

THEMES: Divination, Luck.

CORRESPONDENCES: Earth.

HISTORY AND FOLKLORE: Dice originated at least as early as 1200 B.C.E. in Greece, and possibly earlier in other regions, considering their use in Tibetan, Egyptian, Babylonian, and Assyrian divination methods. Dreaming of a trusted companion throwing dice means that person may prove unfaithful or reckless with your trust. The modern phrase "the luck of the dice" shows that their connection to both divination and luck magick has remained.

SAMPLE APPLICATIONS: I have often found it interesting that people hang stuffed dice from the rearview mirror of the car and can't help but wonder if this has to do with the fortunate connotation they bear. Dice make a handy, portable good-luck charm (I suggest keeping one set aside for this purpose). They also make for easy divination efforts. Think of a question and roll a die. One is a good sign, two is bad, three indicates the need for caution, four suggests that you're not seeing all your options, five says things will get better slowly, and six says move forward confidently. Neat idea: go to a game supply shop, get unique dice like those for role-playing games, and design your own divination system/kit! Refer to any book on numerology for more insights into the potential meanings of the higher numbers.

DILL

THEMES: Anti-magick, Love, Money, Protection, Strength.

CORRESPONDENCES: Earth (seeds), Fire.

HISTORY AND FOLKLORE: Dill had an odd reputation of being an herb both repulsive to witches and used readily by them! In the former case, it seems to turn only negative magick. Romans used the aroma of dill to inspire strength, Greeks used dill seeds as a form of currency, and in France and Spain people carried dill as a overall protective measure. During the Middle Ages cunning folk sometimes added dill to love potions.

SAMPLE APPLICATIONS: One of my favorite uses for dill is in baking bread for a gathering or for sharing among friends. If possible, do this during a waxing-to-full moon, so when eaten, the bread brings everyone vitality, prosperity, and love. Put a sprig of dill in your shoe to keep your funds under tight control (the symbolism here being keeping them well rooted and your spending habits grounded). Hang dill in any area of the home where you don't want random spiritual influences (if you like the aroma, try a sunny window so the warmth releases the scent).

DOG

THEMES: Awareness (alertness), Faithfulness, Friendship, Protection, Psychism, Wisdom.

CORRESPONDENCES: Artemis, Astarte, Fire, Moon.

HISTORY AND FOLKLORE: The dog, one of the first animal companions to humankind, is still known as "man's best friend," and the myths and lore surrounding dogs are plentiful and oddly divergent. For example, although some stories call dogs a fire bringer, others associate them with lunar gods and goddesses such as Artemis. Egyptians venerated dogs as an aspect of Anubis, thus having protective power. This symbolism was mirrored in Rome, where dog images guarded many buildings, and in ancient Persia, where dogs represented wisdom and devotion. Plutarch says dogs represent faithfulness and awareness, while old wives' tales claim they are psychic and can sense spirits.

SAMPLE APPLICATIONS: An old Hittite spell for protection is well worth trying. Find a candle shaped like a dog and put it on a windowsill facing the window. As you light it at nightfall say something like, "Just as your fellows do not allow danger into my home by day, guard against all evil and mal-intent by night." Make sure it isn't too close to curtains and have a bowl of water beneath it for safety reasons; then let it burn all night. (Note: a glass-contained candle with a picture of a dog on it works just as well.) You can repeat this spell anytime you feel the need. Alternatively, place carvings or images of dogs in the four corners of your living space (pick images of the right elemental color).

DOLPHIN

THEMES: Arts, Creativity, Cycles, Guidance, Manifestation, Omens, Prophecy.

CORRESPONDENCES: Aphrodite, Apollo, Isis, Water.

HISTORY AND FOLKLORE: Oceanic tradition and Native American myths both say that dolphins are guides to souls as they move from one life to the next. It is the sacred animal for Aphrodite, Isis, and Apollo, giving the dolphin connections with inventiveness and the arts. Additionally, the word *Delphi* comes from the name Apollo Delphinos, so dolphins are considered prophetic messengers especially in connection with weather changes. Finally, because the dolphin must breach the surface to obtain oxygen, it represents the ongoing energy of life in all its ups and downs.

SAMPLE APPLICATIONS: If you are of the shamanic persuasion, you might wish to commune with the dolphin spirit anytime you need guidance on pressing spiritual matters, especially those that focus on life's routine or cycles. Carrying a carving of a dolphin or small statue (available at nearly any good-sized gift shop these days) inspires creativity. It's an excellent symbol for any artist to keep around the house to overcome blockages and motivate free-flowing imagination.

DOOR/THRESHOLD

THEMES: Choices, Hospitality, Love, Luck, Opportunity, Protection.

CORRESPONDENCES: Janus.

HISTORY AND FOLKLORE: Because of the obvious symbolism of opening and closing, doors and thresholds found their way into hundreds of folk traditions. Charms and prayers were often offered at the threshold of a home to keep it safe or inspire luck for all who dwelled within. For example, to inspire good fortune, always come in through the same door by which you left; to inspire love, bury a braid of your and your lover's hair beneath the threshold (rural United States). To keep a ghost from haunting the home in which it died, open the door after that person's death (England, Ireland, Scotland). Today, the phrase "open-door policy" reflects the door's value as a symbol of welcome and hospitality.

SAMPLE APPLICATIONS: Janus is the gatekeeper who sees forward and backward at all times. This makes any doorway an excellent place to perform magick intended to help with decision making. Or when you need a specific type of energy, go to your door, open it, and welcome that energy inside your home. The reverse is true here too. Take a symbol of what you wish to banish and toss it outside, neatly closing the door on that negativity. To keep guests from arriving at an inopportune time, salt your threshold (just sweep it up afterward when you want company again).

DRUM

THEMES: Dance, Divination, Elements, Energy, Fertility, Focus, Meditation, Messages, Protection, Sexuality, Unity.

CORRESPONDENCES: Earth (note, however, that the sound of the drum may alter this correspondence), Spirit, Winter (China).

HISTORY AND FOLKLORE: Drums are among the most common musical instruments used in religious settings. The sound of a drum repels evil or conveys a message. The surface of a drum symbolizes the sacred circle, and it can become a tool for divination. The sound focuses shamans for their otherworldly journeys (goals vary) and helps witches raise energy. Drums are a common feature in sacred dances to help the dancer achieve altered awareness, and their rhythm often represents fertility or amplified sexuality. Some ancient people even felt that drums could house spirits and offered them rum or other gifts by way of appeasement.

SAMPLE APPLICATIONS: There seems to be a drum revival going on in modern magickal circles these days that is part of the reawakening of what I call the tribal soul. Something about the sound of a drum draws us together, it calls to us with a message of unity even as the circle does, and it is a very effective magickal tool for focus (you don't have to be a great musician to pound out a beat, increase that beat to build energy, then stop to release what you've created).

Making a formal drum is very time-consuming, but serviceable ones can be fashioned from pots, plastic food containers (covered and filled with different levels of water to create varying tones), and the like. Otherwise, watch for a well-made drum in your price range and decorate it with items that magickally mark it as your tool. In using a drum, learn how to blend its voice with your own for best results (you'll find this comes quite naturally when you're in a trance or deep meditative state).

EGG

THEMES: Beauty, Divination, Fertility, Luck, Offering.

CORRESPONDENCES: Earth.

HISTORY AND FOLKLORE: In the world's folklore, the egg had great power and symbolic value. It was from the cosmic egg, for example, that all creation sprang forth. Some writings use an egg to represent the earth or the germ of life itself.

In some European traditions, when one enters a new home, one should break an egg on the threshold as an offering to the house spirit. Similarly, the Maori, Romans, and Slavic peoples buried their dead with eggs as an offering suited for the voyage to the afterlife (the egg was often placed in the navel).

The Romans felt that the shells from any eggs they ate should be completely destroyed, lest a wizard use the remains in a spell against them. In France, eggs were used in magick to ensure a woman's fertility. In Scotland, divination by eggs was quite common, especially on Midsummer's Day and Halloween, and dreaming of broken eggs represents a quarrel, while whole ones are lucky.

SAMPLE APPLICATIONS: You might consider eating eggs as part of a prophetic diet (if you scramble them you can scry the results!) or to improve the fertility of any undertaking. Carry an egg with you for an entire day when you're under the weather, then break it into the earth to break apart the negative energy of sickness. Since beaten eggs make a natural skin toner, try them as part of beauty glamouries, or add an aromatic oil to the blend to better suit the magick at hand.

ELDER

THEMES: Anti-magick, Blessing, Faithfulness, Kindness, Protection, Safety.

CORRESPONDENCES: The Goddess Aspect (flowers), Water.

HISTORY AND FOLKLORE: The Scottish hang elder leaves and branches over their windows or doors to keep the home safe from evil influences. In Russia and the United States the same keeps witches and magick at bay. In the language of flowers, the elder represents compassion, and elder flowers were sometimes scattered at wedding ceremonies to ensure the couple's fealty.

SAMPLE APPLICATIONS: Magick tradition has it that if you gather elder at midnight on April 30 (Beltane eve), it will be more powerful for any workings you use it for. A base of ground elder wood and dried flowers is excellent for goddess incense. Burning this will release the elder's energies into the sacred space or home and honor whatever image of the goddess you follow.

FEATHER

THEMES: Balance, Communication, Divination, Freedom, Glamoury, Omens, Perspective, Strength.

CORRESPONDENCES: Air (other correspondences may be determined by the color of the feather and bird from which it came; for example, an owl feather is sacred to Athena and represents truthfulness).

HISTORY AND FOLKLORE: The earliest uses for feathers were as fetishes for numerous purposes, but often to help connect with a bird totem for perspective. The Greeks developed a complex system of divination based on found feathers (the color, type, and position of the feather all were factors in interpretation). In fact, this was an offshoot of a larger system, auspice, or bird augury. Since the first pens were made from large feathers, there's a strong connection here for using them to symbolize communication and strength. In dream imagery, feathers falling around you denote a life of ease and, by extension, freedom.

SAMPLE APPLICATIONS: Modern magick practitioners often use a feather to disperse incense around the sacred space, to "comb" the auric envelope into balance, or infuse one's personal atmosphere with a specific energy (glamoury). Beyond this, they often appear on or in power pouches, magickal wands, staffs, robes, and other traditional paraphernalia usually to represent the air element in some way. Consider using an old-fashioned quill pen when working on your spellbook or when you need to communicate an idea more effectively and responsibly.

FENNEL

THEMES: Clarity, Insight, Psychism, Purification, Vision.

CORRESPONDENCES: Dionysus, Fire.

HISTORY AND FOLKLORE: Greek legends tell us that fennel bore the spark of fire to earth from Olympus. It was burned in this region during rituals for Dionysus and as a temple purifier. Among folk remedies, it's an herb applied to improve eyesight, which extends metaphysically into the realm of visions and psychism.

SAMPLE APPLICATIONS: Add fennel into your diet just before a spiritual fast to help purify your body, mind, and spirit. Then, when meditating and studying, burn some as part of an incense to improve your spiritual vision and understanding. Nibble a little fennel when you want to speak with clarity and insight.

FIG

THEMES: Awareness, Fertility, Knowledge, Peace; Sexuality, Spirituality, Strength, Wisdom.

CORRESPONDENCES: Dionysus, Fire, Juno, Mithra.

HISTORY AND FOLKLORE: In Islamic tradition figs are sacred as a fruit favored by Muhammad. In Buddhist stories Gautama found enlightenment under the fig tree. Other cultures often depict the fig tree as a knowledge-giver akin to the tree of life. Hebrews considered figs an emblem of peace. Romans held them as sacred to Juno, while the Greeks attributed them to Dionysus and ate the fruit for strength and virility. Seeing figs growing in a dream portends health.

SAMPLE APPLICATIONS: In modern tradition we see figs used most frequently as part of special diets designed to help the spiritual seeker attain deeper insights into his or her Path. Additionally, people might eat figs before spellcraft or rituals to heighten spiritual awareness and the ability to seek wisdom in what they're experiencing. Dried figs can also be carried as a handy magickal charm. Nibble a bite for any of its attributes you wish to internalize.

FINGERNAILS

THEMES: Love, Omens, Power.

CORRESPONDENCES: Earth (physical plane).

HISTORY AND FOLKLORE: Common folklore claims that white spots appearing on your thumbnail mean a gift is coming, on the forefinger they're an omen of friendship, and on the ring finger they portend a message from a lover. If you cut this same nail on Monday you'll hasten the arrival of the news. By far, the most common applications for fingernails in ancient spells was for love charms, but this practice has gone somewhat by the wayside in the interest of nonmanipulation.

SAMPLE APPLICATIONS: It used to be customary to carefully gather nail clippings and save them for spells or burn them, lest another witch use them for ill gain. Modern practitioners continue to sometimes add their own nail clippings to personal power pouches or spell component blends.

The addition of fingernail cuttings to magickal mixtures increases the personal keynote in that effort and therefore amplifies power.

FIRE

THEMES: Clarity, Comprehension, Conscious Mind, Divination, Energy, Focus, Kinship, Motivation, Passion, Protection, Purification, Sexuality.

CORRESPONDENCES: Fire, Hephaestus, Hestia, Lug, South, Spirit, Summer, Sun, Vulcan, Zeus.

HISTORY AND FOLKLORE: The list of deities provided here is terribly short—there are literally hundreds of gods and goddess associated with the fires and the hearth. Perhaps this is why early humans gathered at the fireside (not to mention its protective value), gazed into the fires for insight, and used fire as a cleansing power during times of great duress. Even much later in history, people continued the tradition by way of gathering at ritual fires in a show of common bonds. Today we hear about the fires of passion, cleansing, and spirit and the phrase "put a fire under it" regularly, which helps fire to maintain its ancient symbolic values.

SAMPLE APPLICATIONS: The number of potential applications for fire today is just as diverse (if not more so) than it was in times past. We can burn something in a magickally prepared fire to release its energy (or consume it completely). We can use fire to symbolically shine a light on a situation or to warm a cold shoulder. And we can still gaze into the flame of a fire for visions of the past, present, and future. When you do so, try not to look directly at the flame. Let your vision blur slightly, and then focus on your question. Watch to see how the flame reacts or moves. If it dances joyfully, it's a positive response; dimming is a negative response. If the candle goes out altogether, stop whatever undertaking you asked about immediately; the course you're on isn't a good one and may lead to harm.

FISH

THEMES: Fertility, Miracles, Omens, Prosperity, Providence.

CORRESPONDENCES: Aphrodite, Freyja, Mari, Water.

HISTORY AND FOLKLORE: Among Babylonians, Assyrians, and Phoenicians, the fish was sacred and represented fertility. The Norse ate fish on Friday (the "day of Freyja," a goddess of love) to promote pregnancy! In Welsh tradition and some Oceanic ones, fish are omen bringers. The Christian story of the loaves and the fishes gives this creature strong associations with providence and miracles. Dreaming of catching fish usually means improved prosperity, while swimming with fish symbolizes delving into the mysteries or the intuitive self (water).

SAMPLE APPLICATIONS: Add fish to your diet anytime you want to renew personal virility or as a meat substitute to help augment the insightful, instinctive nature within. For those who are not fond of fish, I recommend a candy substitute (like gummy fish) that you can carry and nibble when you wish to internalize that energy. The sugar in the candy adds "sweetness" to the magick for pleasing results.

FOX

THEMES: Choices, Glamoury, Perspective, Playfulness, Shapeshifting, Wisdom.

CORRESPONDENCES: Dionysus, Moon.

HISTORY AND FOLKLORE: A shapeshifter and playful trickster figure among Native Americans, Japanese, and Chinese, the fox has a somewhat mixed reputation. Europeans appreciated the creature's ability to make swift decisions and considered it wise. The modern term *outfoxed* reminds us it can also represent one's ability to perceive the truth and/or think ahead so as to not fall prey to deception.

SAMPLE APPLICATIONS: If your patron god is Dionysus (who sometimes took the shape of a fox), the fox is a suitable image to have on the altar honoring him. For anyone trying to learn the arts of glamoury or shapeshifting, the fox spirit is an excellent guide. Meditate and visualize the face of a fox slowly transforming from your own, and see how your perceptions change. I also find this meditation helpful anytime I start taking myself too seriously or forgetting how to play. The fox enjoys good fun and can help you rediscover that part of yourself.

FROG

THEMES: Abundance, Fertility, Glamoury, Healing, Prosperity, Shape-shifting, Weather Magick.

CORRESPONDENCES: The Goddess Aspect, Hathor, Isis, Water.

HISTORY AND FOLKLORE: Stories of the frog prince are found throughout Hungary, Norway, Germany, and England, giving the frog associations with shapeshifting and glamoury. Shamans often used frogs as part of healing rituals in which a sickness was transferred to the frog (particularly a cold). This is how the phrase a "frog in your throat" originated. Many cultures regard the frog as a rainmaker and a symbol of fertility or abundance, which is why it was sacred to both Isis and Hathor in Egypt. For the Chinese, frogs represent the archetypal feminine energies (yin) and function as an agent of prosperity.

SAMPLE APPLICATIONS: On the altar a frog is a good symbol to use for the western quarter (I've been successful in finding small frog carvings at New Age shops, science stores, crystal shows, etc., but if you're not so fortunate, a stuffed child's toy will suffice as a focus). Toss a frog-shaped object in water to bring rain or carry it with you to inspire abundance. The frog spirit is also an excellent teacher for those wishing to study the goddess tradition.

GARLIC

THEMES: Courage, Oaths, Protection, Safety, Strength.

CORRESPONDENCES: Fire, Hecate, Muhammad.

HISTORY AND FOLKLORE: The Egyptians so revered this herb that they used it in oath-taking rituals and fed it to the builders of Cheops's pyramid to keep the workers strong. Interestingly enough, Roman soldiers also ate garlic for courage and strength! The herb's potent aroma has given it the reputation of warding off all kinds of evil from vampires to ghosts.

SAMPLE APPLICATIONS: I'm an avid garlic devotee. If you enjoy the flavor, you can add garlic to any protective diet or one to improve personal vitality. Those who have Hecate as a patroness (she is a favored goddess among witches) can plant a clove of garlic at a crossroads as a suitable way to honor her (especially at midnight, which is the figurative crossroad between night and day).

GERANIUM

THEMES: Omens, Protection.

CORRESPONDENCES: Water (may vary with scent).

HISTORY AND FOLKLORE: An old Muslim folktale says that geraniums were created when Muhammad tossed a shirt over a mallow plant to dry. In the language of flowers, it represents an expected meeting. This may be why some ancient witches planted it near the home to foretell the coming of guests. Placing a geranium plant in your window is said to keep insects out of the house.

SAMPLE APPLICATIONS: I'd be tempted to plant blessed geraniums near my doorway to keep out "insects" of the human variety! Note that the geranium petals are edible, so you can steep them in juice or wine to release their energies into the beverage. Since geraniums have various scents (lemon, nutmeg, mint), you can potentially apply the magickal association of their scent to the process at hand. For example, lemon has associations with love, so lemon geranium petals would be an apt component to protect a relationship!

GINGER

THEMES: Communion, Energy, Healing, Love, Offering.

CORRESPONDENCES: Fire.

HISTORY AND FOLKLORE: In the Far East, ginger was used regularly as an offering to help the practitioner commune with the gods. In Melanesia it's a love-producing herb, while in the Philippines it's used to drive away the spirit of sickness. This last idea seems to have translated into other settings, specifically various folk remedies, some of which have proven effective (such as ginger for settling the stomach).

SAMPLE APPLICATIONS: As a zesty spice, ginger adds energy to almost any magickal effort. Drink ginger ale, eat gingerbread cookies, or nibble candied ginger to give yourself an energy boost or to internalize any of ginger's attributes. Heighten other culinary magick by using ginger oil for frying (slice ginger and put it in a bottle of good-quality olive oil in a dark, airtight container). Consider adding ginger to meditative incense for reconnecting with the Sacred or to one designed to increase loving vibrations in and around your home.

GOLD

THEMES: Blessing, Conscious Mind, Control, Happiness, Healing, Leadership, Money, Power, Purity, Wisdom.

CORRESPONDENCES: Fire, the God Aspect, Mithra, South, Sun.

HISTORY AND FOLKLORE: Both the Druids and herbalists of the Middle Ages gathered herbs with a golden tool to honor the plants' sacredness. Folktales talk about chasing after golden geese or other fabulous creatures (such as leprechauns) as an allegory for foolishness. Some people thought gold was a curative, either by consuming it or making it into a suitable amulet, while others felt you could find it in southern streams.

SAMPLE APPLICATIONS: As a metal ruled by the sun, gold confers upon the wearer the sun's blessings, including those of joy, awareness, self-control, authority, and sagacity. It's always been considered a "pure" substance, which is why it appeared on altars and in crowns alike (the latter alludes to a leader's connection with the Divine). Since gold is very costly today, I recommend adding it into your home and wardrobe symbolically (gold-toned fabric, decorations, and the like). A gold-colored candle on your altar is a suitable representation of the god aspect (especially when lit), and if you have Mithra as a patron it is doubly appropriate.

GRAPES

THEMES: Dreams, Fertility, Manifestation, Prosperity, Success.

CORRESPONDENCES: Bacchus, Dionysus, Moon, Water.

HISTORY AND FOLKLORE: Eating grapes purportedly inspires visionary dreams and physical fertility. In fact, Romans kept grapes in the garden specifically to aid with conception. In a dream itself, seeing grapes growing represents your capacity to help fulfill someone else's needs or hopes and achieve personal success.

SAMPLE APPLICATIONS: If you don't really want to conceive, but could use some financial improvements, hang grapes near the area where you balance your checkbook. The number in a bundle symbolically accents energies for abundance. Nibble a few as you work or before you go to bed to receive a dream of how to manifest prosperity. (*See also* Wine.)

GREEN

THEMES: Fairies, Gardening, Growth, Healing, Money, Potential, Youthfulness.

CORRESPONDENCES: Earth, Spring.

HISTORY AND FOLKLORE: The ancients associated green with the energy of growth, as shown in the natural world all around us. Today we also associate this color with money, and the phrase "being green" with youthful outlooks and ecological awareness. Auric healers tell us that green light seems to help the body's natural healing process.

SAMPLE APPLICATIONS: Add green into your wardrobe or living environment whenever you want to work more closely with nature, accent personal growth, attract money, or make yourself more aware of the potential all around you. To increase the effect, do this on Wednesday or the fifth of a month, as these two times are sympathetically aligned with this hue. For anyone born under the sign of Cancer, wearing green is lucky.

HAIR

THEMES: Money, Love, Power, Protection, Unity.

CORRESPONDENCES: Vary by color and personality of bearer.

HISTORY AND FOLKLORE: Tying red ribbons into one's hair is an old shamanic amulet of protection. Similar traditions appear in China, especially to safeguard children. Old wives' tales claim magicians' power lies in their hair—a story that may have connections with Samson. Ancient cunning folk sometimes snitched bits of hair from rivals to gain power over them, in Asia hair was valuable enough to use as money, and in Victorian America young lovers often exchanged a braided lock of hair as a symbol of unity and love.

SAMPLE APPLICATIONS: If you have long hair, clip it up before enacting a magickal procedure and release it with the magick (especially a spell or ritual for prosperity). This increases the power created. Keep a snippet of hair with any personal magickal tool to help key it to your energy signature. Braiding a length of your hair with one from your significant other is a potent spell for unity (be sure the person knows why you're doing this). Keep the braid in a safe place to protect the relationship from outside negative influences.

HAWK

THEMES: Awareness, Clarity, Comprehension, Messages, Omens, Perspective, Reincarnation, Vision.

CORRESPONDENCES: Apollo, Horus, Jupiter, Ra, Sun.

HISTORY AND FOLKLORE: The ancient Egyptians regarded the hawk as a representative of Horus. Images of hawks adorned temples of the sun god and often symbolized the soul in its movement from one life to the next. Romans felt the bird was sacred to Jupiter, and it was revered for its keen sight and awareness. Greeks placed the hawk under Apollo's control, and as such it was a harbinger of his messages. In Persian tales, a great hawk brought the sacred beverage soma to people, an elixir thought to ensure prosperity, longevity, victory, and friendship.

SAMPLE APPLICATIONS: I have found some very nice pieces of jewelry (mainly necklaces) with hawk heads or hawks in flight that can be added to magickal wardrobes for vision and perspective. If you should find a hawk's feather, it is a message from the Divine to be aware (or that you will soon discover your alertness improving). Carry it as a charm or keep it safely with your magickal tools. It works well for dispersing incense around the sacred space, so that your understanding of magickal truths is always clear.

HAWTHORN

THEMES: Anti-magick, Fairies, Hope, Protection.

CORRESPONDENCES: Fire.

HISTORY AND FOLKLORE: Greeks and Romans alike used hawthorn flowers as part of wedding ceremonies to symbolize hope and to protect the couple from malicious magick. Carrying hawthorn protects the bearer from wandering ghosts and storms (England). Where it grows with oak and ash, there you will find fairies.

SAMPLE APPLICATIONS: Except for Beltane (May Day), one should never purposefully cut hawthorn wood for magickal work, but gather branches that nature brings down. The tree is sacred to the goddess and considered protected. Carrying a twig as you go on nature walks may open the world of the fey to you, and burning this wood in incense inspires both hope and protection.

HEARTH

See Oven.

HEATHER

THEMES: Beauty, Glamoury, Luck, Spirits.

CORRESPONDENCES: Isis, Osiris, Venus, Water.

HISTORY AND FOLKLORE: Old Scottish stories tell us that bathing in heather water beneath a full moon makes one lovely. In other parts of Europe a sprig was carried to increase one's good fortune or burned to invoke spirits. Egyptians felt heather was sacred to both Isis and Osiris.

SAMPLE APPLICATIONS: I'm fond of using heather-scented soap in my shower as part of glamoury spells or anytime I just want to feel more attractive. If you'd like to make some magickal powder to enhance your appearance and inspire better luck, simply add a few drops of heather-scented oil to unscented body powder and apply as desired. Sprinkle a little in your shoes so luck walks with you.

HOLEY STONES

THEMES: Blessing, Healing, Luck, Protection.

CORRESPONDENCES: The Goddess Aspect, Odin, Water.

HISTORY AND FOLKLORE: Because, according to a wonderful Norse myth, Odin turned himself into a worm and burrowed through a rock to steal sacred mead that gave anyone who drank it the gift of eloquence, the simple holed rocks found at the seashore are often called Odin's stones. Folk magick has used them for many purposes over the years. Overall they seem to invoke blessings, luck, protection, and health.

SAMPLE APPLICATIONS: Most practitioners recommend stringing these stones through the hole and wearing them to gain the greatest benefit from the energy. I also like to hang larger ones off a magickal walking staff and smaller ones off wands, so that energy "flows" more smoothly through those tools. For healing, it's suggested that you rub the stone slowly over the ailing area so the negative energy slips into the hole. At this point you should either cleanse the stone in salt water or return it to the sea goddess with a thankful heart.

HOLLY

THEMES: Anti-magick, Dreams, Kinship, Luck, Protection, Unity.

CORRESPONDENCES: Fire, Winter.

HISTORY AND FOLKLORE: This evergreen shrub is magickally paired with ivy in European tradition, as noted in pagan songs like "The Holly and the Ivy." Folklore says this greenery shouldn't enter the house before Yule if you wish to inspire good luck and family unity, and it should leave the house by Twelfth Night. A holly sprig, especially if picked on Yule, protects the bearer from witchery and evil spirits.

SAMPLE APPLICATIONS: Holly makes a lovely addition to the Yule altar and temple. Outdoors it can be used year-round as a potent protection against ill-motivated magick or wicked witchery. In modern Wicca, considered a crone's herb, it is suited to eldership rites and mysteries.

On a less lofty level, put a holly leaf under your pillow during the holiday season to invoke sacred dreams. Plant some around the perimeter of your living space to create a protected sphere of energy. And, should you need a little extra luck, bind a piece of holly in a lucky-colored cloth (your choice) with nine knots and carry it with you (the cloth protects you from the thorns).

HONEY

THEMES: Arts, Creativity, Faithfulness, Fertility, Longevity, Love, Offering, Passion.

CORRESPONDENCES: Air/Fire, Artemis, Demeter, Ra, Sun.

HISTORY AND FOLKLORE: Ancient Egyptians said the first honey was born from the tears of Ra, so it's not surprising to see it used there (and in many other parts of the world) as a suitable offering to the god/dess. Greeks felt honey nurtured longevity, Romans ate it for creativity (to inspire the muse), Hindus saw it as a passion food, and the Celts drank honey wine (mead) as part of wedding rituals for fertility, love, and devotion.

SAMPLE APPLICATIONS: Honey is an excellent sugar substitute in our diets, and it certainly offers a myriad of applications in magickal cooking and brewing. Add honey to a specially chosen tea, drizzle it over a bountiful bread, use it as a basting sauce for meat, or brew it into wine! Better still, since honey is thick, you can draw magickal emblems with it as you add it to various preparations, patterning your magickal goal and then eating the sweet energy!

HORN

THEMES: Abundance, Communication, Messages, Protection, Providence.

CORRESPONDENCES: Moon, Water.

HISTORY AND FOLKLORE: Animal horns (which were the predecessors of metal ones) were once used as cups, so they're a suitable water symbol. In ancient times, the sounding of a horn was thought to scare off evil spirits. It was also used as a signal among watchmen and hunters to communicate positions and conditions. The crescent shape mirrors that of the moon, which may be why magick practitioners often used horns to herald lunar rituals. Finally, the horn of plenty supplies all in need with abundance.

SAMPLE APPLICATIONS: Horns are a lovely addition to the magickal altar, because they are able to hold a plethora of symbolic items while maintaining their own symbolic value. Fill one with a libation or offering, a beverage to share, or flowers! I purchased a Norse-style drinking horn at a gift shop and often see them at secondhand stores. Also, many artisans in historical recreation groups like the Society for Creative Anachronism still make customized horns.

ICE

THEMES: Anger, Binding, Imitative Magick, Memory, Protection.

CORRESPONDENCES: Water.

HISTORY AND FOLKLORE: Folk magicians say that if you write something on the surface of ice, you will never forget it. Currently, ice is a common component in imitative magick and binding spells. Dreaming of ice usually implies being in a risky situation; recall the phrase "on thin ice."

SAMPLE APPLICATIONS: Place a symbolic representation of anything you wish to bind in water and freeze it. For as long as that item remains "on ice," any negativity it bears is bound within (especially anger). Carve the image of anything you want to make "disappear" (debts, excess weight, etc.) out of ice and let it melt. Toss the water outside to throw away that energy. When there's frost on your windows, write your "to do" list on them, so you'll remember it!

INCENSE

THEMES: Divination, Meditation, Offering, Prayer, Purification, Worship.

CORRESPONDENCES: Fire/Earth (may also vary by ingredients).

HISTORY AND FOLKLORE: Ancient people around the world used resins, barks, and other plant parts as incense to honor the gods, to aid in meditation, to purify temples, and to symbolize prayers rising to the heavens. A tablet found in Giza dating to 1530 B.C.E. talks of the religious importance of incense, as do the Bible, Eastern writings, and Roman ceremonial treatises for both state and sacred observances (not to mention its use in the Catholic, Anglican, and Orthodox churches). In many settings where incense was used as part of religious rites, people also performed thurifumia, or divination by observation of incense cast on a ritual fire. In Babylonian texts sandalwood and cedar were favored for this. Outside the religious setting this process is called libranomancy.

SAMPLE APPLICATIONS: Use incense in your magick just as the ancients did. Burn sympathetic aromatics to change the energies in and around the sacred space to mirror those of your intention. Whisper your needs into the smoke of ritual incense, so it carries those desires to the four corners of creation. Anytime your home is a little stressful, burn a cleansing incense (like sage) to deter the negativity.

For divination, take an aromatic that symbolizes your question and place it on a fire source. Watch the smoke as you keep your question in mind. Smoke that rises and moves right is an affirmative answer. Smoke that settles or moves left is negative. Swirling smoke represents uncertain futures; proceed with caution. Interpret any symbols, letters, or images that appear in the smoke as you would ink blots or dream imagery.

INK

THEMES: Communication, Divination, Magick, Manifestation.

CORRESPONDENCES: Water (may vary with color).

HISTORY AND FOLKLORE: Since people who knew how to write were often thought to have a kind of mystical power in earlier times, ink bears the symbolism of magick and communication. Taking this one step further, putting something on paper made it "real" and more tangible for people, so ink also represents manifestation. In ancient times, Persians, Arabs, and Greeks alike used ink as a scrying surface or interpreted ink spillings as having portentous meaning. In the language of dreams, red ink portends troubles ahead.

SAMPLE APPLICATIONS: Scent the ink for your Book of Shadows with aromatics that symbolize the section upon which you're working. Or choose a colored ink that similarly represents the energies being created there. Both these options apply to written spells too! When you write down your goal, it makes it more real to your own mind and therefore helps with manifestation—so write it again and again! Remember those corrective, repetitive writings from your school days? Well, the principle holds in magick too. The more you write it, the easier it becomes to integrate that energy in your life.

IRON

THEMES: Anti-magick, Banishing, Binding, Fairies, Protection, Spirits.

CORRESPONDENCES: Fire.

HISTORY AND FOLKLORE: Throughout the world iron is honored as an anti-magick charm that repels not only spells, but also supernatural entities like ghosts, genies, and fairies. So strong was the belief that many ancient priests and priestesses were forbidden to touch the metal for fear it would drain their magick power.

SAMPLE APPLICATIONS: In rituals or spells meant to deter ghosts, take iron to the person's burial spot. This keeps a restless spirit bound where it lies. Sprinkle iron filings around the sacred space or your home anytime you want to banish negativity, turn away mischievous fairies, or buttress protective measures.

IVY

THEMES: Control, Happiness, Love, Luck, Victory.

CORRESPONDENCES: Bacchus, Dionysus, Osiris, Water/Air (clinging ivy).

HISTORY AND FOLKLORE: Greeks crowned the winners of various games with circlets of ivy and placed it on the heads of married couples. Romans held it as sacred to Bacchus, who also wore it on his head. Considering this association with various wine gods around the country, some people felt it could prevent drunkenness (increase self-control), while others associated it with faithfulness because of the plant's ability to endure difficult environments.

SAMPLE APPLICATIONS: Magickally paired with holly for the most potent love magicks, ivy growing around the home keeps it happy and filled with luck. If you're curious about your love life, tuck nine ivy leaves under your pillow to dream about it. For success throughout the day, carry a fresh ivy leaf with you. Release it back to the earth with thanks at the end of the day (just make sure this is domestic ivy, not the poisonous variety).

JADE

THEMES: Death, Gardening, Luck, Prayer, Spirits, Weather Magick.

CORRESPONDENCES: The God Aspect, Water.

HISTORY AND FOLKLORE: The Chinese prize jade as representing the yang forces of the universe, which may be why this mineral was sometimes fashioned into prayer gongs, given as gifts to newlyweds, and carried or rubbed for good fortune. There and in Mexico, Egypt, and even among Native Americans, pieces of this stone were placed with bodies to protect the spirit of the dead. Tibetans and Burmans sometimes toss it into water to invoke rain or snow. Jade is also often given the attributes of love, victory, power, and wisdom.

SAMPLE APPLICATIONS: For love, look for a piece of jade fashioned into a butterfly, the most traditional form for a charm. Alternatively, if you can find small jade beads, string them into a wind chime, so they can ring out positive vibrations throughout your home. Modern magickal gardeners often swear by jade's ability to improve yield (they bury it around the perimeter of the garden for this purpose—but green jade is best).

KEY

THEMES: Anti-magick, Binding, Leadership, Longevity, Magick, Opportunity, Power, Protection, Spirituality.

CORRESPONDENCES: Athena, Hecate, Ishtar, Spirit.

HISTORY AND FOLKLORE: Keys represent the entryway to the afterlife, which is why many ancient gods and goddesses were associated with keys or had keys as part of their costume. Folklore follows this pattern by giving keys great power, specifically for obtaining magick or finding the path to spiritual awakening. Carrying a key protects against the evil eye (Germany), hanging an iron one in any region acts as an anti-magick charm (Norway), giving one to a child "locks" them into a long life (China), and keys have a sympathetic effect of opening or closing a particular energy, like helping with birth (e.g., Sweden, Rome, Serbia).

SAMPLE APPLICATIONS: In reviewing the spells and lore of keys, it seems "old" keys have more power than new ones. You can often find these at secondhand stores or flea markets. Just take care to cleanse the token once you find one you like (bathe it in salt water or pass it through sage smoke). After that, leave it on your altar to represent an ongoing "open" door that leads to Spirit. Bury an old key as part of a binding spell and carry one to heighten your magickal power, to protect you against unwanted enchantments, or to help create an opportunity. I often hang one off my magickal walking stick, and if you collect several different-sized keys of varying base metals, they can even be made into protective wind chimes.

KNIFE

THEMES: Anti-magick, Divination, Protection.

CORRESPONDENCES: Fire, the God Aspect.

HISTORY AND FOLKLORE: Since some of the first knives were crafted of iron, they were considered a powerful ally against evil magick. Placing one beneath a window or burying one by the door safeguards a home against unwanted intrusions (spiritual or otherwise). Ancient magicians often drew the sacred circle with a ritual knife (athame) and used it to represent the god aspect of the Sacred. Throwing, spinning, or scrying the reflective surface of a knife was sometimes used as a form of divination.

SAMPLE APPLICATIONS: If you have a butter knife in the house, you have a handy magickal tool. You can use this to scribe magickal emblems in the air when calling the circle (or just to attract energy). You can gaze upon its surface like a crystal ball for insights into the past and future. Get some inexpensive knives at a secondhand shop and bury them around your living space for protection (polish them first so they reflect negativity). Keep one special knife for harvesting or chopping magickal herbs used in potions, spells, and rituals. Dip it in salt and rinse it each time you use it, so the tool is always free of residual energy.

KNOTS

THEMES: Binding, Freedom, Healing, Love, Protection, Unity, Weather Magick.

CORRESPONDENCES: Buddha, Earth (especially square knots), Vishnu.

HISTORY AND FOLKLORE: The knot's obvious symbolic value was used regularly by folk magicians for binding spells, especially those to bind sickness and malevolence. The Finnish, Laplanders, Egyptians, and Syrians (among others) all used knotted ropes to invoke or bind wind and rain.

In India, knots are one of the symbols of both Vishnu and Buddha, and knots are tied into newlyweds' clothing to mark their union. This very ancient tradition, which has variants in Rome, Russia, and Europe, is how we come by the phrase "tying the knot" to describe a marriage. Conversely, untying a knot represents a release. Interestingly, the word for *magician* in Russian and Hebrew translates as "knot tier," and in both Indonesian and Aramaic, the word for *amulet* or *charm* is the same as "knot."

SAMPLE APPLICATIONS: The beauty of knot magick lies in its universal symbolic value and simplicity. You can make a knot out of anything from a paper towel to an electrical cord if need be! For example, if you want to bind negative energy, take an old electrical cord, knot it three times, and then dispose of it properly. If you're feeling creative, get a book on knot tying and look at the visual or symbolic value of different kinds of knots. Slip knots, for example, can capture a type of energy and then make it disappear with a quick tug! Fishermen's knots might be tied for bountiful "catches" in a literal or figurative sense, and square knots are the perfect vehicle for earth-centered magick.

LAVA STONE

THEMES: Abundance, Control, Healing, Protection.

CORRESPONDENCES: Fire, Pele.

HISTORY AND FOLKLORE: The magickal use of the lava stone was somewhat limited in ancient times to regions where volcanic activity existed, for example, Hawaii. There, lava stone was sacred to the volcano goddess, Pele, who guarded it jealously. One was not allowed to take a stone without her permission (or without leaving a gift in its place). Once properly obtained, however, the stone brought the goddess's assurance of abundance, health, and protection.

SAMPLE APPLICATIONS: Since lava comes from deep within the earth, it bears a powerful combination of fire and earth energies (fire being predominant). Placing lava stones around you when working magick creates an excellent psychic shield, the fire protecting and the earth holding that protective energy in place. And since the "fire" in this stone has already cooled, it might be a good charm to carry to keep a heated temper or volatile situation under control.

LAVENDER

THEMES: Beauty, Health, Longevity, Love, Manifestation, Peace, Purification, Sleep.

CORRESPONDENCES: Saturn, Summer.

HISTORY AND FOLKLORE: King Solomon sprinkled lavender flowers throughout the temple to purify and perfume it. Early pagans often used lavender as part of midsummer rituals and to promote manifestation. Romans used lavender in their baths for beauty, it was a popular component in the love potions of the Middle Ages, and just smelling lavender is said to increase one's life span.

SAMPLE APPLICATIONS: Add lavender to magickal sachets during the fall months to protect the members of your family from colds, or dab some oil on winter scarves for a similar protective effect. Lavender oil applied to the temples (or flowers added to dream pillows) promotes a restful night's sleep. Place lavender on your summer altar, or give it to a loved one as a magickal token of your affection. To improve the effect, candy some of the flowers and nibble them so love stays sweet!

LEAD

THEMES: Divination, Energy, Protection, Purity, Spellcraft, Spirits.

CORRESPONDENCES: Earth.

HISTORY AND FOLKLORE: In Vedic tradition lead is considered protective against demons and ghosts. Anything placed within a lead box will retain its purity. The Greeks often inscribed spells on lead so the magick would last as long as the metal. Melted lead dripped into water and then observed is an old form of divination.

SAMPLE APPLICATIONS: Considering that lead even keeps Superman's prying eyes away, this might be an excellent component for privacy magick. If you find a lead-lined box (like those of old smoking stands), consider storing your magickal tools and components in it to safeguard the purity of their energy. Add a bit of lead as a component to any magickal procedure (except those items you plan to consume) where you need enduring results (note: use caution; lead is poisonous).

LEAF

THEMES: Anti-magick, Energy, Health, Protection, Spellcraft, Weather Magick.

CORRESPONDENCES: Air/Earth.

HISTORY AND FOLKLORE: Much of the folklore of leaves depends upon the plant from which they originate. In general, folk magicians located specific leaves and then used them as charms, amulets, and divinatory aids. Sometimes spells would be written on a leaf and the leaf burned to release the energy (Europe). Tossing leaves on water brings rain or wind. Catching a falling oak leaf before it hits the ground in autumn protects you from colds (Germany). Binding carefully chosen leaves (those known for protective powers) to the house will keep it safe from magickal influences until the leaves dry.

SAMPLE APPLICATIONS: I see no reason not to follow the Germanic example. Go out to where there are oak trees early in the autumn and try to catch a leaf. If you do, wax it to preserve its protective power (place it inside some waxed paper, wax side down, and iron). If the leaf crumbles at any time, the magick has dissipated. Just release the pieces to the wind with a wish for ongoing health, perhaps by way of an incantation like, "This leaf I found and carried, to earth I now release. May health remain and sickness cease!"

LEMON

THEMES: Faithfulness, Friendship, Imitative Magick, Love, Purification

CORRESPONDENCES: Moon, Water.

HISTORY AND FOLKLORE: In England and Italy lemons were often used as poppets: the name of a person was attached, and whatever was done to the lemon was carried to that individual for boon or bane. During the Middle Ages, lemon flowers represented fidelity, love, and friendship. Because of its astringent value, lemon juice is often part of purification rituals to this day.

SAMPLE APPLICATIONS: If you need to cleanse a component or tool that's not harmed by water, lemon juice and water is an excellent choice. I frequently add lemon rind powder to incense aimed at improving relationships. Finally, a lemon may substitute for a poppet if you don't have time to make one. To use it for this purpose, just treat the lemon in a manner that symbolizes your goal. For example, to safeguard love, put the lemon in a little warm nest somewhere safe. To the nest add images of yourself and your loved one. When the lemon starts to dry out, replace it with a new one so love stays ever fresh (or perhaps use one of the plastic lemons filled with juice for longevity)!

LETTUCE

THEMES: Anxiety, Fertility, Health, Money, Peace.

CORRESPONDENCES: Min, Moon.

HISTORY AND FOLKLORE: Egyptians offered lettuce to the god Min and considered it a symbol of fertility (oddly, some superstitions in England claim just the opposite effect occurs—sterility in women). The emperor Augustus revered wild lettuce because it cured his severe illness once. Some folk remedies recommend lettuce to calm the nerves.

SAMPLE APPLICATIONS: The modern applications for lettuce have changed, most emphasizing its color and leafy nature—specifically as a money-attracting food. Take a nice-sized lettuce leaf and wrap it around a silver coin, saying, "Silver and gold, mine to hold, constraints cease, money increase!" Put this in a dry, safe spot. By the time the lettuce leaf dries, you should begin seeing improvements. At this time, give the coin to a charitable cause to bless someone else.

Anytime you're under undue stress, add a small leafy salad into your diet once a day (perhaps with a creamy dressing to help smooth things over). This is also a good way to connect with lunar energies, both the lettuce and cream-based dressing being associated with the moon.

LODESTONE

THEMES: Energy, Faithfulness, Purity, Sexuality, Strength, Unity.

CORRESPONDENCES: North.

HISTORY AND FOLKLORE: The ancients often gave lodestone to newly married couples to maintain their faithfulness and virtue. Perhaps this is why it's sometimes called the loving stone (China) or kissing stone (India). Alexander the Great provided his troops with pieces of lodestone to protect them from evil spirits and provide strength, and Assyrians rubbed the stone over their bodies to improve sexual performance.

SAMPLE APPLICATIONS: Magickally paired to iron for obvious reasons, lodestone attracts whatever energy you specify through your magickal methods. It's associated with the northern quarter of the magick circle because of the magnet's ability to always point due north. Some magicians recommend anointing your lodestone with linseed oil and burying it in the earth for three days to augment its attractive power. Magnets are suitable gifts to exchange at handfasting or wedding rituals.

The easiest way to use lodestone in your magick is in the form of refrigerator magnets. Find one that represents your desire, and put it on the refrigerator with a piece of paper detailing that desire. Each time you see it, recite your goal out loud until it manifests. Burn the paper afterward with thanks. Alternatively, find a plain magnet, paint it a color that represents your desire, and carry it with you to attract that energy.

LOTUS

THEMES: Balance, Beauty, Congeniality, Creativity, Fertility, Happiness, Law, Longevity, Peace, Prosperity, Purity, Spirituality.

CORRESPONDENCES: The Goddess Aspect, Isis, Lakshmi, Mithra, Osiris, Sun, Vishnu, Water.

HISTORY AND FOLKLORE: Peoples in the Far East consider the lotus the flower of life and a symbol of spiritual laws, fertility, prosperity, joy, longevity, purity, and the goddess's creative force, which may be why its roots are often made into soups or side dishes. Egyptians felt the lotus improved reproductive ability, and they also used it in mummification rituals to please the spirits of the dead. Assyrians also worshiped the flower, connecting it to the sun, as did Egyptians. This connection is seen again in the story of Hercules, who borrowed a golden cup of the sun shaped like a lotus for one of his adventures.

SAMPLE APPLICATIONS: Following Eastern tradition, the most potent time to work with lotus as a component is at dawn, which represents both hope and the light of awareness awakening in the human soul. In verbal or written charms the word *lotus* is a synonym for beauty (blossoming like a lotus, for example), and wearing lotus oil is said to improve one's comeliness within and without. Burning lotus incense is an excellent way to augment your awareness of the goddess and draw her blessings into the sacred space, while keeping the living flower around represents a lovely blend of god and goddess to encourage balance and harmony in your life and home.

MARIGOLD

THEMES: Awareness, Death, Dreams, Fairies, Omens, Vision.

CORRESPONDENCES: Fire, Sun.

HISTORY AND FOLKLORE: Ancient lore says rubbing marigold petals on your eyelids endows you with the gift of vision. In many parts of Wales and England, the marigold's petals are observed as a weather omen (if they're not open by seven, it will rain by eleven). Mexicans use marigolds in rituals for the dead, often sprinkling the petals on walkways to show spirits the way home, while Gypsies carry a marigold if they wish to see the fey.

SAMPLE APPLICATIONS: Some practitioners feel this flower is best gathered when the moon is in Virgo, when the sun is in Leo, or during the month of August to retain the most effectiveness for magick. To inspire visions or augment your spiritual awareness, dice up some marigold petals and add them to scrambled eggs, fried rice, or breads. Make sure you stir this blend clockwise to draw that energy to yourself. Or put some petals under your pillow to bring visionary dreams. Petals from a marigold that remains closed might be used for invocatory rain incense, and marigolds continue to make a suitable decoration for Summerland rituals.

MARJORAM

THEMES: Banishing, Clarity, Conscious Mind, Happiness, Health, Hope, Love, Protection.

CORRESPONDENCES: Air, Aphrodite, Spring.

HISTORY AND FOLKLORE: Greeks said this herb was sacred to Aphrodite, which is why it appeared in wedding rituals. This member of the mint family was nearly indispensable to the medieval apothecary, especially to alleviate melancholy and augment the conscious mind. In England, marjoram tea was considered an excellent spring tonic bearing the hope of the season to the drinker, while Germans used the herb to banish ghosts and other spirits.

SAMPLE APPLICATIONS: During the Middle Ages people often scattered marjoram on the floor to improve the aroma of an area and chase away negativity. Since marjoram is still readily available today, it may hold merit in your home or sacred space as part of a protective ritual or spell.

This is especially true if you feel your relationship with a loved one is in some type of danger.

Drink a cup of marjoram tea (about 1 teaspoon herb to 1 cup water) anytime you need to think more clearly. If you're pondering matters of the heart, add honey or sugar to bring sweetness to that situation. Stir the potion clockwise for positive energy or counterclockwise to turn away any lingering shadows that hinder communications.

MASK

THEMES: Gardening, Health, Imitative Magick, Spirits, Weather Magick, Worship.

CORRESPONDENCES: Vary by goal and imagery.

HISTORY AND FOLKLORE: Masks were utilized around the world as part of magickal procedures for health, spirit worship, imitative magick, weather magick, farming rites, and much more. Effectively the wearer of the mask both honored and became what he or she represented in the ritual, making this a very effective tool for glamoury as well.

SAMPLE APPLICATIONS: The ancients made masks out of many materials ranging from wood and gems to precious metals and plant parts. We can do likewise in making our own masks, so that the final image inspires all the right mental and spiritual responses for effective manifestation. I recommend cardboard as a base medium (it's cheap and readily available). Cut the mask so it represents your intention (like a radiant sun for improved weather). Then wear it while working your magick.

For glamoury, I would suggest visualizing a mask instead of actually making one, primarily because the energy of the visualization can stay with you until you remove it. In this case, rather than assembling the mask part by part physically, you assemble it in your imagination, putting it on your face before going out into whatever situation it's designed for.

MEAD

THEMES: Arts, Communication, Creativity, Divination, Health, Longevity, Offering, Strength, Travel.

CORRESPONDENCES: Odin, Water/Fire (alcohol).

HISTORY AND FOLKLORE: A sacred drink to many cultures, mead adorned altars across the world as a fitting offering to the gods and goddesses. Norse tradition says that mead is given to the soul upon death to ensure everlasting life, and those who drink mead are assured of artistic creativity, eloquence, and divinatory skills. In both Germany and Scotland, mead endowed the drinker with strength, and the Argonauts were thought to pour mead upon the waters to ensure safe travel. During the Middle Ages mead was revered as a health preserver.

SAMPLE APPLICATIONS: As an avid brewer, I really enjoy using mead in magick. For those who may not have time to make it from scratch, I suggest adding some warm honey and sympathetic herbs to a dry wine for similar symbolism. You can sip a bit just before having important discussions or when you feel weak, pour some out as a libation before your vacation for a safe, pleasant trip, and share a cup in the ritual space to encourage effective communication between the gathered members.

MEAT

THEMES: Awareness, Grounding, Kindness, Prosperity, Victory.

CORRESPONDENCES: Apollo (poultry), Earth, Isis (cow/beef).

HISTORY AND FOLKLORE: Scandinavian legend speaks of a cow mother who birthed the gods themselves. Isis sometimes bore the head of a cow in artistic rendering, Persians had a red cow that symbolized dawn, and the Celts used pork as part of victory feasts. The Greeks and Romans used the rooster to symbolize awareness, because it greets the dawn, and turkey is a "giveaway" bird among Native Americans that reminds us of the importance of kindness. Overall, meat gained the reputation of being a prosperity food, because for many years only the more affluent could afford meat for the entire family regularly.

SAMPLE APPLICATIONS: If you are a vegetarian, the best way to invoke meat's energy in your life is to share it with others in need. This gesture of kindness will return threefold. If you seek success in a specific endeavor, you might try blessing a bit of pork and consuming it at dawn to mark a fresh start filled with victorious energy. Small bits of meat are a suitable offering for Isis (these are best given back to nature after your ritual). And to encourage an ongoing flow of money, try keeping dried meat in your pocket and nibbling it periodically throughout the week! For those of you who are vegetarians, how about some type of fresh green vegetable slices instead? The green color accents your prosperous goal.

MILK

THEMES: Abundance, Fairies, Fertility, Health, Providence.

CORRESPONDENCES: Dionysus, the Goddess Aspect, Hathor, Min, Moon, Water, Zeus.

HISTORY AND FOLKLORE: Since all cultures rely on mother's milk as a first food, it's not surprising that milk is associated with the Mother of creation. Its nutritive quality has given it strong associations with health in many settings. Both Greeks and Egyptians believed milk was a suitable offering to the gods and that it promoted fertility. In Europe, milk, especially sweetened milk, is a favorite food of the fairy folk and a suitable gift to keep them from doing any mischief. The phrase "milk and honey" has come to represent abundance.

SAMPLE APPLICATIONS: For any lunar observance or one honoring the goddess, milk is an excellent beverage for the ritual cup (or if you prefer, try a vanilla milkshake, which maintains the symbolism through color). Since most of us have milk in our diets daily, take a moment to focus on the attribute you most need from this substance before drinking it or adding it to foods. Keep your goal in mind as you consume the milk and internalize that energy. You might wish to add an incantation like, "Mother goddess flow, with health and providence where this milk now goes!"

MINT

THEMES: Anxiety, Blessing, Congeniality, Conscious Mind, Faith, Happiness, Hospitality, Jealousy, Learning, Offering, Spirituality.

CORRESPONDENCES: Air.

HISTORY AND FOLKLORE: The ancient Hebrews sometimes paid tithes with mint, while in Greece it was considered a good herb to cure jealousy, improve congeniality, and bless the temples to the gods. Pliny said that wearing mint on your head would improve your capacity to study, which indirectly indicates that the aroma activates the conscious mind. In an odd dichotomy, mint was favored in the Middle Ages to decrease stress. Romans bathed in mint for strength and health and wore it to celebrate victories. Bolivians picked it on St. John's Day for joy, and stories of Muhammad claim he said, "Mint is religion."

SAMPLE APPLICATIONS: Mint is a readily available herb and one that grows nicely in a window box; I recommend keeping some growing in your home. It will act as an ongoing welcome to guests. And considering how much stress we all have these days and that nearly everyone could use a little extra blessing or success, having this herb "growing" can only improve those kinds of energies in your living space. Nibble a bite to lift your spirits or improve your ability to communicate a compliment effectively. Break a leaf and smell it when you need a clear head. Add a mint leaf to anti-anxiety teas, or burn it in incense for relaxation.

MIRROR

THEMES: Astral Realm, Banishing, Beauty, Binding, Divination, Glamoury, Protection, Spirits, Truth.

CORRESPONDENCES: Buddha, Dionysus, Moon.

HISTORY AND FOLKLORE: The ancients often felt that reflective surfaces could capture spirits and wandering souls. A variety of gods and goddesses are associated with mirrors, of which some reflect the true nature of the individual who looks into them, some represent the essence of truth or the god/dess, some reveal events, and some warn of being overly consumed with superficial beauty (e.g., Narcissus).

In Japan, a mirror facing outward from a home is said to protect all within from evil. The Greeks seemed to concur in that a mirror was used to protect Perseus from Medusa. Cabbalists used seven mirrors for divination, each of which was made out of a different polished metal. Finally, in France people often tried to chase away nasty storms using a mirror pointed in their direction!

SAMPLE APPLICATIONS: Witches still often use mirrors for scrying, the mirror's surface representing a doorway into the astral realm. The process is very similar to scrying by crystals except that the surface of the mirror is sometimes anointed with oil or the back painted black to improve the visual effect.

Mirrors are an effective focus for glamoury spells, since they deal so directly with self-images. For something along these lines you might take a cue from Snow White's incantation of "Mirror, mirror on the wall..." Carry a small handheld mirror to encourage truthfulness with yourself and others. This can also be used to collect excess negativity like an amulet. When the mirror seems "full," or like it's not helping anymore, break it to discharge the negative energy, then sweep up the pieces counterclockwise and use them in a protective witch bottle near your home.

MISTLETOE

THEMES: Divination, Health, Longevity, Love, Peace, Protection, Spirits.

CORRESPONDENCES: Air, Apollo, Sun.

HISTORY AND FOLKLORE: The most sacred of herbs to the Druids, mistletoe was revered by various ancient peoples for its purported healing qualities. In Celtic tradition, carrying a sprig brings good luck, while in Africa, Italy, and Scandinavia it's regarded as protective. In the practice of "water witching," the most potent divining rod is one cut from mistletoe, especially on Midsummer's Day, which is the best time to harvest any magickal herb. And we all know the Yule tradition of kissing beneath the mistletoe, giving the herb associations with love. This tradition actually dates back to an ancient Roman festival called Saturnalia, which took place on the winter solstice.

SAMPLE APPLICATIONS: If you're fortunate to find mistletoe growing in an old oak (and sometimes a willow), knock it down using a stone. Picking it by hand is said to bring bad luck. Or you can buy some extra during the Yule season and keep it tucked near your doorway to keep out unwanted spirits. I hang a piece of mistletoe in my dining room as a symbol of peace (read: no fighting at the table, kids), following the Teutonic custom that says when two armies met beneath this herb, they had to put down all weapons and cease fighting that day.

MOON

THEMES: Creativity, Cycles, Dreams, Fertility, Healing, Imagination, Luck, Magick, Miracles (blue moon), Money, Omens, Potential, Shapeshifting, Spellcraft, Transformation.

CORRESPONDENCES: Artemis, Diana, the Goddess Aspect, Hecate, Water.

HISTORY AND FOLKLORE: Going to the temple at the first sign of a crescent moon was traditional in the Roman worship of Diana, a lunar goddess. In Greece, the moon represented Hecate, the patroness of witches, which may be why it was felt that witches gained power from the moon. In Romanian and Gypsy tradition, creatures like werewolves are governed by the moon, which may have some bearing on why a full moon is still considered a most powerful aid for shapeshifting exercises.

Many cultures based the timing of religious observances on the moon, and they often observed its appearance to make predictions about the future (especially weather). For example, European lore says that should you happen to see the moon (especially a full moon) over your right shoulder, make a wish! This wish should manifest by the next full moon. Throughout this region the moon was an important part of remedial magick too, most often the waning moon, so that sickness would shrink.

SAMPLE APPLICATIONS: Many modern spells still mention using the moon's phase as a timing consideration. Cast your spell during a waxing moon for steady progress, the full moon for maturation and manifestation, and the waning moon for banishing or decrease.

Each of these phases emphasizes a different aspect of the goddess that you might want to meditate on as the moon waxes and wanes. At the crescent moon think of the youthful, energetic goddess and reclaim her exuberance and potential. At the full moon focus on the mother, who gave us life and who helps us reach personal maturity. Come the waxing moon, think of the crone, who is wise and understands magickal mysteries.

MOONSTONE

THEMES: Fertility, Gardening, Growth, Luck, Prophecy.

CORRESPONDENCES: Moon, Water.

HISTORY AND FOLKLORE: Having a moonstone in one's mouth at the full moon aids in telling the future (Rome). In India, a moonstone is carried to increase the bearer's love, passion, or luck, and putting one in the garden makes plants fruitful. Moonstones are considered a most fortunate charm for those born in June.

SAMPLE APPLICATIONS: In modern Wicca, the high priestess of a group may wear a moonstone ring or headpiece to denote her position and connection with "intuitive" energies necessary for that job. I personally like to use the surface of a moonstone for scrying or wear one to inspire a little extra luck. Find tiny tumbled moonstones and place them in the bottom of flowerpots or around your garden to inspire lush growth. By extension, keep this stone nearby when meditating on matters of personal or spiritual growth.

MOUSE

THEMES: Clarity, Luck, Money, Omens, Resourcefulness.

CORRESPONDENCES: Earth, Moon (white mouse).

HISTORY AND FOLKLORE: A mouse is an attribute of both Zeus and Apollo. Bohemians regard white mice as a fortunate sign of forthcoming luck, but in Germany mice fleeing from an area warn of disaster or war. Various folktales speak of mice as a witch animal and a symbol of frugality, detail-mindedness, or resourcefulness.

SAMPLE APPLICATIONS: Even if you can't find a mouse carving, stuffed animal, or picture, you're likely to have another mouse around the house to use—the one by your computer! Draw a dollar sign on it, so that each time you work with it, you help energize your capacity to think clearly and prudently about finances (perhaps especially when working on a budget program!).

MUSTARD

THEMES: Astral Realm, Faith, Health, Passion.

CORRESPONDENCES: Apollo, Fire.

HISTORY AND FOLKLORE: Because of its use in folk remedies, mustard was considered sacred to Apollo, a god of medicine. Sometimes the flowers were dried and carried as a health amulet in Rome, while rabbinical and early Christian tradition used it as a symbol of faith. Hindus felt that eating mustard seed allowed for travel through the air (perhaps astral projection), and they also used it as an aphrodisiac.

SAMPLE APPLICATIONS: Mustard's amuletic nature makes it good to sprinkle around any space to keep everyone within healthy and inspired with faith. Its lovely golden color gives it fiery energy, and in paste form it can be applied to magickal fire masks or used to mark "fire"-related tools. Since a mustard paste is helpful to colds, try applying one so it creates a magickal pattern for wellness. Chant or sing a magickal song as you go, so the energy can follow that pattern and help the healing process along.

NASTURTIUM

THEMES: Luck, Victory.

CORRESPONDENCES: Fire.

HISTORY AND FOLKLORE: In the language of flowers, the nasturtium represents victory or faithfulness to one's country. Some say carrying the petals encourages luck.

SAMPLE APPLICATIONS: The nasturtium is an edible flower that is high in vitamin C and tastes peppery. Place an open flower (washed) on a plate and fill it with your favorite noodle or tuna salad (this allows you to combine various symbols together—for example, the fish salad represents abundant success!). Or try the stems steamed in soup to "warm up" a little luck.

NETTLE

THEMES: Anti-magick, Courage, Energy, Protection, Strength.

CORRESPONDENCES: Fire, Thor.

HISTORY AND FOLKLORE: Pliny advocated sugared nettles for vitality. In Norse tradition, it represents bravery and is sacred to Thor. Germans regard nettle seed as an aphrodisiac, and in folktales nettles are used to create a magickal shirt that dispels powerful curses. In magick traditions the "stinging" nature of nettle is interpreted as protective, so people carry it as an amulet.

SAMPLE APPLICATIONS: Nettle is magickally paired with yarrow to banish fear or with houseleeks to attract a good catch when fishing! Make it into a potion by steeping some in warm water beneath a waning moon (to banish or decrease), and then keep this mixture in an airtight, dark bottle. Sprinkle it around anytime you feel that magick is being used to harm you. Do this moving counterclockwise around your living space saying, "Away from me all negativity . . . stay, stay . . . away, away!" If it's easier, dip a broom in the tincture and sweep the bad energy out of your house moving from the end farthest from the door forward. Close the door on your troubles afterward. (Note: If you plan to use nettles for courage or energy, prepare the potion during a waxing moon instead.)

NUMBERS

THEMES: Divination, Healing, Psychism.

CORRESPONDENCES: Varies by number.

HISTORY AND FOLKLORE: The art of divining by numbers, or numerology, was practiced in Egypt, Arabia, and throughout the Roman world. Pythagoreans believed numbers had a mystical nature, and in some parts of the world specific numbers were reserved for the gods.

Folk magicians used the numbers three, four, seven, nine, and thirteen in their art to time the date of a working, to determine the number of times an incantation should be repeated, and sometimes the number of ingredients to use in a spell or potion. In particular, numbers seem to have significance for healing magick (the number of days over which the magick is applied) and in determining a person's psychic potential (by the date of birth or their ranking in the family).

SAMPLE APPLICATIONS: Since this information is covered in Part One of this book (with other examples in History/Folklore here), what I'd like to provide here are some additional correspondences for your reference:

One: In Arabic tradition the number of god. Similarly in Egypt this was Ra's number, so if you have Ra as a patron, this is a good number to use in spellcraft, rituals, and the like. Mystically this is the number of unity, authority, and sun magick.

Two: The number of the moon and the goddess. Use two to enhance magick for beauty, truth, instinct, cooperative efforts, friendship, and relationships.

Three: This number represents both humankind's and the divine triune nature. When divining by dice, getting three of the same roll is considered very lucky, and that fortunate energy seems to surround this number. After all, three's a charm! Use three to augment harmony, balance, and purpose.

Four: Egyptians and Babylonians honored the number four as symbolic of fulfillment. In other parts of the world it represents the four corners of creation, the direction, the watchtowers, and the earth. Use four in magick focused on completion, foundations, and development.

Five: The protective star of Wicca (pentagram) has five points, four of which represent one element and the last the practitioner. Use this number in magick directed toward appreciating diversity, improving awareness, remaining accountable, and/or augmenting your spiritual senses.

Six: The Star of David has six points, and to this day double triangles are regarded as having protective power. Magickally speaking, six is perfectly suited to protective magick, as well as inspiring creativity, manifestation, and fidelity.

Seven: Seven is a sacred number in many traditions. It's magickally alligned with energy for harmony, spiritual awareness, understanding lunar mysteries, and/or fine-tuning one's chakras.

Eight: The Egyptians felt this number, as a double four, represented rebirth. In Judaic tradition, eight symbolizes justice and liberation. For magick, use eight to increase your physical energy, leadership abilities, or to help manifest dramatic transformations.

Nine: As three times three, nine represents fulfillment and completion. We see this number regularly in folk medicine, in degreed mystery traditions, and even in the traditional magick circle that is drawn nine inches across. Magickally, nine renews vitality, psychism, and power, and stresses the magick user's responsibility to his or her community.

NUTMEG

THEMES: Awareness, Clarity, Comprehension, Conscious Mind, Health, Learning, Love, Memory, Passion, Psychism.

CORRESPONDENCES: Fire.

HISTORY AND FOLKLORE: Ancient people felt nutmeg was good "brain" food because of its resemblance to a human brain. Alternatively, wearing it like a necklace prevents aches and pains along with other minor ailments. Romans used nutmeg as a strewing aromatic for festivals (scattering it on floors and roadways), in medieval France it appears as an ingredient in love potions, and Arabic tradition considers nutmeg as an aphrodisiac. Adding a pinch to psychic incense increases awareness.

SAMPLE APPLICATIONS: A cup of nutmeg tea, when prepared with intention, still makes a great potion to hone one's mind and bring warmth to an ailing relationship. Since nutmeg berries are very small and durable, they make excellent charms—just make sure to bless and empower them for whichever attribute you most need, wrap them in a suitably colored cloth, and carry the token regularly to manifest that energy. For example, for psychism you might energize the berry by a full moon's light and then wrap it in silver or yellow cloth to accent intuitive, creative senses.

OAK

THEMES: Abundance, Blessing, Communion, Fertility, Gardening, Luck, Oracles, Spirits, Worship.

CORRESPONDENCES: Athena, Fire, Jupiter, Odin, Thor, Zeus.

HISTORY AND FOLKLORE: The oak is perhaps the most celebrated of trees in ancient history. Greeks listened to the sound of oak leaves to know the future, Romans gave honored guests a wreath of oak, and Druids conducted sacred rituals among the oaks. The tree even appears in legends of King Arthur and as the wood that shaped Jason's Argo! So precious was this holy wood that even the ashes weren't wasted—they were sprinkled on the land to encourage fruitfulness.

SAMPLE APPLICATIONS: The fruit of an oak tree (acorn) may be carried as a simple, sturdy good-luck charm. It attracts the blessings of the god/dess and overall improvements. The Bible tells us that Abraham met angels beneath an oak tree, so this might be a suitable spot to meditate when you wish to commune with spirits. At Yule, this is the traditional wood to use for your Yule log—never let the whole log burn away, however, or you'll burn away your luck. A small piece of oak makes a very suitable kindling for any ritual fire, especially those for wedding rituals, where oak embers represent fertility (Rome). Make sure to gather the ashes afterward and put a pinch or two into each of your plant pots or around the garden for lush flowering.

OATS

THEMES: Abundance, Beauty, Fertility, Gardening, Money, Providence.

CORRESPONDENCES: Autumn, Ceres, Demeter, Earth.

HISTORY AND FOLKLORE: Throughout much of Europe, the last oat sheaf in the field is diligently harvested and preserved as representing this grain's essential spirit. Keeping this token safe from one year to the next planting season ensures the land and its people of fertility. Additionally, because oats are a foundational grain food, they can symbolize never wanting for food or financial stability.

SAMPLE APPLICATIONS: Oats find their way into our homes in cereals, so you probably have some on hand right now. Try roasting some plain oats (to heat up the magick) and brew it into a coffeelike potion for personal abundance in any form. If you live near a farm, see if you can gather some of the remnants of the harvest for your autumn altar. Keep at least one of these bits after your ritual until next year, so that the god/dess continues to provide for you and your family year-round.

Make a warm oatmeal paste with a few drops of rose oil in it to enhance both internal and external beauty. Apply this to your face, first drawing symbols that represent your goal, then filling in any empty spots (oatmeal is an excellent natural conditioner). Wash it off after it cools, and let the energy shine!

OBSIDIAN

THEMES: Divination, Grounding, Vision.

CORRESPONDENCES: Fire.

HISTORY AND FOLKLORE: This volcanic glass is actually a variety of quartz, and it became a favored material for ritual tools and other ceremonial implements. Dr. John Dee, a seer who served Queen Elizabeth in the 1500s, used an obsidian mirror for scrying. In Mexico, it is sacred to the god Tezcatlipoca, who uses an obsidian mirror to see all things in the world at one time.

SAMPLE APPLICATIONS: Some modern practitioners tell me that when they need to settle their mind and spirit, holding this stone seems to bring them back to earth. Since this is the case, should you wish to use obsidian in any visionary magick, I'd recommend putting it in a pouch or on a surface where it remains untouched.

OLIVE

THEMES: Fertility, Happiness, Health, Peace, Protection, Safety, Wisdom.

CORRESPONDENCES: Apollo, Athena, Fides, Fire, Poseidon, Zeus.

HISTORY AND FOLKLORE: When a heavenly war broke out to see who would be the patron god or goddess of Greece, Athena won for her gift of the olive tree. In this region the olive represented wisdom, fertility, and safety. An olive branch in the home or carried with one protects from witchcraft and harsh storms. The Roman goddess Pax, whose role is that of bringing harmony, is shown holding an olive branch, a symbol of peace. The oil from olives was used to light temples throughout the ancient world, and Romans in particular felt that olive oil was the key to a joyful, healthy life.

SAMPLE APPLICATIONS: Olive oil is one of the best bases for making aromatic oils for anointing and personal perfume or cologne. For this, simply warm one cup of oil and add one teaspoon each of the desired herbs. Strain it when it reaches the desired aromatic strength. Store it in a dark, airtight container, labeled with its magickal purpose (and any significant timing requirements). (Note: If the oil ever gets cloudy, throw it out and make a fresh batch.)

Nibble on an olive for peace, protection, or wisdom. Write your wish on paper, stuff it into an olive, and bury this for growing joy, fruitfulness (productivity), or well-being. Use spiced olive oil for pantry magick when you want to create a smooth path by which your energy can flow.

ONION

THEMES: Cleansing, Courage, Luck, Oaths, Omens, Purification, Strength.

CORRESPONDENCES: Fire, Isis, Moon.

HISTORY AND FOLKLORE: Egyptians included onions as part of oath-taking rituals, and Alexander the Great believed that onions endowed one with bravery and vitality. Many people also associate onions with luck. In some areas dreaming of them is lucky, while in others burning them draws improved good fortune. In old England and Germany, the growth of onions was often observed as a prognostication about relationships or the weather. Carrying a bit of red onion in your pocket protects from sickness, and placing them above a threshold cleanses everyone who enters of any illness that threatens (southern United States).

SAMPLE APPLICATIONS: Really, any form of onion will work effectively for magick, from fresh chives to dried, chopped onion. Use what's most convenient for your situation. Use the dried form for sachets and other pocket magicks and the fresh when you want a fast, zesty addition. Food magick and growing some small white onions in windowsill boxes are the easiest ways to incorporate the onion's energy.

ONYX

THEMES: Balance, Love, Passion, Protection.

CORRESPONDENCES: Fire.

HISTORY AND FOLKLORE: In Arabic tradition, onyx represents love and passion, while in India people wear it to cool lusty intentions. Some ancient writings recommend wearing it to protect yourself from the evil eye, and in Burma people used pieces of it as household fetishes.

SAMPLE APPLICATIONS: Any of the aforementioned uses are perfectly suited to modern magick, especially since onyx is easy to come by and inexpensive. However, I would like to propose one more application. Since the onyx is layered black and white, it might make an excellent stone for promoting balance and symmetry in your life in all matters. For this purpose, hold the stone in both hands and visualize its being filled with rainbow-colored light (including white and black). Continue until it feels warm, and then carry it as a charm.

ORANGE

THEMES: Abundance, Anxiety, Faithfulness, Happiness, Love, Purity.

CORRESPONDENCES: Fire, Hera, Zeus.

HISTORY AND FOLKLORE: Because the orange tree is a type of evergreen, the ancients considered it a symbol of abundance. In Greek mythology, Hera received an orange from Zeus on their wedding day, giving the fruit associations with love and commitment. The medievals used the aroma of oranges or orange blossoms to lift spirits and ease tension. In the Far East, people consume oranges for purity. This association remained in the Victorian language of flowers, where the orange blossom represents chastity.

SAMPLE APPLICATIONS: From a magickal standpoint, since the color and the fruit bear the same name, you can use them interchangeably (remember, a symbol is as powerful as what it represents). You can candy the rinds of oranges for a long-lasting magickal treat that inspires productivity or enjoy the flowers in orange pekoe tea to decrease anxiety. Add powdered orange rings to incense prepared for love or devotion, and use the fresh fruit to decorate your altar during solar/fire rituals (consuming them as a postritual food to internalize the magick).

ORCHID

THEMES: Fertility, Friendship, Kinship, Love, Passion, Sexuality.

CORRESPONDENCES: The God Aspect, Water.

HISTORY AND FOLKLORE: In China orchids are the flower of friendship, while in Turkey the roots were used as a passion enhancer. This second use might come from the myth that says orchids are the food of satyrs, which is why they also found their way into various spells for sexuality (particularly for male "performance").

SAMPLE APPLICATIONS: Orchids are edible, so if you think your love life needs a boost, you might want to try nibbling a petal or two while thinking lusty thoughts! Dried flowers can be added to magickal incense or potpourri for kinship, friendship, love, or romance (make sure you blend with other appropriate ingredients to accent your goal). Drop a fresh orchid as a decorative touch into a love potion's glass to express your intentions.

OVEN/HEARTH

THEMES: Congeniality, Divination, Health, Hospitality, Kinship, Love, Luck, Providence, Unity.

CORRESPONDENCES: Fire, Hestia, Sun.

HISTORY AND FOLKLORE: A tremendous amount of superstition surrounds the hearth, which is considered the heart of the home. Our modern saying "Keep the home fires burning" bears witness to this truth and reminds us that the flame here is that of love and family unity.

If the hearth fire goes out, it represents the loss of love in the home, waning health, or bad luck. Homemakers in Europe would often observe the fires or cinders of the hearth to divine the future. In the Far

East, many people have small shrines in their kitchens to honor the hearth gods and goddesses who watch over the home and provide for the family's needs. In England there was a similar custom for a small fairy called a Hob, who oversees the pantry.

SAMPLE APPLICATIONS: The hearth is among the most important places for folk magicians or kitchen witches. Thanks to modern technology, most people don't have to worry about the fire going out (read: pilot light), so the symbolism for ongoing warmth is already there just waiting for you to activate it through intention and focus. Also, as the social center (you might think it's the living room, but watch to see where people gravitate during a party!), the kitchen stove is the perfect "altar" from which to prepare and cast spells that create an ambiance of welcome for all those who visit your home.

OWL

THEMES: Messages, Omens, Spirituality, Truth, Wisdom.

CORRESPONDENCES: Air, Athena.

HISTORY AND FOLKLORE: Greek art depicts Athena with an owl as a constant companion, giving the creature strong associations with wisdom. In this part of the world, the owl's hooting is carefully observed as an omen, often one foretelling death. This ominous feeling is mirrored in various settings, including Scotland, Wales, and Newfoundland, where the portentous meaning changes, but still speaks of ill fortune.

In Native American tradition, this predictive ability was given a unique twist: the bird acts as an early warning system so people can prepare. This is likely due to the owl's ability to bear the spirit of a deceased shaman. Among the Hopi, if one finds an owl feather, it represents the need to be truthful.

SAMPLE APPLICATIONS: Should you discover that you have an owl as a totem or spirit guide, you can anticipate your magick studies taking on whole new dimensions. These birds always bear a bit of mysticism in their wings, and they make us more fully aware of our spiritual nature and our capacity to look beyond surface reality. If you find an owl feather, it's an excellent talisman for being true to yourself and inspiring wisdom in all your words and deeds. Keep owl images around you when you're in need of insights or messages from the Sacred.

PAPER

THEMES: Communication, Manifestation, Memory, Organization, Spell-craft, Wishcraft (and much more).

CORRESPONDENCES: Earth/Air.

HISTORY AND FOLKLORE: The importance of paper to folk traditions can be traced to the superstitions surrounding the art of writing as a magickal or mystical ability. When paper became available, it was much easier to use than stone or skins for scribing spells. And since the world's greatest histories and tales were diligently recorded by religious people and bards from the time papyrus came into being, it also symbolizes effective communication and remembrance.

SAMPLE APPLICATIONS: I have a saying in my house: "If it's not written down, it doesn't exist." I'm an inveterate note writer, and I use paper in nearly every spell for organization or improved memory retention because of the potent associated symbolism (for me, anyway). The nice thing about paper as a component is it's inexpensive and relatively flexible for nearly any type of magick you want to perform. You can write or paint on it (for manifestation), carry it for "pocket magick," freeze it (binding energy), burn it (releasing a prayer), put it in a box or bottle (wish magick), bury it (growth or grounding), crumple or stomp on it (banishing or overcoming), tear it (dispersing or diminishing), tie it (halting energy), and so forth. So get creative!

PARSLEY

THEMES: Death, Love, Luck, Protection, Spirits.

CORRESPONDENCES: Air, Aphrodite, Venus.

HISTORY AND FOLKLORE: A sacred herb for the dead, parsley could often be found adorning graves in Greece and Rome or neatly tucked into articles of clothing to protect the bearer from wandering spirits. Oddly enough, it was also sacred to two goddesses of love, making it an ingredient in many romance mixtures. Old European tradition tells us that if you need parsley, don't accept it as a gift or it will upset your luck.

SAMPLE APPLICATIONS: Modern magicians still consider parsley a good herb to use in rituals for death or when working with spirits of any kind. Sprinkle fresh diced parsley around the sacred space to keep it safe and filled with love. Also, follow the restaurant custom of putting parsley on each meal plate to freshen the breath and keep our words filled with adoration.

PEACH

THEMES: Divination, Fertility, Longevity, Passion, Prosperity, Protection, Spirituality, Truth.

CORRESPONDENCES: The Goddess Aspect, Water.

HISTORY AND FOLKLORE: The Chinese regard peaches as a fruit of longevity, prosperity, yin energies, and fertility. Taoists consider the peach sacred and mystically helpful. Some carry a peach branch to protect themselves against evil spirits. Peachwood can be used as an effective divining rod, a peach with a leaf still attached represents honesty, and Albertus Magnus (1200–1280) recommended peaches as a passion enhancer.

SAMPLE APPLICATIONS: Consider drying a peach pit to use in power pouches or other forms of pocket magick to encourage the peach's attributes in your daily life. These can be decorated or scented to further illustrate your magickal goals. Add peaches to any magickal diet for mystical insights and wisdom in your magickal arts. Fresh peaches especially are an excellent fruit to eat when you wish to focus on your positive, feminine powers and draw them out.

PEARL

THEMES: Beauty, Health, Protection, Weather Magick.

CORRESPONDENCES: Aphrodite, Diana, Freyja, Isis, Lakshmi, Moon, Poseidon, Venus, Water.

HISTORY AND FOLKLORE: In Saxon folklore, the pearl was formed by Freyja's tears, which is likely why it was a favored component in some forms of love magick. In the Far East, it was once thought that pearls swallowed dragon-generated raindrops, causing the radiant sphere to grow. This may be why the Chinese regard pearls as both fire amulets and serviceable for weather magick! Hindus consider them powerful protective charms, in Borneo every ninth pearl harvested is fed with rice so that more pearls will grow in its place, and in the Middle Ages pearl milk was considered an overall health tonic and powdered pearls were added to beauty aids.

SAMPLE APPLICATIONS: For modern magick users, the least costly form of pearl may be mother-of-pearl or freshwater pearls, both of which you can often buy at gem shows or New Age outlets. I recommend the former for any spell or ritual in which you want to use pearl as a disposable component (like crushing the mother of pearl and scattering it on open water as a wish for love to find you). Wear a pearl to safeguard yourself from unfavorable weather, keep one in your home to protect it from fire, and rub one gently over your temples while visualizing your aura filled with pearly light to improve comeliness.

PEPPER

THEMES: Money, Offering, Passion, Protection.

CORRESPONDENCES: Fire, the God Aspect, the Goddess Aspect.

HISTORY AND FOLKLORE: Pepper was so valuable in the ancient world that it sometimes paid ransoms! Once the spice hit the trade routes, it was widely used as a panacea or an aphrodisiac. In Madagascar, pepper became an offering for the god and goddess aspects in their roles as father and mother of all things.

SAMPLE APPLICATIONS: I recommend fresh peppers or freshly ground peppercorns, if possible, for magick. The herb's fiery nature is strongest in these forms. Hang whole chili peppers near your doorway to keep unwanted visitors (especially old significant others) from arriving or in the pantry to safeguard your magickal potions and edibles. Carry a pep-percorn in your pocket to attract enough money with which to pay bills, and sprinkle pepper on magickal passion foods.

PINE

THEMES: Banishing, Happiness, Health, Longevity, Love, Purification, Strength, Victory.

CORRESPONDENCES: Air, Poseidon.

HISTORY AND FOLKLORE: Many ancient people, including those of China and Japan, regarded the pine as a tree that represented life and the immutable human soul. When magickally paired with the vine, pine becomes a symbol of love (Rome). Romans also ate pine nuts for strength. In Greece, the winners of the Isthmian games received a wreath of pine. Nowadays we revere pine oil as an effective purification herb that banishes negative energy.

SAMPLE APPLICATIONS: Pine wood and needles make an excellent base for nearly any magickal incense, especially those for cleansing, success, and vitality. Pine needles can be used whole, but burn better if you grind them first.

Follow Japanese custom and bring pine sprigs into your home to inspire happiness. Or sprinkle pine needles around the sacred space to keep it free of negativity. Small pine cones make great health amulets that inspire physical strength and radiate protection. For this purpose, you may wish to dab the pine cone periodically with fresh pine oil to keep the magick active.

POPPET

THEMES: Concealment, Cooperation, Imitative Magick, Manifestation, Protection, Transformation, and many others.

CORRESPONDENCES: Various.

HISTORY AND FOLKLORE: The first poppets were often made from clay, wax, or hardened dough. Other base materials included wood, corncobs, lemons, and stuffed cloth. In China, a woman who wished to conceive carried the poppet of a baby near her stomach, while in Borneo baby poppets were placed in cradles to fool fairy folk and other spirits who might intend children harm. Europeans made poppets out of wheat sheaves to protect the spirit of the grain from one season to the next, or they used the images for disease transference (often burning or burying the doll afterward in a mock death).

SAMPLE APPLICATIONS: For the magick of the poppet to work, the poppet must somehow physically resemble the desired goal. For example, if you wish to conceal something, hide a representation of that item inside the poppet. If you wish to encourage cooperation in a group of people, make a poppet for each person and place them in a circle in a safe place. If the poppet represents you, and you want to make a positive change, simply change the clothing the poppet wears or any items it carries to similarly transform its energy. Bear in mind that if you want the poppet to get rid of something, the poppet itself should likewise disappear after you're done with it. Similarly, if you're trying to manifest a particular desire, have the doll mimic that desire as already fulfilled in the way you position it, clothe it, and so on.

POTATO

THEMES: Passion, Perspective, Poppet Magick, Sexuality, Vision.

CORRESPONDENCES: Earth.

HISTORY AND FOLKLORE: Because the potato is a member of the nightshade family, it fell in and out of favor with folk magicians. When it was being used, the most common applications were for health, to cure impotency, or improve passion. After new potatoes are gathered for the first time, those eating of them should make a wish.

SAMPLE APPLICATIONS: Because potatoes are easily carved into specific shapes using common kitchen utensils, they make a very effective poppet substitute. After you create the desired shape, attach a piece of paper with your need written upon it and bury the potato. To supplement common medical remedies, rub a potato on an afflicted area and throw it away. This symbolically collects and discards any associated negative energy (this seems especially useful with wart removal). Because potatoes grow underground, you might want to consider using them in magickal procedures during a waning or dark moon, the time that farmers recommend planting this vegetable for hearty growth!

Scalloped potatoes are a good addition to passion platters (the creamy consistency smoothes the way for loving exchange). Finally, because potatoes have so many "eyes," you might want to consider this a component that could help with perspective or vision.

PRIMROSE

THEMES: Abundance, Beauty, Fertility, Productivity, Resourcefulness.

CORRESPONDENCES: Frey, Freyja.

HISTORY AND FOLKLORE: During the 1600s, people loved to candy primroses, make them into salads, and mingle them into potages perhaps based on the idea that primrose somehow opened the gates of heaven to souls. In Norse tradition the primrose was sacred to Frey and Freyja as a symbol of abundance, beauty, and fertility.

SAMPLE APPLICATIONS: Steep primroses picked before ten in the morning in warm water and wash your face in this potion as part of any spell to enhance inner and outer beauty. Grow primroses around your house to attract abundance (make sure to twine them so they grow clockwise). Keep freshly cut primroses in any area where you have to work for resourcefulness and productivity.

PUMICE

See Lava Stone.

PURPLE

THEMES: Balance, Leadership, Power, Psychism, Purification, Spirituality, Wisdom.

CORRESPONDENCES: Moon, Spring, Water.

HISTORY AND FOLKLORE: The Latin *purpura* means "purple," "purple dye," or "the purple fish." This last definition refers to the mollusk from which people originally got purple dye; it was rare, so purple those days was very expensive. Because of its steep price, only the rich could afford the color purple and thus it became a symbol of nobility or high rank. In our ancient past it also represented unity among people, which may be why many rulers donned purple vestments—it was their job to maintain community harmony. In Christian tradition it's associated with the Lenten season (cleansing), and in Japan it's the color of magickal power.

SAMPLE APPLICATIONS: In esoteric traditions, purple signifies mystical wisdom and spiritual insights and is strongly aligned with the crown chakra. Use this color in visualizations to deepen the trance state, center yourself, and open your psychic senses. Add purple highlights into your wardrobe for sagacious decision making and strong leadership skills. Bathe in water with a hint of purple food coloring for auric cleansing and purification (or you can use an aromatic that comes from purple flowers). For a really interesting effect, try adding some purple glitter to the surface of the water and meditate.

QUARTZ

THEMES: Clarity, Divination, Energy, Healing, Vision, Weather Magick.

CORRESPONDENCES: Spirit, Water, Winter.

HISTORY AND FOLKLORE: Ancient myths say that the quartz crystal formed out of solidified ice. Consequently, quartz has strong associations with weather magick, especially in Oceanic cultures. In shamanic traditions, quartz was considered a living stone and was even fed deer's blood to maintain its potency for divination and healing. The Chinese feel that quartz pleases the spirits and gods when given as an offering, and the Japanese feel this stone bears the power and perfection of white dragons.

SAMPLE APPLICATIONS: Magick practitioners value quartz as one of the best stones for scrying. For this purpose, wash the crystal in salt water, and then place it on a dark surface in front of you. Breathe deeply while thinking of a question and watch for images, clouds, or colors to appear on the surface. Make notes of what you see and interpret it afterward. Movement up or to the right is generally a positive response, while that down and to the left is negative.

For spellcraft and charms, carry a blessed crystal to improve your spiritual or physical energy. Place tiny quartz crystals around any area where you want improved clarity (like in a potted plant at your office desk). Because of the quartz's unique ability to hold energy (note its use in watches), it can absorb any type of magick you wish to place within it. One way to achieve this is by whispering to the stone a short phrase or work that represents your goal (like love, prosperity, or peace) three times. Repeat this phrase once to activate the stone while you hold it in your hand.

In the ritual space, natural quartz wands can represent the god aspect and a tumbled sphere can represent the goddess and the moon. Shamans also turn to quartz as a guiding spirit to help them communicate with other members of the mineral world. Finally, dog owners may want to keep a rose quartz in their pet's bed to help them overcome bad habits!

RABBIT

THEMES: Fertility, Imagination, Longevity, Luck, Messages, Passion, Peace, Productivity, Resourcefulness.

CORRESPONDENCES: Aphrodite, Buddha, Eros, Freyja, the Goddess Aspect, Moon, Spring.

HISTORY AND FOLKLORE: The symbolism of the rabbit changes dramatically from setting to setting. Among some Native American tribes it's a type of trickster, in others the cottontail rabbit stole fire from the sun for humankind, and in still others it is a messenger from the gods! Throughout ancient Rome and much of Europe the rabbit is a symbol of fertility and passion because of the number of young it bears. The Chinese include white rabbits in their lunar festivals, because of a myth that says a hare lives on the moon (this myth appears in Mexico, Japan, and South Africa too). They also associate rabbits with feminine power, longevity, spirituality (white rabbits), luck, and peace (red rabbits).

The Celts and Teutons associated rabbits with lunar gods and goddesses, particularly Oestra, after whom Easter is named. This is why we have an Easter bunny! Other nearly universal attributes given this creature include craftiness and quickness.

SAMPLE APPLICATIONS: I like to stock up on marshmallow bunnies during the Easter holiday. That way I have some ready-made symbolic edibles to use in magick for internalizing any of the rabbit's attributes that I most need. If you wish to conceive, the image of a red rabbit placed in your bedroom on the night of a full moon makes for some powerful supportive energies (if the cycle timing is correct). Alternatively, put the image near a project to which you'd like to bring a little luck or productivity. To release your imagination or improve your receptivity to nature's and the god/dess's messages, make a rabbit mask and don it during procedures aimed at similar goals.

RAIN

See Water.

RASPBERRY

THEMES: Forgiveness, Love, Passion, Protection.

CORRESPONDENCES: The Goddess Aspect, Venus, Water.

HISTORY AND FOLKLORE: Raspberry is a fruit of Venus, giving it associations with love and passion. In an odd dichotomy, it's also considered a forgiving fruit and one able to entrap negativity in its thorns. This latter attribute is why raspberry branches were sometimes hung on homes after a death has occurred: they keep wandering ghosts out. Raspberry leaf tea is a common remedy for "woman's problems," which makes this fruit sacred to the goddess aspect.

SAMPLE APPLICATIONS: When you've been angry with someone you love, feed each other raspberries and accept forgiveness into yourself. Get creative here, folks, and certainly let nature take its course in how your forgiveness ritual develops! I'm fortunate to have a raspberry bush in my yard, so I can nibble a berry or two anytime I want to improve self-love. If you can grow one nearby, slowly train the brambles so they encircle sacred spaces for protection (like a magickal garden). And when you don't have the fruit, you still have your lips and tongue with which to make the "Bronx cheer." Although some might think you silly, moving backward while doing this would be an effective form of banishing and protection!

RATTLE

THEMES: Communion, Dance, Focus, Meditation, Protection, Weather Magick.

CORRESPONDENCES: Vary by design. Generally those attached to a staff align with the God Aspect, and those shaped out of shells or other hollows that mimic a womb align with the Goddess Aspect.

HISTORY AND FOLKLORE: The rattles of old were not simply handheld percussion instruments. Some were attached to ritual garb, while others were fastened to a staff or body part to accompany sacred dances. In this respect, the rattle acts like the drum to focus the dancer's attention, deepen his or her trance state, and improve the resulting communion with the spirits being invoked.

The sound of a rattle seems to have connotations similar to those of a bell for chasing away evil spirits (particularly those of illness). Also because many bear a rainlike sound, it is a common implement in sympathetic and imitative magick to bring rain. In this case the rattle might be constructed out of corn and grain kernels for sympathy with the crops.

SAMPLE APPLICATIONS: The number of materials used in traditional rattle making was amazing, including seeds, animal hooves, metal cones, bits of semiprecious metal, and fruit shells. Following in this creative tradition, the modern magician has even more options! Try sealable food containers filled part way with popcorn or dried beans, for example (this would be very suited to magick aimed at providence or frugality). You could also save a gourd from Halloween and let it dry for a serviceable rattle, or simply purchase a child's rattle. Really, any form is fine, as long as it has meaning to you (such as using the child's rattle as a protective tool in a child's room).

Sound your rattle counterclockwise around your home anytime the "bad vibes" start overtaking that space (traditionally this is done two times a year, spring and fall). Or shake it rhythmically to improve your meditative focus.

RAVEN

See Crow.

RED

THEMES: Energy, Luck, Magick, Power, Protection, Purification.

CORRESPONDENCES: Aries, Fire, South.

HISTORY AND FOLKLORE: As the color of life's blood, red was favored among many ancient cultures for power and protection, including those of Japan and India. For example, tying a bit of red string to a person's clothing or hair kept him or her safe from sickness, ghosts, and fairy folk! In contrast, in Europe mages and certain fairy folk wore red hats as a sign of magickal power. In many esoteric traditions red represents the element of fire and the southern quarter of creation. It's often worn for safety or to improve energy levels.

SAMPLE APPLICATIONS: If your birth sign is Aries, red is considered a very lucky color for you. Add red highlights to your environment and wardrobe anytime you're feeling listless or unmotivated. Carve an emblem for personal power into a red candle and burn this every day until the emblem melts away to manifest the magick. Make sure to keep the remaining wax for other similar spells or to seal personal letters and magickal papers with a keynote of power.

If you're feeling psychically assaulted, visualize your aura filled with sparkling red light. This has a natural side effect of increasing your energy levels, which helps combat any attacks, and it also creates a protective sphere against any incoming negativity.

RICE

THEMES: Fertility, Longevity, Luck, Protection, Providence.

CORRESPONDENCES: Air/Water/Earth (varies depending on source).

HISTORY AND FOLKLORE: In Bali, rice is so important that it is believed to bear a soul. In other parts of the world the word *rice* actually means "staff of life," much as Westerners view bread. This reverence is portrayed powerfully in Ceylon, where diviners must be consulted, prayers said, and proper propitiation made before a rice field can be planted.

In Japan, people eat rice on their birthday much as we eat cake for luck, fertility, and longevity. There, to waste rice is considered a terrible sin because it is a sacred food, essential to all feasts, the family altar, as a strewing food to chase off evil spirits, and the making of sake (rice wine), which also has ritualistic importance in this culture.

SAMPLE APPLICATIONS: According to Eastern tradition, if you wish to cultivate joy and abundance, eat red rice, which you can get by cooking the rice with red beans. Cook and eat purposefully! In protection rites, place rice around the sacred circle (or anoint the area with sake instead).

RING

THEMES: Balance, Cycles, Divination, Equality, Faithfulness, Focus, Friendship, Leadership, Love, Oaths, Power, Protection.

CORRESPONDENCES: Moon (silver), Sun (gold).

HISTORY AND FOLKLORE: Rings were among the first pieces of jewelry to be used as amulets, their function being determined by the type of metal, stones, and designs in the rings themselves. In Celtic tradition, rings were often given by overlords to their warriors as a sign of loyalty. In various other settings leaders wore a special ring (often a signet) as a mark of authority and power.

The tradition of exchanging wedding rings comes from Rome, where the ring represented eternity, the sun, and the sacred circle of life. Even before that, however, rings were sometimes given to those who served the god/dess wholly (this later translated into the ring given to nuns upon taking final vows). Later in the Victorian era, wedding bands became part of love divinations and spells.

SAMPLE APPLICATIONS: There's a saying in Wicca today: a witch without jewelry might as well be naked. Though meant humorously, it seems true that many witches and neo-pagans use jewelry both as a symbol of their life's Path and for directing magickal energy. For the latter purpose, your rings should be carefully chosen. To determine the best ring for your goal, follow the ancients' wisdom—consider the metal, stones, and imagery.

For those of us who can't buy a new ring every time we want to carry magick with us, there are many other ways to put rings to work. Bless and energize those you already have for specific functions in your life and then wear them regularly. Take larger rings (like hula hoops) and put them around items that need protection. Visualize rings of a suitable color pouring down over your head and settling in your stomach region for focus and an improved sense of balance. For written spellcraft, use the image of circles linked together as part of a spell for connection or networking.

ROSE

THEMES: Death, Enlightenment, Fairies, Friendship, Happiness, Love, Oaths, Offering, Omens, Passion, Prayer, Purity, Reincarnation.

CORRESPONDENCES: Aphrodite, Bacchus, Eros, Demeter, Isis, Muhammad, Venus, Vishnu, Water.

HISTORY AND FOLKLORE: Greek legend tells us that roses were born from Aphrodite's blood when her foot got pricked by a thorn, but the Greeks were certainly not the first or last civilization to include this flower in myth and lore. It's been the queen of flowers for over three thousand years. Ancient stories say that Cleopatra welcomed Mark Anthony with thousands of rose petals as a sign of her love. In Rome and surrounding regions, the rose not only represented romance, but also joy and passion.

In Greece, any oath or information shared beneath a hanging rose was considered binding and secret. Teutonic tradition says roses are protected by fairy folk. Arabs consider them sacred to Muhammad, and they were favored by Vishnu in India. Some regions of Europe consider the rose a funerary flower, while in others its petals are observed for omens (often about a relationship).

In much of the Orient, the rose is the goddess's flower, which is why goddess images often receive showers of rose petals as an offering. The idea of a prayer "rosary" comes from the fact that the beads were originally made of rose petals, and roses are Mary's flowers. Golden roses represent spiritual perfection, white roses purity, yellow ones friendship, and eight-petaled roses signify reincarnation.

SAMPLE APPLICATIONS: There aren't many magickal procedures that won't benefit from the rose's loving energy, since one of magick's rules is: "Love is the law, Love under will." I personally enjoy roses as an altar decoration just for their beauty. I grow them in the yard, but always remember to ask the fairy folk's permission before picking, lest I incur bad luck!

It is relatively easy to make rose-scented oils, teas, and potions for magickal use simply by steeping the freshly picked petals in warm (*not* hot) oil or water until they become translucent. Repeat with fresh petals until you're happy with the scent, then store in a dark, airtight container that's suitably labeled. Roses are edible and the hips yield high amounts of vitamin C, making them serviceable physically as well as metaphysically!

ROSEMARY

THEMES: Banishing, Beauty, Conscious Mind, Death, Dreams, Fairies, Health, Learning, Knowledge, Memory, Purification, Shapeshifting, Success, Youthfulness.

CORRESPONDENCES: Sun.

HISTORY AND FOLKLORE: Since early times, rosemary symbolized remembrance, devotion, and friendship, which is why it was often seen in funeral displays. Greek students carried rosemary or wore it in their hair to improve study skills. In this region you could often find rosemary sprinkled on temple floors to banish evil spirits and, more pragmatically, to purify the air.

In the Netherlands and Sicily, if one wishes to see the wee people, one simply watches a rosemary bush carefully. Should you befriend one of these devas, they will teach you the art of shapeshifting! The Welsh believe that cooking with a spoon made from rosemary wood improves the healthy quality of food and that smelling it invokes youthful energy. During the Middle Ages, sleeping with rosemary under your pillow was believed to ensure sweet dreams, and in Hungary, rosemary was traditionally added to beautifying preparations.

SAMPLE APPLICATIONS: A very handy pantry spice, rosemary is nearly as flexible in magick as are roses! When you're using rosemary in relationship spells, it seems to be somewhat paired to honey and/or oranges for the most potent results. I combine all three together with a hint of garlic for a meat glaze that energizes, tickles taste buds, and warms the heart!

Rosemary burns effectively in incense, but don't add too much of it. The aroma can overwhelm your other ingredients. Burn this anytime you're trying to learn something new or difficult. Alternatively, dab rosemary oil on the pages of your Book of Shadows to better remember those pages.

ROWAN

THEMES: Anti-magick, Divination, Magick, Protection, Psychism, Spirits.

CORRESPONDENCES: Fire, the Goddess Aspect, Moon.

HISTORY AND FOLKLORE: In Celtic tradition, the rowan represents magick, very likely due to the fact that the word *runa,* from which it gets its name, means "charm"! The Irish took this meaning fairly literally, adding rowan wood to ritual fires for invoking spirits. In an odd dichotomy, one of the most ancient anti-magick charms seen throughout Europe is the binding of two rowan branches with red thread to make an equidistant cross. This same charm often got used for protection from ghosts. There is some evidence suggesting that the Druids used rowan in divination, perhaps in the form of rods.

SAMPLE APPLICATIONS: One rather lovely custom you can follow if you own a home is planting a rowan tree on your property. This keeps the house and its inhabitants under the protection of the goddess. Alternatively, carry rowan berries as an anti-magick charm or make them into a magick-enhancing jelly (make sure you remove the seeds). Rowan leaves and bark make a good base for incense when combined with other ingredients for divinatory ability, psychism, or protection. Finally, if you find a fallen rowan branch, you might want to make a set of runes for yourself from it. Slice the branch in half-inch pieces and carefully sand the cut surfaces. Carve or paint the runic images on the wood, and then varnish both sides for easy handling. This makes a very durable divination system that speaks with nature's voice.

RUNES

THEMES: Arts, Communication, Creativity, Divination, Magick, Protection, Wishcraft.

CORRESPONDENCES: Vary by rune symbol.

HISTORY AND FOLKLORE: Runes were among the early forms of written language in Scandinavian tradition that later got adapted in Italy and Germany and some other European countries. Those that most people see on the market today come from the Germanic collection called the *Elder Futhark*.

From what we can tell, the runes helped to mark people's lands and personal goods. More than that, however, the belief exists that the symbols themselves evoke magickal energy. This idea may have originated in the legend that says Odin created the runes for magick, sacrificing his one eye to ensure their power. Another tale concludes that the Norse god Braggi learned this magickal language from his consort, which made him the greatest poet ever known.

SAMPLE APPLICATIONS: Look to a divination book or book about runes to learn their symbolic value. Then you can paint them on magickal tools, use them in written spellcraft, write using runic "code" in your Book of Shadows, carve the symbols into candles for manifesting their energies, and so on. And, of course, you can buy or make a set for yourself to use in divination.

If you live near a beach, draw a rune that represents your need in the sand before high tide and let the waters wash that wish to the four corners of creation. If you want your magick to grow, lightly carve a rune in tree bark so the magick grows with the tree (not too deeply— you don't want to harm the tree). When you feel the need for safety, draw the *algiz* rune (it looks like a capital Y with the center line extended upward) in the air with your strong hand visualizing it as brilliant white light. Do this in all four directions to set up a temporary sphere of protection.

SAGE

THEMES: Dreams, Health, Law, Longevity, Purification, Wisdom, Wishcraft.

CORRESPONDENCES: Air, Zeus.

HISTORY AND FOLKLORE: It is said that sage was named after Saga, the wise seer of Frigg, giving it strong associations with wisdom. Sage was one of the favored remedial spices in China, Greece, Rome, and most of Europe. Medieval writers even called it the "healer of all ills." In Greece specifically, people ate sage to improve the mind, while Romans consumed it to promote fertility. Carrying a sage leaf brings positive legal judgments (rural United States) and helps manifest wishes, and eating it in May increases longevity. Among the Apache, brushing the aura of a person with sage is said to chase away bad dreams.

SAMPLE APPLICATIONS: Among my favorite pantry spices, sage finds its way mostly into cooking magick in my home or into herb bundles for purification and protection. For the latter, take pieces of freshly dried sage (about twelve inches long) and bind them together tightly, crisscrossing string and knotting it as you go. When you tie each knot, focus on the kind of energy you want the sage to release when it's burned. By the way, since chicken is associated with health and sage is a perfect herb for seasoning it, combine the two into a healthy soup, stew, or magickal main dish.

SALIVA

THEMES: Banishing, Healing, Luck, Magick, Oaths, Power, Strength, Vision.

CORRESPONDENCES: Water.

HISTORY AND FOLKLORE: Ancient folk healers in Italy, Israel, and China trusted in the power of saliva for assisting in healing rites. Next to blood, saliva ranked second as the bodily fluid used to boost magick's power—be it to banish demons, offset bad luck, produce visions, or improve physical strength. In Scotland it wasn't uncommon to seal a promise with saliva or by spitting, and even the Qu'ran mentions spitting four times as a way of getting rid of bad thoughts.

SAMPLE APPLICATIONS: Turning and spitting behind oneself may not be acceptable etiquette, but it is effective magick for turning away negativity. If you feel awkward, remember that most mothers still use saliva as a quick cleanser for dirt or minor scratches (much to many children's objections).

Any magickal implement that you want to mark with your energy signature can be anointed with a bit of your saliva. To increase the overall power in spell components, add a drop of saliva to them (this is akin to how the ancient warriors spat into their hands for strength and might).

SALT

THEMES: Banishing, Congeniality, Fear, Hospitality, Money, Oaths, Purification, Reincarnation.

CORRESPONDENCES: The Goddess Aspect, Osiris, Poseidon, Water/ Earth.

HISTORY AND FOLKLORE: Because of its connection with the sea, salt often represented rebirth and cleansing in ancient cultures. The Hebrews had offerings of salt, and one of the ancient Hebrew names for the goddess translates as "salt." Among medieval people, salt was favored for banishing spirits and consecrating religious items, and Arabs swore oaths by salt, especially when guests came into the home. These oaths represented hospitality and courtesy on everyone's part.

In ancient Rome, soldiers were commonly paid in salt, which is how we come by the phrase "a man worth his salt." Persians used salt to rid themselves of fear, and in several Native American traditions salt was so important that it was personified as a spirit, often called the Salt Mother.

SAMPLE APPLICATIONS: Salt is another incredibly useful component in many different forms of magick. When mixed with iron filings or garlic and sprinkled around a home, you can be assured no ghostly guests will intrude. Or simply sprinkle salt on the earth in any area where evil or negative energy exists as part of banishing rites.

Put a little salt on both sides of your threshold to welcome guests. As they pass it, all negativity will be collected and kept neatly outside. Or add salt to foods prepared specifically to increase your financial flow, and use some salt water for bathing when you're doing any form of ritual cleansing.

Tools that won't be harmed by a little salt do well to sit in a pile of it for a while, or a saltwater solution, to rid them of any random energies. If you do this regularly, your tools and components will always be clean vessels through which magick flows unhindered. By the way, most magicians seem to prefer sea salt over commercial brands. You can find this at many natural food stores.

SALVE

THEMES: Forgiveness, Healing, Imitative Magick.

CORRESPONDENCES: Vary with ingredients.

HISTORY AND FOLKLORE: During the Middle Ages salves were used for an interesting type of sympathetic magick. When individuals injured themselves on a knife or other tool, salve was applied to *both* the tool and the wound in the belief that by forgiving and healing the implement, the wound would heal faster! Also many salves throughout the ages were prepared based on the purported magickal efficacy of the herbal components.

SAMPLE APPLICATIONS: Homemade salves have a wonderfully long shelf life in which to preserve any magick you place within. Begin by choosing up to three herbs that represent your goal. Steep one teaspoon of each of these in one cup of warm oil, bearing in mind your goal as you work. When the aroma grows strong, strain the oil and add one cup of melted candle wax to the mixture (hint: choose a harmonious magickal color for the wax, or perhaps save wax from spell candles for improved energy). Let this cool slightly and then beat the mixture with a fork until it's completely cooled (the final texture is like cold cream). Apply to yourself or magickal tools and the sacred space as desired. If you like the aroma, dab a bit on lightbulbs so you can "turn on" the magick!

SHELLS

THEMES: Choices, Cycles, Dance, Divination, Imagination, Oracles, Protection, Transformation, Wishcraft.

CORRESPONDENCES: Mari, Poseidon, Water, West, and all water-dwelling gods/goddesses.

HISTORY AND FOLKLORE: As a gift from the earth's womb and the sea goddess, shells were often carried as protective amulets, specifically against the evil eye and wandering spirits. In China and Japan, the shells from turtles were often used for a type of divination called plastromancy. Various shamanic traditions adopted a similar custom using small cast shells. In one such system, an abalone shell represented outcomes, cowrie shells symbolized a decision, and spirals were equated with cycles or time. In Africa cowrie shells were used for a binary divination system (yes-no).

The casting of shells carried over into Greece and Rome, where oracles sometimes cast shells to gain insight into specific questions. Finally, shells were often used as percussion instruments for sacred dances.

SAMPLE APPLICATIONS: Shells make a perfect accent to the western quarter of the sacred circle or a water-focused wand to represent the water element. Carrying one will help you "go with the flow" more and tap into your intuitive, imaginative self. I also keep a few seashells around my home for protection and a gentle reminder of life's ever moving cycle and our ability to grow and change (like that of the water from which the shells come).

To use a shell in wishcraft, you will need to go to a place with running water, preferably water that eventually moves into a lake or ocean. Hold the shell tightly and visualize your wish, and then toss it into the ocean with a hopeful heart. By the way, most magicians recommend finding your shells over buying them, because you can then suitably thank the waters for their abundant gifts. However, if you don't live near a beach, buying shells will do. Just soak them in salt water to refresh their energy.

SHOES

THEMES: Divination, Dreams, Fertility, Leadership, Luck, Magick, Safety, Sexuality, Travel, Worship, and others (depending on what gets put in or done with the shoes).

CORRESPONDENCES: Aphrodite, the Goddess Aspect, Isis.

HISTORY AND FOLKLORE: The Egyptians and Greeks considered shoes as an emblem of sexuality (often female). This is likely how our custom of tossing shoes after a newly married couple or tying them to a car got started. The Egyptians used shoes for an interesting form of divination in which the soles of an enemy's shoes were scrutinized for insights, and they also exchanged shoes at property transfers or a change of leadership.

Shoes represented quick movement in Rome, which explains their appearance on warrior's shields. In Japan wearing new shoes brings luck (in the United States we put a penny in penny loafers for similar reasons). In some religious traditions removing one's shoes is a way of respecting the sacred space. Finally, thanks to *The Wizard of Oz* we know that wearing ruby slippers inspires magick, and clicking our heels together three times will always bring us home!

SAMPLE APPLICATIONS: Some magick practitioners like to work barefooted, because it helps keep them in closer contact with earth and the earth element. On the other hand, shoes figure predominantly in portable magick such as putting a lucky item in your shoe so luck walks with you. Some examples here include a specially prepared herbal powder or perhaps a bay leaf if you're seeking strength.

Placing one's shoes in the form of a T (Thor's hammer) attracts sweet dreams and protective energy. To encourage more luck, always put the right shoe on before the left. At Yule, consider putting out a special shoe for Santa—the power of tradition should never be overlooked in folk magick, and this action helps attract pleasant surprises!

SILVER

THEMES: Awareness, Creativity, Dreams, Faith, Fate, Imagination, Insight, Magick, Meditation, Protection, Psychism, Spirituality, Success.

CORRESPONDENCES: Diana, the Goddess Aspect, Isis, Moon, Water.

HISTORY AND FOLKLORE: Second only to gold as a metal used for religious purposes, silver was favored for making protective bells for ritual vestments by several cultures, including the Hebrews. In Muslim regions, charms were sometimes inscribed in silver, while the priests and priestesses at Delphi used silver to represent overcoming obstacles and purity. Folk tradition tells us silver is necessary for killing certain unnatural creatures like werewolves. This may be why we see so many protective silver amulets in diverse settings including China, France, and the United States.

A person's fate might be described using silver, as seen in the phrase "born with a silver spoon." Gypsies predicted the future if given a piece of silver, and because of its associations with the moon, it is still favored as a very magically oriented metal that bears lunar attributes.

SAMPLE APPLICATIONS: Silver bells are an excellent tool for invoking the goddess during spells or rituals or for opening psychic pathways to your intuitive self. Wearing silver jewelry when honoring the full moon is quite common among modern witches, as is the custom of a high priestess donning a silver headpiece to denote her connection with the goddess. Sleep with a silver coin beneath your pillow to inspire psychic dreams or meditate with it over your third eye to improve your spiritual awareness and imaginative ability.

In spells that call for special lunar timing, a piece of silver can be substituted as a moon emblem. Keep a piece of silver next to any project to which you want to bring success. I personally suggest getting your silver at a coin or jewelry shop so you know it's fairly pure.

SNAKE (SERPENT)

THEMES: Balance, Concealment, Glamoury, Health, Magick, Protection, Reincarnation, Sexuality, Shapeshifting, Transformation, Wisdom.

CORRESPONDENCES: Apollo, Earth, Zeus.

HISTORY AND FOLKLORE: The snake has somewhat ambivalent symbolism, having been regarded with both fear and reverence. This dichotomy is actually very helpful in folk magick, because the snake becomes a perfect representation of balance—both male and female, vitality and death.

Egyptians made cobras a symbol of leadership and power. Mithraic tradition sees snakes as protective companions. Greeks and Romans seemed to agree, often keeping snakes as pets to bring health and fertility into the home. Similarly, snakes abiding in a field were often left alone in the belief they would bring abundant harvests.

The Athenic temples also often kept a snake as a guardian, symbolizing both magick and wisdom. Cretans observed how the snake shed its skin and began associating snakes with reincarnation and the immutable soul. Hindus see it as a reminder of the power that comes from uniting masculine and feminine energies, the Hopi honor it as an emblem of the moon and fecundity, and in parts of Africa snakes are sacred because they bear the souls of dead ancestors.

SAMPLE APPLICATIONS: I must confess that I'm a little uneasy around snakes, so I often defer to a stuffed or rubber model if needed for magickal symbolism. From a shamanic perspective, the snake spirit is an excellent guide to understanding and unlocking our sexuality and improving yin-yang balance and its associated power. I've also found that meditating on the manner in which a snake sheds its skin is a good way to work on personal transformations or glamoury (seeing yourself changing out of one "skin" into another).

SOIL

THEMES: Abundance, Divination, Gardening, Growth, Health, Fertility, Oaths, Protection, Providence.

CORRESPONDENCES: Earth, Gaia, the Goddess Aspect.

HISTORY AND FOLKLORE: As the key component of Mother Earth, soil has long been revered by folk magicians. Soil nurtures, it brings forth fruit, and sustains all life. Consequently, numerous rituals were developed to ensure the land's richness and prepare it to receive seed.

In Slavic regions oaths are sworn by placing one hand on the earth. Some European lore suggests that soil gathered from near a church or graveyard and carried is a protective amulet (symbolically overcoming death). Various other cultures, including those of Russia, Scotland, West Africa, Burma, and India, use dirt or soil for geomantic divination. Beyond this, soil became a vehicle for folk healers, who might bury a patient in a mock death to fool the spirit of sickness or apply warm clay to a wound to ease pain.

SAMPLE APPLICATIONS: The nice thing about soil is that you can always get a pinch or two easily! For magick, however, I suggest finding a rich soil that shows signs of healthy life. This encourages manifestation. Plant a seed that corresponds with your magickal goals in a pot of earth and tend it. Each time you water the seed and weed the soil, keep your goal in mind. Whisper it to the soil, and maybe even play magickal music in the room where the planter is! By so doing, you're giving positive energy to your goals. The soil takes care of nurturing things along in nature's gentle way. By the time the seed sprouts, you should see some tangible results.

SPIDER

THEMES: Communication, Creativity, Cycles, Fate, Luck, Money, Shapeshifting.

CORRESPONDENCES: Air/Earth, Athena, Ishtar, Spirit.

HISTORY AND FOLKLORE: Egyptians, Greeks, Norse, Hindus, and Babylonians alike had myths about a spider goddess who weaves people's fates. The center of the spiderweb represents the meeting of all places and times. From there, the network of life and its cycles reaches out in all directions. And the spider's eight legs represent the Wheel of the Year.

In Japan, the spider spirit has the power of shapeshifting. Other Oceanic cultures consider this being a creative force who also gifted humankind with fire. Native Americans credit the spider with devising the first alphabet, and the Hopi specifically say that the spider embodies earth medicine.

SAMPLE APPLICATIONS: Folk magicians know that it is very bad luck to kill a spider; doing so cuts off money. So when you find one around your house, whisper your financial needs to it and then gently release it outside so it can bear your needs to all creation.

In visualization, focusing on the image of a spiderweb is good for communicating messages over a long distance or drawing creative energy to yourself. For the second, see yourself as the center of the web. Over each fiber energy can flow in toward you (see this as light carried on the thread). Stay with that imagery until you feel filled to overflowing and then go right to your creative tasks.

SQUARE

THEMES: Elements, Faithfulness, Grounding, Organization, Safety, Truth.

CORRESPONDENCES: Air (right side), Earth (top, and the whole shape), Fire (bottom), Water (left side).

HISTORY AND FOLKLORE: The square represents the four corners of creation. Because of the square's foundational nature, it has also often symbolized truth, integrity, order, faithfulness, and safety. Meanwhile, a square within a square becomes an emblem of the outer world and inner world, of the coresidence of both the temporal and spiritual within all things.

SAMPLE APPLICATIONS: I find it interesting that many modern magicians choose to house magickal tools in a decorative square box—it seems the protective energies of the square are rooted deeply in our subconscious. You may be able to use this in visualizations for psychic safety by seeing yourself in a mirrored or radiant light box (make sure it has three dimensions so it covers above and below too).

When you feel flights of fancy distracting you, bring more squares into your environment in everything from fabric patterns to picture frames. Or draw a square on a piece of paper using brown for the top edge, yellow for the left edge, red for the bottom and blue for the right. As you make each mark, beginning with the yellow, say in turn: "By air, by fire, by water, by earth, my thoughts remain grounded and firm." Carry this drawing with you.

SQUIRREL

THEMES: Meditation, Persistence, Playfulness, Resourcefulness, Spirituality, Strength, Weather Magick.

CORRESPONDENCES: Earth/Air.

HISTORY AND FOLKLORE: The squirrel is a bit of a mischief maker in Norse mythology, but it is also a welcome rain bringer. Buddhists have a far nicer image, seeing the squirrel as a symbol of spiritual strength that often comes through meditation. Mayans depicted the squirrel as a persistent gatherer-planter and one who is always prepared.

SAMPLE APPLICATIONS: The modern phrase "squirreling something away for a rainy day" says much about the squirrel's influence for magickal purposes. For shamanic work, the squirrel spirit can teach you much about frugality and careful use of your resources. If you listen patiently (squirrel spirits can get distracted), you may also get some good hints for your meditations!

If you need to learn something from the squirrel or tap its attributes, the easiest way is by giving the creature a gift of nuts. Hold the nuts in your hands and imagine your need, then sprinkle them on the ground moving clockwise (to generate positive energy), possibly adding an incantation like, "A gift given is a gift received, in this magick I believe, I open myself to receive!"

STAR

THEMES: Divination, Fate, Gardening, Guidance, Hope, Imagination, Omens, Oracles, Prophecy, Psychism, Reincarnation, Spirits, Wishcraft.

CORRESPONDENCES: Fire/Air, the God Aspect (morning star), the Goddess Aspect (evening star), North (the north star only).

HISTORY AND FOLKLORE: The number of beliefs about stars is staggering. Astrology emerged in Babylon somewhere around 2000 B.C.E. as a mapping system that helped guide people to distant places and as a system for predicting the outcomes of wars and other important matters. Astrology underwent some changes depending on the culture, but eventually got used to assist farmers in timing the planting and reaping of crops. Natal astrology (developed about two thousand years ago) still exists today as a popular divinatory and predictive method.

Islamic children had a true star that was thought to guide their destiny. In Native American traditions a star may be a spirit, the soul of an ancestor watching over the tribe, or the embodiment of god and goddess (morning and evening stars, respectively). The custom of wishing on stars appears in Malaysia (for love), Europe, Sicily, Laos, and the United States and likely originated in animistic nature worship.

SAMPLE APPLICATIONS: Every night my daughter watches out the window waiting to hang her wishes on the first star she sees. It's a charming custom and one well worth trying regularly. Keep these wishes simple, maintain hope in your heart, and see what happens!

Consider patterning your garden in the image of a star so that everything grown in it inspires hope, your imaginative sense, and your ability to understand nature's omens. Carry a silver star energized by the light of a full moon to help you manifest your psychic self in everyday life or use it as a spell component in magick aimed at better understanding your purpose in life. (Note: An inexpensive source of various colored stars can be found in the form of children's reward stickers!)

STATUARY

THEMES: Communion, Divination, Faith, Imitative Magick, Offering, Poppet Magick, Prophecy, Worship.

CORRESPONDENCES: Vary by image.

HISTORY AND FOLKLORE: Around the world ancient peoples used statues to represent their gods, goddesses, and important spirits. They placed these statues in public places to invoke divine protection, on their altars to inspire faith, and in temples where worshipers could come and leave offerings or commune with an image of the god/dess. Some rather interesting bits of magick resulted from this. For example, in Greece people would go to temples dedicated to Hermes, whisper a question in the god's ear, then go outside. The first phrase heard after that was considered the god's answer! In other parts of the world, small statues were sometimes used as an effective substitute for a poppet, receiving clothing or being acted upon in the manner desired for manifesting the magick!

SAMPLE APPLICATIONS: There is no reason not to follow our ancestors' lead on this. Use statues to represent gods, goddesses, or spirits with whom you wish a closer rapport. Decorate these seasonally and leave small, suitable offerings before them in times of need. Pray or meditate nearby to invoke the attention of that Being. By the way, you can often buy statuary at secondhand shops, but if these don't have what you want

I suggest lawn and garden shops or nurseries instead. There are also some mail-order catalogues that carry multicultural god and goddess images, like Tuscano, and on-line services like those offered at www.statue.com and archaeologic.com.

STRAWBERRY

THEMES: Fairies, Fertility, Love, Passion.

CORRESPONDENCES: Freyja, Water.

HISTORY AND FOLKLORE: Because they are sacred to the goddess of marriage and childbirth, it's not surprising to discover that strawberries have fertile, loving energy. Among Bavarians it's believed that fairies hide in strawberry patches!

SAMPLE APPLICATIONS: Old tidbits of folk magick recommend gathering strawberries on Lammas (August 1) to receive the maximum magickal benefit from the fruit. I personally believe that strawberries should be magickally paired with chocolate for a luscious, love-food dessert! Nibble on them to improve self-love too. Dried strawberry leaves can be carried as charms to attract more love into your life or to inspire visits by the wee folk.

STRING

THEMES: Binding, Fate, Freedom, Grounding, Guidance, Memory.

CORRESPONDENCES: Earth.

HISTORY AND FOLKLORE: The lore of string is closely tied (excuse the pun) to myths about fate and the magick of knots. For example, various gods and goddesses are depicted as fashioning destiny from string or yarn, and the children's game of cat's cradle has many mystical overtones. In this game—which appeared in Europe, Africa, South America, the Arctic, and Pacific regions—string is woven together into a pattern. Each pattern (depending on the culture) represented a story, a net with which to capture the sun or animals, or the web of life itself. Today, the symbolism behind string remains. We talk about cutting apron strings, tying a string to our finger so we never forget, and the silver cord that binds our soul to the body in the astral realm so we can safely find our way back.

SAMPLE APPLICATIONS: When a problem arises, write it on a piece of paper. Fold this in on itself and bind it with string to also bind the difficulty. To liberate yourself from a situation, visualize yourself bound to it by an energy string and then neatly cut that string in your imagination. For memory retention, name your string after what needs to be memorized and knot it as you speak. Tuck this someplace where you will notice it regularly. If string isn't available, try colored ribbons, yarn, sewing thread, or even curtain cords.

SUN

THEMES: Blessing, Conscious Mind, Energy, Enlightenment, Growth, Happiness, Hope, Leadership, Learning, Protection, Strength, Success.

CORRESPONDENCES: Apollo, Fire, the God Aspect, Osiris, Summer.

HISTORY AND FOLKLORE: As the most predominant object in the sky, the sun was very likely the first heavenly sphere worshiped. Many ancient pagan, shamanic, and druidic rituals honored the sun's movement through the sky or were designed to give it strength over darkness (especially in winter). Folk traditions tell us that when the sun shines on special occasions, it's a sign of divine favor and that following the natural movement of the sun in baking and other daily tasks encourages success.

SAMPLE APPLICATIONS: In modern magick traditions, the sun is considered predominantly masculine in nature, bearing the attributes that accentuate leadership, strength, learning, blessing, energy, vitality, growth, and the conscious mind. The easiest way to apply the sun's energy to your magick is to work while it's shining! To augment the effect even more, add yellow-or gold-colored components and ritual garb, which honor the sun, to the process.

When you feel a little drained of energy, take a moment and let your face bask in the rays of a bright sun (this is actually healthy for limited periods). When you need hope, watch a sunrise; reach out your hands, let the light saturate every cell of your being, and then go into the day refreshed.

SUNFLOWER

THEMES: Faithfulness, Growth, Truth.

CORRESPONDENCES: Apollo, Demeter, Fire, Sun.

HISTORY AND FOLKLORE: The Incas worshiped sunflowers as a suitable representative of the sacred sun. Similarly, Aztec priestesses wore them as crowns during special rituals to honor the gods. Greek mythology tells us that a sea nymph was so constant in her devotion to the sun that she became this lovely yellow flower that always turns to face the solar disk.

SAMPLE APPLICATIONS: Folk magicians sometimes use sunflowers in magick for personal growth and attainment, because they have very long sturdy roots that help the flower grow tall! It is also a favored component in truth-telling, simply by sleeping with the flower beneath one's pillow. Sprinkle sunflower petals around the sacred space for fire festivals or anytime you're working with solar energies, or eat sunflower seeds to internalize the radiant power of the sun and the devoted nature of this flower.

TANSY

THEMES: Beauty, Fertility, Health, Longevity, Purification, Reincarnation.

CORRESPONDENCES: The Goddess Aspect, Water.

HISTORY AND FOLKLORE: Some myths say that tansy was presented to Ganymede to make him immortal. Over time, this gave the tansy strong associations with the immortality of the human soul.

SAMPLE APPLICATIONS: Today many magicians use tansy as a purifying element in women's rituals. It's also carried to banish headaches (smell it for this purpose). A magickally prepared poultice of tansy flowers rubbed on the belly improves the chances of conception, and applied to the face it enhances beauty.

TATTOO

THEMES: Anti-magick, Community, Courage, Kinship, Love, Protection, Safety, Strength, Success, Unity.

CORRESPONDENCES: Fire (may vary by marking).

HISTORY AND FOLKLORE: The art of tattooing has a long history dating back to the Egyptians. There and in many tribal societies tattoos helped mark a person's community, family, personal accomplishments, and much more. Beyond that, many tattoos (temporary or permanent) bestowed magickal power on the wearer. When young people prepared for a hunting rite of passage, they received special markings for courage and success.

When the Celts went into battle, they wore woad to frighten the enemy and give themselves strength. In parts of India and New Zealand it's considered unseemly to go before the deity without a tattoo, and in Burma women wear tattoos on their lips as a love charm.

SAMPLE APPLICATIONS: Tattooing has regained a lot of attention today as a way of setting oneself apart from the crowd. If you wish to get a tattoo to mark your magickal Path, you can certainly do so. I know some groups whose members even get the same tattoo to denote their unity and focus. For those like me, however, who don't like the idea of needles, I suggest washable body paints as a viable alternative. Paint the image of your goal on yourself and keep it safe until the magick manifests!

TEA

THEMES: Awareness, Congeniality, Divination, Enlightenment, Faithfulness, Meditation, Prayer.

CORRESPONDENCES: Water/Fire.

HISTORY AND FOLKLORE: There's a wonderful story from China about a Zen monk who meditated by himself seeking enlightenment. Sadly, after nine faithful years he fell asleep. When he woke up he was so ashamed that he tore off his eyelids. Where they landed on the ground, the first tea plant blossomed, so no other devoted followers would nod off again!

Gypsies and other fortune-tellers have often turned to tea leaves for insights, and it is a favored beverage for treating illness.

SAMPLE APPLICATIONS: Tea has a friendly demeanor and is a good beverage to drink periodically to enhance this attribute in yourself. Enjoy any type of herbal tea just prior to meditation (simply match the flavor to your meditative goals), or add a couple of pinches of dry tea to your incense for awareness.

To divine with tea leaves, you'll have to get some loose tea and steep it. Drink carefully while thinking of a question. When there's about one teaspoon of liquid left, swirl it three times clockwise and then gently tip over the cup. Right it and look to see what patterns develop. Those appearing near the center of the cup are more intimate and current. So if, for example, you see a heart here, it portends love on the horizon, while a ring at the edge of the cup represents a commitment in the future.

THYME

THEMES: Courage, Dreams, Fairies, Fear, Happiness, Hope, Purification, Strength.

CORRESPONDENCES: Water.

HISTORY AND FOLKLORE: Throughout European folk traditions thyme represents strength, attracts fairies, and banishes the fears of anyone who carries a fresh sprig. Sprinkling it around any space drives off evil spirits and lifts depression.

SAMPLE APPLICATIONS: Magickally paired with rosemary, thyme evokes magickal dreams, often of relationships. Many modern practitioners like to add a bit of thyme to purification incense, following the Greek tradition of burning it in the temples. Beyond this, it's an effective herb for pantry magick to internalize the energy of joy and renewed hope.

TIDES

THEMES: Abundance, Fertility, Healing, Meditation, Prosperity, Tenacity, Transformation.

CORRESPONDENCES: The Goddess Aspect, Water.

HISTORY AND FOLKLORE: A lot of lore is associated with tides in seafaring communities. In Brittany, for example, sowing seed at high tide brings fertility. Similarly, in Norse tradition the early morning tide represented abundance, prenoon tides brought growth and prosperity, and midday tides represented the will. Following suit, the tide at dusk brings transformation, evening tides are fertile, night tides augment awareness, midnight tides heal, and premorning tides improve meditative abilities.

SAMPLE APPLICATIONS: If you're fortunate enough to live in an area that experiences tidal fluctuation, you can use this rhythm as a foundation for timing your spells and rituals. Definitely go to the beach for these, as being close to the water energizes the work. As the tide is coming in (or moving out, depending on the symbolic value) draw an image in the sand of what you want to manifest, and let the water do the rest!

TIN

THEMES: Luck, Travel.

CORRESPONDENCES: Air, Moon, Thor.

HISTORY AND FOLKLORE: Ancient alchemists tell us that the best day for using tin as a component is Thursday ("Thor's day"). Carrying tin promotes good fortune, and, when necessary, the color makes it a suitable substitute for silver.

SAMPLE APPLICATIONS: Wrap a dollar bill around a bit of tin to improve your luck with money. If you're one of those folks who has unending car problems, tin is a great automobile amulet that also seems to help avert breakdowns. For this purpose I recommend putting it in the trunk with your emergency kit (kind of like taking an umbrella so it won't rain!).

TOMATO

THEMES: Love.

CORRESPONDENCES: Water.

HISTORY AND FOLKLORE: It took a while for the tomato to become part of culinary arts because it was associated with the deadly nightshade. However, over time it became known as the "love apple" and has been part of magickal love and romance menus ever since.

SAMPLE APPLICATIONS: To this day Italian witches use tomatoes and tomato sauce as a gentle nudge to star-crossed lovers (you'll notice many ingredients in traditional spaghetti sauce have love correspondences!). Also because of the red color, tomato sauce and juice are a suitable blood substitute, especially in old love spells. If you grow tomatoes in your magickal garden, they'll deter bug infestation and inspire loving energies in all the vegetables/flowers. You can also can, dry, or freeze spiritually augmented tomatoes to preserve their energy for another time when it's needed.

TRIANGLE

THEMES: Balance, Banishing, Growth, Knowledge.

CORRESPONDENCES: Fire, the God Aspect, the Goddess Aspect.

HISTORY AND FOLKLORE: The ancient goddess had three aspects: maiden, mother, and crone. This idea explains part of the triangle's symbolic value—to this day cauldrons still have three legs set in a triangular pattern!

Hindus use a downward pointing triangle for the feminine aspect, interlocking triangles as creative force, and an upward red triangle as the *tattvas* (elemental symbol) that represents fire and the masculine principle. By using this last image, the practitioner learns to control and invoke the fire element and its associated deity. Greeks seemed to follow suit, except the fire triangle bore no color. In this region the word for pyramid (a triangle in three dimensions) means spirit or active thought.

SAMPLE APPLICATIONS: Folk magicians sometimes wrote their spells so they formed a point-down triangle for banishing ("Abracadabra" being a notable example for sickness) or point-upward for growth-related energies. This pattern is still fully functional for modern folk magick.

Abracadabra
abracadabr
abracadab
abracada
abracad
abraca
abrac
abra
abr
ab
a

It's interesting that a masculine element (fire) is so strongly associated with a feminine emblem. This makes the triangle a good shape to focus on in meditations where you're balancing your feminine and masculine attributes.

TURQUOISE

THEMES: Congeniality, Fear, Goals, Imitative Magick, Protection, Safety, Travel, Weather Magick.

CORRESPONDENCES: Buddha, Hathor, Water or Earth (varies by writer).

HISTORY AND FOLKLORE: As early as the thirteenth century we see turquoise being worn by travelers—humans and horses alike—as a protective amulet. For many years it was considered a man's stone, often as a sign of social standing. In Persia, where the stone originates, it is a talisman of luck, courage, and safety. The Pueblo Indians often carved animal images in this stone for sympathetic/imitative magick, and the Apache consider it a shaman's stone suited to weather magick and marksmanship on the hunt.

SAMPLE APPLICATIONS: In our mobile society, turquoise is among the most valuable stones to keep in your magickal contingent. Add it to a portable altar for your car or suitcase.

Find a ring with a turquoise set into it to improve your congeniality and overall social demeanor, or put a piece of turquoise on top of a paper with your personal goals listed on it for good luck and to help speed manifestation. To bring a gentle rain, take a handful of tiny turquoise stones and sprinkle them on a liquid surface saying, "Moisture drawn from the seas, rain come to me!" If you don't want to lose them, put them in a rain stick made from a cardboard tube closed at both ends. Shake this gently while dancing clockwise to draw the rain, counterclockwise to turn it away.

TURTLE (TORTOISE)

THEMES: Creativity, Divination, Longevity, Messages, Providence, Strength, Tenacity.

CORRESPONDENCES: Aphrodite, Vishnu, Water/Earth.

HISTORY AND FOLKLORE: Hindu mythology shows the world resting on the back of a giant tortoise. Here, the creature symbolizes the creative power of water and the provision of earth. In China the turtle's four feet are the four quarters of creation, and the animal represents long life, tenacity, and strength. In China and Japan, turtle shells were often used for divination by heating them till they cracked and then interpreting the lines. This tradition may have evolved because the Japanese consider turtles divine emissaries.

SAMPLE APPLICATIONS: When you feel you may have need of divine assistance in the future, visualize that need being carried by a turtle across the waters to a heavenly land. The tortoise spirit will make sure the message is delivered safely. To draw upon the turtle's other attributes, I've found the small soapstone carvings available at many Eastern-style gift shops to be quite affordable and magickally appealing. They have a very soft texture which encourages rubbing—this, in turn, puts energy into the stone, specifically the energy of your thoughts at that moment.

UMBRELLA

THEMES: Leadership, Power, Protection, Unity.

CORRESPONDENCES: Buddha, Sun.

HISTORY AND FOLKLORE: Though a symbol of the god's power and leadership and the solar wheel in India and Mexico, some people believe the design for these originated from the sphere depicted over Buddha's head called the *da-cha*. White umbrellas were part of Greek rituals for the sun and in marriage rites of Africa, likely alluding to purity, protection, and the unity afforded by the sacred circle.

SAMPLE APPLICATIONS: Since it's really easy to get a variety of umbrellas today, these could prove really fun for spring and summer rituals. During spring, choose elementally colored ones, put them at the four quarters of the sacred space, and play the sounds of rainfall in the background. Come summer, twirl brightly colored umbrellas while you dance around a ritual fire. Paint a wish on them, so that as they spin clockwise they generate energy for bringing that goal to fruition!

VANILLA

THEMES: Happiness, Love, Passion, Sexuality.

CORRESPONDENCES: Water.

HISTORY AND FOLKLORE: An old Central American myth tells us of a young goddess who turned herself into the vanilla bean to give pleasure and joy to the mortal man she loved. It has remained an herb strongly related to love and relationships in modern magick circles.

SAMPLE APPLICATIONS: Stick a fresh vanilla bean in your sugar jar for sweet love! Vanilla also takes well to oils and vinegars, so it's easy to make all kinds of culinary additives that are filled with exciting, warm energy.

To ensure that love will always walk with you, stick a vanilla bean in some body powder and leave it there until the aroma is pleasing. Sprinkle this in your shoes daily saying, "Love from me, love find me, love be with me."

VIOLET

THEMES: Anxiety, Death, Faithfulness, Forgiveness, Jealousy, Protection, Sleep, Spirits.

CORRESPONDENCES: Water, Zeus.

HISTORY AND FOLKLORE: Violets bear the folk name of heartsease, which is why violets have been used in magick to ease the pain that comes with losing a loved one or when love goes awry. Greek and Roman myths often say this flower is the result of jealousy, yet the Greeks sometimes wore the petals to offset anger or improve sleep! In another odd twist, we find these flowers adorning babies' beds and newlyweds' rooms in old

Germany, which may have been a way of trying to protect these areas from ghosts. In the language of flowers, the violet represents devotion.

SAMPLE APPLICATIONS: Violet-scented potpourri and incense are marvelous for people experiencing a lot of stress. Violet calms and comforts the vibrations throughout your environment. Should you find yourself suffering a case of the "green-eyed" meanies, try tucking a violet in your pocket or shoe to deter that negative behavior. At the end of the day it's best to tear this petal up and return it to the earth, so as to disperse the negativity. By the way, violets are edible, so nibble a few petals before bed or steep them in tea saying, "Violet, violet, 'tis the end of day, bring me safe to sleep, come what may." This spell improves sleep, and keeps you safe from wandering spirits until dawn.

WALNUT

THEMES: Anti-magick, Conscious Mind, Fertility, Learning, Wishcraft, Worship.

CORRESPONDENCES: Fire, Jupiter, Sun, Zeus.

HISTORY AND FOLKLORE: The Greeks and Romans served walnuts at weddings for fertility. Conversely, should one wish not to bear children, Romanian lore recommends burying walnuts, one per year. *Strege* (Italian witches) sometimes met beneath the boughs of this tree to worship, yet many European customs instruct keeping walnuts around as an anti-magick charm! Finally, in the doctrine of signatures (which says an object's appearance is a clue to its function) walnuts are recommended for mental healing and enhancement.

SAMPLE APPLICATIONS: Anytime you're studying your magick notes, keep a handful of walnuts nearby to maintain mental keenness. Carry one with you to turn away unwanted magicks, or place them in any area where you want to attract fertility in literal or figurative terms.

A fun form of wishcraft uses the walnut shell. For this, split a walnut in half, keeping both halves of the shell intact, and remove the meat. Put a small piece of paper with your wish written on it inside the shell and close the halves around it. Tie it closed with a suitably colored ribbon, knotting the ribbon three times (adding an incantation, if desired, at this time), and leave this undisturbed in a safe place until the wish manifests. Then burn the tied shell on a ritual fire, giving thanks.

WAND

THEMES: Goals, Magick, Power, Transformation.

CORRESPONDENCES: Air.

HISTORY AND FOLKLORE: The rod with which Moses struck the rock and obtained water was a kind of magickal wand. In fact, the mere variety of wands in various cultural settings is pretty amazing, ranging from the shamanic talking sticks to staves and rulers' batons. Fairies are also often depicted bearing a wand, denoting their connection to magick.

Speaking of fairies, the most telling tale showing the wand's symbolic value is "Cinderella." In it the fairy godmother transforms a serving girl into a princess through the power of hope and a little magick!

SAMPLE APPLICATIONS: No matter how simple or complex, wands represent magickal power and proficiency. The point at the top neatly directs energy where you want it to go, so it reaches the goal with more accuracy. If you can, I highly suggest making your own out of a fallen branch. Decorate it with a few crystals (quartz is a good choice) and perhaps a handhold. Then, as you're weaving a spell, hold it in your strong hand and visualize the energy of your magick being directed through your arm, through the wood, and, amplified by the crystals, outward—beaming toward its mark!

WATER

THEMES: Beauty, Blessing, Creativity, Fertility, Happiness, Healing, Peace, Purification, Weather Magick.

CORRESPONDENCES: Mari, Mithra, Poseidon, Water.

HISTORY AND FOLKLORE: The world's mythology is filled with stories of life originating in a cosmic sea filled with the power of the gods. Meanwhile on land, wells were regarded as having indwelling spirits that could be appeased (Europe), which is how we come by one popular wishing tradition!

The idea of blessing people or animals with sacred water appears in Saudi Arabia, Germany, Macedonia, and Wales. Divination by water seems nearly as popular, appearing in Babylonia, Greece, India, Israel, and much of Europe. Beyond this there's a great deal of folk magick centered around using water for healing (to cleanse), to improve relationships (fertility, peace, and joy), and to attract or banish storms.

SAMPLE APPLICATIONS: The great attraction of working with water in folk magick is that it comes in many forms, including dew, rain, snow, ice, steam, and tears! If you use any of the alternate forms, however, the theme of the magick should somehow denote the change in state (like frozen water barring fertility instead of augmenting it).

Personally, I love dancing in a gentle rainstorm to receive blessings and rinse away the tensions of the moment. It really releases the inner child too! Or try gathering dew on May 1 and washing in it. This is said to bring out your true beauty. Use water moving away from you to carry things out of your life, and water flowing toward you to bear its power into the moment.

WHALE

THEMES: Death, Magick, Psychism, Reincarnation, Spirituality.

CORRESPONDENCES: Earth, Water.

HISTORY AND FOLKLORE: In the biblical story of Jonah and the whale, this great creature's belly represents the land of the dead. Arctic and Arabian lore says the earth rests on the back of a great whale and earthquakes are caused by the shaking of its tail. In Russia the story is pretty similar, except that four whales (one for each direction) hold the earth. In Norse tradition witches ride whales, and as such they represent the birthing of magickal power. Oceanic cultures regard whales as the preferred mounts for the sea gods.

SAMPLE APPLICATIONS: Because of the whale's association with magick, some modern practitioners regard a whale totem or a dream about whales as representing growing psychic abilities. From a shamanic vantage point, the creature is a marvelous guide in discovering your spiritual self. Because of the mingling of earth and water energies, those wishing to develop a stronger awareness of earth as a global community would do well to carry the image of a whale with them. To awaken or augment your magickal abilities, try visualizing yourself on the back of a great whale being caught in a spray of sparkling light from its blowhole. Welcome this light and its energy into every cell of your being.

WHITE

THEMES: Death, Luck, Magick, Offering, Protection, Purity, Safety.

CORRESPONDENCES: Air, Moon, Spirit, Winter.

HISTORY AND FOLKLORE: In various tribal societies, only white creatures were considered suitable to offer to the gods, likely alluding to a kind of purity represented by the color. Also, white animals were thought to have magickal power. Wrapping yourself or an object in the skin of such a creature would afford great protection and luck (this has translated into the use of white cloth for similar goals in modern practices).

In the Far East, white is the color of mourning. In many other settings it is the sacred color of the goddess, but may also represent Spirit in all its forms and power.

SAMPLE APPLICATIONS: A white candle on your altar is a perfect symbol for the god/dess, especially when lit. Other round, white objects are a suitable representation for the moon in your sacred space. Wear white or carry white-colored stones when you feel the need for additional protection, during those moments when you want your intentions to remain virtuous, for a little extra good fortune, or to augment your magickal awareness.

WILLOW

THEMES: Beauty, Death, Divination, Health, Love, Magick, Providence, Safety.

CORRESPONDENCES: Artemis, Diana, Hecate, Hera, Moon, Water.

HISTORY AND FOLKLORE: Among the many types of trees used for water witching (dowsing), people in the Far East consider the willow the tree of immortality. In Greek tradition, any souls who bore a bit of willow on them during their afterlife journey would always arrive in the land of the dead safely.

At the advent of spring, Romanians hang willow to ensure providence and good health. European folk tradition recommends carrying willow to attract love, while the Gypsies keep it as a charm that enhances one's beauty.

SAMPLE APPLICATIONS: One of my favorite trees for as long as I can recall, the willow is a gracious lady. Many modern practitioners believe that the word *witch* may have originated with the willow, because of the tree's flexibility (magick's aim is to bend and change) and its strong connections with magick charms. Consequently, I recommend willow wood for homemade wands and rune sets and ground willow as an all-purpose magickal incense base.

If you're interested in learning the willow's lessons, take one of its long tresses and wrap it gently around your waist. Stand and meditate beneath the tree, breathing deeply. Open your awareness and see if you receive mental images or feelings—these are messages from the willow.

WIND

THEMES: Communication, Comprehension, Fertility, Guidance, Healing, Knowledge, Learning, Luck, Messages, Motivation, Omens, Oracles, Spirits, Travel, Wishcraft.

CORRESPONDENCES: Air, East, Spirit (others depending on direction of the wind), Zeus.

HISTORY AND FOLKLORE: The wind is moody, changeable, and elusive, which is likely why many ancient peoples associated it with ghosts or the Great Spirit. In Hebrew tradition the wind is fertile and productive, Native Americans speak of it inhabiting the four corners of creation, and Arabs specialized in knot magick to contain or release the winds.

In Chile, Greece, and Tibet, people observed the winds for omens and signs. Greeks, in particular, watched the ancient oak at Donada, listening to the wind rustling through its leaves. This sound would be interpreted by the oracle on duty.

SAMPLE APPLICATIONS: Wind magick offers many alternatives for the modern practitioner, since each direction from which the wind comes changes the energies it bears. The eastern winds bring air energies (communication, hope), southern winds bear fire energy (passion, warmth, power), western winds convey water energy (emotions, love, healing), and northern winds contain earth energy (grounding, growth). So if you know which direction the wind is blowing from, you can release light objects (seeds, flower petals, rice, bread crumbs, and the like) to the winds with wishes and desires.

For luck when you travel, take a coin and toss it toward the direction the wind is blowing from. This will ensure a safe, enjoyable excursion. To get the winds to change (and thereby your fortune), toss a beryl stone in the direction you'd like the winds to come from while whistling. And finally, don't forget to get out and walk with the wind at your back regularly for good health, motivation, and effortless living.

WINE

THEMES: Blessing, Creativity, Fellowship, Happiness, Healing, Hospitality, Love, Oaths, Offering, Oracles, Unity.

CORRESPONDENCES: Bacchus, Dionysus, Thor (red wine), Water/Fire.

HISTORY AND FOLKLORE: Wine appeared on altars across the world as a suitable offering to the Sacred Powers. Greeks played a game with wine, and if any spilled they'd interpret the splashings! Some oracles in this region sometimes imbibed wine before pronouncing prophecies. It's interesting to learn that the Greeks felt that Dionysus was so much a part of grapes that each time wine was poured out, he was there to join the celebration!

During the Middle Ages healers favored wine as a base for remedies, because it was healthier than drinking water and covered the taste of less pleasant herbs.

SAMPLE APPLICATIONS: I enjoy making wine for special personal and magickal occasions. By choosing the fruits and spices according to metaphysical associations, the results are tasty and energized. For those who don't have as much time, choose your wine's color according to your goal, then flavor it with suitable herbs, juices, or ginger ale for uplifting energy.

During harvest festivals sprinkle wine around the circle to mark the sacred space. Leave a chalice of wine on the altar for the god/dess and pour it out in libation as part of your ritual or spell. Sip a bit with friends to facilitate friendship and unity, or just leave a corked bottle somewhere in the house where the energy within can slowly age to perfection!

WOODRUFF

THEMES: Banishing, Congeniality, Money, Protection.

CORRESPONDENCES: Fire, Spring.

HISTORY AND FOLKLORE: Romans used woodruff to honor the coming of spring and the goddess Flora, from whom we get the word *flower*. European lore says carrying this wood or its flowers improves congeniality, and growing the tree or keeping snippets around the house attracts money and protective energy. This is why churches often hung blossoming woodruff during spring festivals. It banished evil spirits.

SAMPLE APPLICATIONS: Add a sprig of woodruff to your May Day bowl and decorate the sacred space with the lovely flowers. After the tree stops flowering, bits of branches, bark, and wood make a good base for incense, especially for burning in conjunction with magick to protect your finances. Alternatively, use a piece of woodruff as a component in sociability spells.

WORDS

THEMES: Banishing, Binding, Blessing, Communication, Comprehension, Courage, Manifestation, Memory, Power, Protection, Victory.

CORRESPONDENCES: Air.

HISTORY AND FOLKLORE: Words have power, and the ancients were intimately aware of this. A deathbed curse from someone was among the worst kind of magickally empowered words, for example. Yet one could turn away the evil eye or garner various other positive abilities by speaking the right words in the proper magickal sequence!

Egyptians considered speech divinely inspired. The Bible says God spoke the universe into being, and Japanese warriors had a shout of power that was said to give them victory in battle. To this day, children recite various lessons to commit them to memory and internalize the power of that knowledge.

SAMPLE APPLICATIONS: Throughout this book you've seen examples of incantations, chants, and affirmations to help your magick along. Now's the time to try creating one or two yourself. Think of something positive you'd like to bring to your life or develop inwardly. Make a little rhyme that emphasizes that goal—keep it short so you can recite it anytime, anywhere. Consider if there's a number that coincides with that goal (such as two for partnership), then repeat the incantation/chant/affirmation that number of times. Each time you think to do this, the energy in the air within and around you changes to mirror your goal and helps manifest the magick!

YELLOW

THEMES: Communication, Congeniality, Creativity, Faith, Fertility, Friendship, Leadership, Strength, Travel.

CORRESPONDENCES: Fire, Sun/Air.

HISTORY AND FOLKLORE: As an alternative to gold, it's not surprising to find yellow having many of the characteristics of that metal. Pale yellow, however, is more strongly associated with the air element, while vibrant yellow is equated with fire. The ancient European mages tell us that yellow is a lucky color for those born under the signs of Libra or Taurus, while Chinese mages favored yellow-colored paper upon which to inscribe their spells. They felt this improved the spell's potency.

SAMPLE APPLICATIONS: In modern times it's become a custom to give yellow roses as a sign of friendship, so that hue can become part of any friendship spell. You can certainly try the Chinese approach and see if the vibrations of this color improve the results of your written spellcraft. Beyond that, surround yourself with yellow highlights when you need a creative or charismatic boost. For faith and communication, keep the tones softer, such as the pale yellow glow of a candle or pastel yellow-colored decorations.

CHAPTER 5

Modern Components

In the last chapter, we examined many of the traditional components that magicians throughout history have used in their art. But what about modern practitioners? Of course we continue to use many of the components suggested by our ancestors and frequently honor the metaphysical correspondences those items were given in the ancient past with little variance. Be that as it may, our world is changing very rapidly. Technology has brought innovations that our forebears never even imagined, but certainly would have used if given the chance! See, the folk magician was always a pragmatist: if it worked, was readily available, and suited the task, it got used!

With that utilitarian tradition in mind, this chapter gives you fun ideas about how to use modern gadgets, foods, stones, and other items in magickal constructs. Again, this refocuses your attention on the potential in and around the sacred space of the home. Just because something is "newfangled" doesn't mean it's counterproductive to magick. In fact, because these things are around us all the time, their symbolic value may be more potent than traditional components to which we've had less exposure!

Note, however, that it would be impossible to include all the possible modern goodies in a book of this size. What follows is just a brief sampling intended to provide some examples that, in turn, will tantalize your imagination and creativity.

For the most part, modern items haven't had time to develop much in the way of history or folklore, so those sections cannot be provided here. Since I have no real precedence upon which to build, the associations listed under both "Themes" and "Correspondences" are purely personally devised. If you feel other themes or correspondences are more suitable because of personal experience, pay close attention to that inner voice. It is far more dependable than any book or author.

AIR CONDITIONER

THEMES: Anger, Clarity, Forgiveness, Messages.

CORRESPONDENCES: Air, East, Summer, Wind Gods and Goddesses.

SAMPLE APPLICATIONS: Turn on your air conditioner anytime you're working magick to cool down a heated situation. The symbolism is very powerful, and the cool air adds a sensory dimension to the effort. Beyond this, having a gust of cool air aimed in our direction improves clarity, so we can resolve the issues that led to being angry.

To convey a message to someone, hang an aromatic bundle whose scent symbolizes your missive in front of the air conditioner before turning it on. Once activated, the aroma will continue to convey your feelings until the air conditioner is turned off (note: this works best for people inside the building, since windows aren't opened to allow the aromatic magick to waft outside).

BALLOONS

THEMES: Anxiety, Happiness, Hope, Playfulness, Wishcraft, Youthfulness.

CORRESPONDENCES: Air.

SAMPLE APPLICATIONS: In contemporary settings balloons represent happy occasions. So when you feel a little depressed, consider blowing up a few and enjoying the youthful gaiety. Or visualize your tensions being lifted away in a hot-air balloon moving far into the distant sky. Conversely, envision a balloon popping over your head and spilling a rainbow of hope into your heart chakra.

Get a friend to help you with this wish spell. Blow up a balloon whose color sympathizes with your desire. Paint a symbol on the balloon that also represents that goal. Then to keep magick afloat, take turns tapping the balloon to keep it in the air. Each tap increases the energy you put toward manifesting that wish. (Note: some people recommend releasing the balloon to the winds with your wish, but the plastic material can be quite harmful to animals and birds. This is an earth-friendly alternative.)

BARBECUE

THEMES: Abundance, Banishing, Comprehension, Divination, Guidance, Kinship, Offering, Prayer, Providence, Purification, Wishcraft.

CORRESPONDENCES: Fire, Hearth Gods and Goddesses, Summer.

SAMPLE APPLICATIONS: From the time the snow melts here until it flies again, my back yard becomes an ongoing fire festival! I love to grill and blend in a little magick as I go (it's really interesting to see how the energy affects the whole neighborhood as it's carried on the aromas). The smoke effectively carries away negativity, the light banishes any shadows and improves awareness, the fire purifies, and the scent conveys our wishes!

Your barbecue is a modern version of the tribal fire and can be used in much the same way (in fact, for outdoor gatherings this is really fun). I do recommend preparing the grill without chemical lighting fluid for magickal goals, however. And save burning any herbs that don't mingle with your food for after the cooking process has been finished; then toss a handful of charged aromatics on the lingering coals.

BATTERIES

THEMES: Control, Energy, Manifestation, Motivation, Potential, Power, Resourcefulness, Tenacity.

CORRESPONDENCES: Fire.

SAMPLE APPLICATIONS: Batteries have a lot in common with quartz in that they can hold whatever energy you put into them. For this purpose I suggest using a *nearly* dead battery. One that's fully charged leaves less room for your spiritual "charging," and one that's completely dead has all the wrong symbolic connotations. In particular, small batteries are great for pocket magick aimed at boosting or regulating personal energy. Combined with a handheld flashlight or other item that you can turn on, the symbolism becomes one of manifestation and moving the energy where you want it to go.

BLACKTOP

THEMES: Concealment, Fellowship, Forgiveness, Peace, Shapeshifting, Transformation, Travel.

CORRESPONDENCES: Earth.

SAMPLE APPLICATIONS: Blacktop smoothes over a rough road allowing us to move from place to place freely and engage in fellowship with one another. The smooth texture implies peace and forgiveness (because it goes over bumps like a salve). For those readers wishing to even out rough edges in their personality or minimally conceal them on a specific occasion, this is a nice component to carry as a charm (just pick up a piece near the road and put it in a power pouch or other magickal blend).

The transformative quality of blacktop may also provide a good vehicle to help with shapeshifting work. Visualize your aura being covered with the liquid form and taking on the shape desired. (Note: I'd recommend using it only for a black-colored creature.)

BLENDER/MIXER/FOOD PROCESSOR

THEMES: Cooperation, Cycles, Energy, Equality, Transformation.

CORRESPONDENCES: Air/Fire.

SAMPLE APPLICATIONS: Blenders transform food from one form to another. So if you put in a mixture that conveys the theme of what you want to change, the mixing process supports that goal. It also gives whole new meaning to the phrase "whipping something up"!

In most blenders, the blades move clockwise generating positive energy. The constant circular motion also represents cycles. Finally, since everything that goes into the mixer comes out in equal-sized portions, it's a good tool to use in magick for fostering cooperation and fair treatment.

BRICK

THEMES: Binding, Grounding, Protection, Strength.

CORRESPONDENCES: Earth.

SAMPLE APPLICATIONS: Bricks represent a kind of strength and resiliency. Their shape and function also symbolize the earth and its foundational powers. Carry a piece of brick with you to keep one foot on the ground or to improve physical strength. Alternatively, take a symbol of something from which you wish protection and surround it with brick for safety and to bind that negative energy neatly inside.

BUBBLES

THEMES: Creativity, Divination, Happiness, Hope, Imagination, Playfulness, Youthfulness.

CORRESPONDENCES: Air/Water, Moon.

SAMPLE APPLICATIONS: The luminescent sphere created by a bubble makes it an excellent representation of a full moon floating upward into the sky. Focus on this sphere and catch it when it returns to earth to likewise recapture your playful, imaginative, creative spirit. Or speak your problems into the bubbles as you blow them. When they fly away, they'll take those difficulties away with them.

I have a friend who likes to scry the surface of her dish soap bubbles (talk about accomplishing two things at once!). She says to try this yourself, simply place a candle or two nearby so they shine a gentle light on the water's surface without dripping into the sink. Watch for images or shapes to appear in the bubbles' configuration. This works in the bathtub too!

BUTTER

THEMES: Congeniality, Prosperity.

CORRESPONDENCES: Earth.

SAMPLE APPLICATIONS In ancient times, only the upper classes could afford butter, making it a food through which you can literally spread abundance into your life. Additionally, taking a cue from the modern phrase "buttering someone up," this edible makes a good medium through which one may either internalize better feelings toward others or try and inspire congeniality from others. To add to the magick, scratch a name or symbol in a piece of toast before eating it so you can "apply" the magick to where it's most needed before consuming.

CAMERA

THEMES: Clarity, Communication, Messages, Perspective, Spirits.

CORRESPONDENCES: Spirit.

SAMPLE APPLICATIONS: When cameras were first presented to more primitive peoples, they considered them "soul stealers." It's interesting that many modern ghost hunters claim that spirits do, indeed, show up on film even in the absence of any other signs of haunting!

A picture is worth "a thousand words," giving cameras strong associations with our ability to communicate things effectively. Part of this comes from the camera's ability to clarify an image and provide better perspective. In order to put this idea to use in a magickal setting, mindfully create a set that represents your goals and take pictures of it from various angles (consider chanting, singing, or adding an incantation while you work). Get the photos developed, and then leave one or two snapshots in a visible place to continually remind yourself of the energies created.

CHOCOLATE

THEMES: Blessing, Forgiveness, Happiness, Imitative Magick, Kindness, Love, Passion.

CORRESPONDENCES: Water.

SAMPLE APPLICATIONS: Good chocolate is the ultimate soul food for many people, and its taste seems to incite love, passion, joy, and numerous other positive emotions. Better still, since chocolate melts, solidifies, and freezes well, it makes a wonderful vehicle for imitative magick. You want to internalize love? Get or make a chocolate heart. For forgiveness, give the heart to the one from whom forgiveness is needed (ever notice how often we apologize with flowers and chocolates?). And when someone is feeling down, offer a bit of chocolate and watch the mood change! Okay, so part of the magick here is thanks to sugar, but the chemical magick that happens within our bodies shouldn't be overlooked or underrated. It helps the internalization process along!

CLOCK (OR TIMER)

THEMES: Death, Fate, Healing, Manifestation, Memory, Omens, Spellcraft.

CORRESPONDENCE: Earth.

SAMPLE APPLICATIONS: As a symbol of time, clocks gathered some folk-lore that we can consider for modern magick. Specifically the random chiming of a clock on off-times often portended ill events like death.

We may also consider aphorisms like "Time heals all wounds" and "All things in good time" for symbolic value. In this case, one might arrange for an alarm clock to sound at the end of a healing spell or as part of magick aimed at speedy manifestation (the alarm has similar symbolism to bells with the additional implications of being a gentle reminder of something or promptness).

COASTERS

THEMES: Balance, Cycles, Elements, Protection, Spellcraft.

CORRESPONDENCES: Earth, Spirit.

SAMPLE APPLICATIONS: You have two things to consider in looking to coasters for magickal functions: their form and application. First, most coasters are round, so they represent the sacred circle and associated energies. Second, coasters balance cups and provide protection to surfaces. Putting this into a functional scenario, paint the coaster with the four elemental colors and put glasses full of magickal potions on top of them to keep the energy moving! Or paint the image of your goal on the coaster and use it with any beverage to provide an extra magickal boost. Protective coasters can be stored in an area where their sphere of safety is most needed.

COFFEE

THEMES: Awareness, Clarity, Comprehension, Conscious Mind, Divination, Fellowship, Focus, Learning, Tenacity, Zeal.

CORRESPONDENCES: Fire/Water.

SAMPLE APPLICATIONS: Coffee's stimulating effect is well known. We drink a cup to wake ourselves up, to pay attention, to stay with long or difficult projects, to provide an extra burst of energy in the last mile, and so forth. Beyond that, we often gather socially over this beverage. All these things combine to make coffee something that can easily be adapted into a magickal potion, especially now that gourmet (flavored) coffees are available on supermarket shelves. Choose vanilla to improve loving feelings between two people sharing coffee together, try zesty cinnamon for energy plus, or perhaps orange coffee to inspire devotion. Don't forget to stir clockwise when charging your coffee to draw positive energy into the beverage.

Some very creative people have learned how to scry their coffee simply by adding a bit of cream and swirling it clockwise. Keep your question in mind while you do this and see what images, letters, and shapes appear. Compare these to tea-leaf images for interpretation values.

Finally, if you're not a coffee lover, you can use the energy in coffee beans or grounds by adding them to power pouches, incense, charms, and amulets instead. In fact, in a ritual aimed at improving personal energy, you could even use coffee beans to mark the perimeter of the sacred space.

COMPUTER

THEMES: Communication, Community, Knowledge, Memory, Unity.

CORRESPONDENCES: Vary depending on part.

SAMPLE APPLICATIONS: Computers and the Internet have changed the face of the world and made us a truly global community. Through this amazing tool we can learn about new things and communicate over long distances, not to mention write books like this one! Since computers work on electricity, there's no reason you can't piggyback magickal energy on your next e-mail, or pour it into a special file to open up later when you need it most. I know groups who hold ritual over the Net, and many people use leftover computer parts as spell components (like old memory chips for remembrance!).

CONCRETE

THEMES: Binding, Conscious Mind, Faith, Grounding, Longevity, Oaths, Strength.

CORRESPONDENCES: Earth.

SAMPLE APPLICATIONS: Concrete has connotations similar to brick in strength and blacktop in coverage. Many modern phrases tell us more about this component's magickal potential. If we write something in concrete, for example, it's a symbolic statement of a long-lasting record. This means concrete is an interesting medium for oaths and to promote the longevity of beloved projects. Similarly, if something is sealed in concrete, it's pretty well there to stay, barring the absence of explosives—so considering this as a binding force is reasonable. Finally, if our faith is as sure as concrete, it's built on strong foundations, so carrying a bit of concrete in our power pouch to support our belief structures has merit.

CORRECTION FLUID

THEMES: Banishing, Concealment, Forgiveness, Protection.

CORRESPONDENCES: Water.

SAMPLE APPLICATIONS: An all-purpose correcting agent, correction fluid can be put on written spells to conceal something secret, banish what was visible, protect what's beneath it, or "forgive" the mistake made. Because this is a liquid, you can add small amounts of herbal tinctures and oils to the blend to accent the effect.

COUPON

THEMES: Choices, Divination, Money, Resourcefulness, Wisdom.

CORRESPONDENCES: Earth.

SAMPLE APPLICATIONS: Many Sundays you can find me merrily clipping coupons and blessing them for prosperity. To make these into a divination system, simply pick out a minimum of thirteen with products or images that reflect a diversity of human experiences. For example, a coupon for Joy dish detergent can represent happiness and/or positive outcomes! Lay these face down, mix them up, and then think of a question. Close your eyes and pick up a coupon to get a response (then buy this item and use it to release the energy in your life!). Carry blessed coupons (perhaps dabbed with a bit of patchouli oil for prosperity) in your wallet to keep money where it belongs.

CRACKERS

THEMES: Guidance, Health, Providence, Resourcefulness, Transformation, Travel, Wishcraft.

CORRESPONDENCES: Earth.

SAMPLE APPLICATIONS: Crackers are the modern version of ancient journey cakes, being durable, long lasting, and easily portable. Better still, supermarkets carry a variety of flavors that you can choose to better suit your goal (like a garlic flavor for protection while traveling). To use crackers for wishcraft, simply hold them in your hands while thinking of your desire. Grasp the crackers more and more tightly to instill them with your wish, then release the crumbs to the earth and the winds so the magick begins.

DENTAL FLOSS

THEMES: Banishing, Binding, Communication, Freedom.

CORRESPONDENCES: Air.

SAMPLE APPLICATIONS: Don't have any thread or string handy? Dental floss is a perfectly suitable substitute to use for knot magick, binding and releasing. Bless minty dental floss before using it to sweeten and energize your words. If you're going to be talking about intuitive matters, charge the package by a full moon and for logical/rational conversations bless it in sunlight. Or focus on a particularly sticky situation while you're using it so that you can literally "loosen" things up!

DOLL

THEMES: Cooperation, Imitative Magick, Love, Messages, Poppet Magick, Protection, Shapeshifting.

CORRESPONDENCES: The God Aspect, the Goddess Aspect (varies by design).

SAMPLE APPLICATIONS: Dolls are basically modern poppets and perfectly suited to similar functions. The amazing variety of dolls on the market now also makes them very useful as personalized god/dess images that you can dress and adorn to suit the season, the goal of your magick, or that god/dess's attributes.

For imitative magick, use the doll as a model for what you want to happen. For example, if you're interviewing for a specific type of job, pick a doll that resembles you somehow and dress it in clothing suited to that job. Leave this on your altar while you're interviewing! You can also keep the doll safely stored in that outfit to improve your ability to adjust to the new situation once the position is acquired.

DUCT TAPE

THEMES: Balance, Binding, Control, Equality, Miracles, Persistence, Strength, Tenacity.

CORRESPONDENCES: Moon, Spirit.

SAMPLE APPLICATIONS: There's a joke in the New Age community that duct tape is really the Force—light on one side, dark on the other, and miraculous in its power. As an all-purpose utility item, duct tape is hard to beat, and keeping bits around to help with magickal projects is wise. Carry an energized roll with you everywhere. Symbolically this will help keep you in balance or improve strength. Use small pieces wrapped around symbolic objects to bind negative influences, or put a piece on the bottom of your shoe so you'll persevere when walking in difficult situations. On a purely pragmatic level, use the blessed tape as a temporary fix when your ritual robes tear, when your muffler falls off on the way to a gathering, and the like.

ELECTRICITY

THEMES: Control, Energy, Focus, Guidance, Manifestation, Messages, Potential, Power.

CORRESPONDENCES: Fire, Sun.

SAMPLE APPLICATIONS: In the marvelous invention of electricity you have the perfect symbol through which to "turn on" your magickal juice! Anything that has a switch can become a focus for power. Simply choose the object for its meaning to the magick (possibly add an aromatic touch, like dabbing the item with oil, if safe to do so), concentrate on your goal, and flick the switch to release the energy! For visualization purposes you could see yourself figuratively plugging into an astral outlet to recharge internal batteries when they get low or to give your magick an extra boost. To reverse the effect (e.g., bind energy) consider using a dead electrical cord as a component to likewise deaden the energy you're trying to banish or bind.

EYEGLASSES

THEMES: Awareness, Clarity, Comprehension, Conscious Mind, Insight, Knowledge, Learning, Memory, Organization, Vision.

CORRESPONDENCES: Air, Fire.

SAMPLE APPLICATIONS: For those who don't wear eyeglasses, sunglasses are a viable substitute that might offer even more symbolic options because they come in a variety of colors and styles. For example, if you want to rid yourself of unhealthy illusions, get a cheap pair of rose-colored glasses and crush them during your spell or ritual to destroy that energy. Or dab the corners of the glasses with a suitable oil that matches your magickal goals (like rosemary and/or sandalwood to improve your memory and psychic skills, respectively, when studying spells).

FAN

THEMES: Choices, Communication, Healing, Motivation, Purification, Transformation, Weather Magick.

CORRESPONDENCES: Air, East, Summer.

SAMPLE APPLICATIONS: Both handheld fans and electrical ones may be used, but the advantage of handheld versions is that their location in the sacred space need not be limited by an electrical outlet! Place a paper fan (like those found at Eastern import shops) in the eastern quarter of your ritual space to welcome the element of air. Use this same fan to disperse incense into the winds with your desires or to cleanse any unwanted energies from the area. Turn on a fan when you need a "fresh wind"—turn your back to it and let the transformational air give you a nudge in the right direction. Finally, when you wish to raise a gentle wind, whistle into a fan's air slowly and steadily. It's been said since ancient times that witches have the power to whistle up the winds; all you're adding here is a little sympathetic support.

FLUORITE

THEMES: Anxiety, Balance, Conscious Mind, Learning, Meditation, Perspective, Spirituality.

CORRESPONDENCES: Water/Earth.

SAMPLE APPLICATIONS: The fluorite's blue-to-purple tones align it with the water element, making this an excellent touchstone to soothe stress and bring our emotions back into balance. Its natural shape is that of a pyramid, which provides a connection to earth and its foundations— thereby stressing the rational mind. If you work at an office, keep a fluorite pyramid on your desk as an anti-anxiety amulet that will also keep your wits keen.

Modern shamans say that one should wear fluorite to understand life's lessons or to attract those lessons you most need to undertake for personal growth. Alternatively, some auric healers like to use this stone for alleviating stress.

FOOD-STORAGE CONTAINER

THEMES: Energy, Longevity, Organization, Protection, Providence, Resourcefulness.

CORRESPONDENCES: Earth (but may change with content).

SAMPLE APPLICATIONS: Whatever you put inside a food-storage container symbolically (and often literally) gets an extended shelf life. So if you want to bring longevity to a project, put an image of that project in the container and keep it there until you feel the magickal support is no longer needed. Or neatly store away something to which you've added magickal energy in an airtight container—this makes a great "toolbox" for components (especially herbs), keeping their powers preserved and fresh for when you most need them. Finally, to preserve your finances and other resources, put loose change in a container. When it's full, donate at least half to a good cause (so the energy returns to you threefold), and leave a seed coin in the container so prosperity remains with you.

GEODE

THEMES: Concealment, Dreams, Fairies, Focus, Guidance, Meditation, Potential, Psychism, Spirits, Unity.

CORRESPONDENCES: Earth (may vary by stone).

SAMPLE APPLICATIONS: Geodes have a natural womb shape, making them a good representation of the goddess and the earth mother. Keep one around to direct energy into during earth-healing rituals or when you're meditating on the goddess within. Some people feel that geodes have a unique indwelling stone spirit whose power and attributes are amplified by the size of the crystal grouping and the type of stone.

To use a geode to promote unity, turn it upright (like a bowl) and place small slips of paper inside bearing the names of the people to whom you wish to bring harmony. Conversely, to conceal yourself or an item from unwanted eyes, put a piece of paper indicating what you're hiding *underneath* a geode turned upside down (so the hollow covers the paper). The intense energy of the crystals blurs any attempt at discovery until you're ready to reveal what's inside!

GLASSES AND CUPS

THEMES: Blessing, Cooperation, Forgiveness, Perspective, Unity.

CORRESPONDENCES: Bacchus, Dionysus, the Goddess Aspect, Water, West.

SAMPLE APPLICATIONS: Another natural womb symbol, glasses and cups are an updated version of the chalice and may be used in exactly the same way (*see* Chapter 4, Chalice). If filled with wine, these are very good tools to use in honoring gods of the vine like Bacchus and Dionysus.

Beyond the traditional symbolism, the modern phrase about whether a person sees a glass "half empty or half full" is a way of describing our perspectives. So you could fill a glass with a beverage and drink it to internalize a fresh outlook on any situation (try and match the beverage to the theme of the situation for best results).

GLUE

THEMES: Binding, Control, Faithfulness, Friendship, Grounding, Love, Tenacity.

CORRESPONDENCES: Earth.

SAMPLE APPLICATIONS: Glue and glue sticks are among the great, easy, and inexpensive fasteners available to the creative witch. You want a crystal's energy to stay somewhere specific? Glue it in place! Want to improve your devotion toward someone? Glue a picture of that person to something you carry with you regularly.

HAMMER/GAVEL

THEMES: Banishing, Choices, Freedom, Justice, Law, Persistence, Strength.

CORRESPONDENCES: Fire.

SAMPLE APPLICATIONS: A symbol of justice, decision making, firmness, and strength, hammering is a way to signal the beginning or end of spells aimed at any of these themes. Just as a bell sounds out your intention, the resonance of a hammer or gavel pounds out your desire to the universe. The vibrations change the energy in the air in and around you too, mirroring your intention and speeding manifestation.

HEATER

THEMES: Congeniality, Friendship, Kindness, Love, Motivation, Passion.

CORRESPONDENCES: Fire.

SAMPLE APPLICATIONS: Another symbol of the hearth, heaters are a handy non-flame-producing form of fire that can warm up a cold heart, inspire passion or friendship, and put a figurative "fire" underneath you when you're lingering. For example, if you place the name of someone you've had an argument with in an ice cube, then let that melt in front of the heater, it helps begin the healing process by melting the coldness that stands between you. Or for motivation in a specific situation, put your feet up to a heater before going out for a few minutes and let the warm toasty energy get you moving!

INTERCOM

THEMES: Awareness, Communication, Cooperation, Learning, Messages, Protection, Truth.

CORRESPONDENCES: Air.

SAMPLE APPLICATIONS: One of the handiest inventions for magick users with children, intercoms allow us to communicate, protect, and send important messages to areas of the sacred home that we couldn't ordinarily reach. Extending this idea, you can chant, incant spells, and sing magickal songs over this system to send whatever type of energy you desire throughout the house simultaneously.

KITE

THEMES: Freedom, Goals, Hope, Success, Wishcraft, Youthfulness.

CORRESPONDENCES: Air, Spring.

SAMPLE APPLICATIONS: There's nothing that brings out the child within more than a lovely spring afternoon spent flying a kite. Paint the image of your goals or wishes on the kite, and then release it to the winds to begin manifesting that energy. The higher the kite reaches toward the heavens, the greater the power of the spell. Then as you reel the kite back in, visualize the energy created returning to you threefold!

KIWI

THEMES: Abundance, Fertility, Growth, Love, Luck, Money.

CORRESPONDENCES: Water.

SAMPLE APPLICATIONS: The sheer number of seeds in kiwi fruit gives it symbolic connections with abundance and prosperity. The color also makes it a good-luck or growth food. To use kiwi in love diets, I suggest blending it with a bit of sweet cream to augment the energy.

LAMP

THEMES: Awareness, Banishing, Comprehension, Creativity, Energy, Enlightenment, Hope, Learning, Truth, Vision, Wisdom.

CORRESPONDENCES: Fire (lava lamps are Fire and Water), Sun.

SAMPLE APPLICATIONS: Lamps directly relate to candles in their symbolic value and are a suitable, fire-safe substitute for them (*see* Chapter 4, Candle). The advantage to using lamps is that you can choose a colored lightbulb to represent your intention and you don't need a match to activate the energy! I personally like to dab essential oils on lightbulbs (the aroma represents my need), and then turn the lights on to release the magick into my home.

MACARONI AND CHEESE

THEMES: Congeniality, Friendship, Kinship, Love, Youthfulness.

CORRESPONDENCES: Apollo, Earth.

SAMPLE APPLICATIONS: Both ingredients in this meal have some ancient roots. Cheese was used for physical vitality and love in Greece, where it was believed that Apollo gifted humankind with this edible. Noodles appear in Far Eastern diets, being consumed for longevity and prosperity. Mixed together, the noodles provide a solid foundation in which the magick of the cheese can grow.

One of many comfort foods in my home, alongside pizza rolls and ice cream, macaroni and cheese awakens my inner child and inspires warm feelings toward others. To change the meaning, however, all you need do is make this meal from scratch and change the cheese base. For energy or cleansing, for example, try a pepper cheese. To increase the effect, cut the cheese into small symbolic portions whose shape represents your goals before you melt it (warming then releases the energy).

MAGNIFYING GLASS

THEMES: Abundance, Awareness, Clarity, Comprehension, Growth, Learning, Perspective, Potential, Truth, Weather Magick.

CORRESPONDENCES: Fire.

SAMPLE APPLICATIONS: You can consider using a magnifying glass in weather magick designed to attract a little extra sunlight. For this, take the magnifying glass outside and catch light in it. Turn this light in the direction where you wish sun to appear for a time. Focus on your goal as you work.

Besides this, any symbol that you place under a magnifying glass during spellcraft gets "focused" on—the power is expanded and augmented by the magnifying nature of the tool.

MAIL

THEMES: Communication, Fellowship, Friendship, Happiness, Hope, Kinship, Messages.

CORRESPONDENCES: Air.

SAMPLE APPLICATIONS: Mail yourself magickal letters that indicate the energies you wish to attract to your home. When they arrive, taking them in the house welcomes that energy! Dab specially prepared oils on letters to friends and loved ones, so your magick quietly blesses them when the notes arrive. Or fold a little bit of glitter into the envelope like fairy dust to bring joy into any moment.

MICA

THEMES: Anti-magick, Divination, Protection, Psychism.

CORRESPONDENCES: Air, Moon.

SAMPLE APPLICATIONS: The sheen of mica gives it a suitable surface for scrying and also makes it a handy substitute for any lunar component. Since it flakes off easily, you can gather several small pieces to use in pocket magick, carrying it with you or putting it in dream pillows to improve your psychic powers. By extension, the reflective surface of mica creates the potential for reflecting back negativity and unwanted magick.

MICROWAVE

THEMES: Cycles, Energy, Manifestation, Transformation, Zeal.

CORRESPONDENCES: Fire.

SAMPLE APPLICATIONS: Anytime you want to speed up the manifestation of any spell, put the microwave-safe components inside and stimulate the magick! Since the tray turns clockwise (mine does anyway), it naturally generates positive energy and represents cycles. Beyond this, you can "nuke" any potion or magickal meal to increase personal zeal, since microwaving excites the molecules of your magick!

PEANUT BUTTER

THEMES: Binding, Fertility, Tenacity.

CORRESPONDENCES: Earth, the God Aspect.

SAMPLE APPLICATIONS: Peanuts are a natural emblem of the god aspect, especially when still in the shell. When creamed into peanut butter, the sticky nature of this food gives it strong correlations with persistence or binding. For example, if you need to be more resolute in changing a personal habit, draw a symbol of what you hope to achieve in peanut butter on bread using a knife. Eat to internalize both the transformation and the positive, tenacious energy!

PEN

THEMES: Communication, Divination, Goals, Love, Magick, Memory, Messages, Oaths, Organization, Power, Spirits.

CORRESPONDENCES: Fire/Water (can vary by color).

SAMPLE APPLICATIONS: For centuries, those who knew how to write were considered to have a kind of magickal power, whether or not they were mages! We can use this association in modern magick by choosing the pens for our spells and spellbooks according to their color association. Or we can write in different styles that suit the mood of the magick. Bless a special pen and carry it to improve written communication skills, your memory, and organizational ability.

PIZZA

THEMES: Cooperation, Cycles, Equality, Friendship, Grounding, Peace.

CORRESPONDENCES: Spirit.

SAMPLE APPLICATIONS: There are so many ways to top a pizza that this food's variety makes it nearly as diverse and multifaceted as Spirit in energy! This is also what makes pizza a very flexible food for pantry magick. Just by altering the toppings (and the patterns you make with them), you can transform the energy you create to likewise change a particular cycle or foster other types of positive energy. For best results, remove the pieces clockwise when cultivating a positive, counterclockwise when banishing a negative.

POTATO CHIPS

THEMES: Grounding.

CORRESPONDENCES: Earth.

SAMPLE APPLICATIONS: I'm a junk food junkie and often find myself turning to potato chips after spellcraft or rituals. The crunchy nature brings me back down to earth, and the flavor quells the small hunger pangs that magickal procedures often leave behind.

PRETZELS

THEMES: Cycles, Goals, Grounding, Providence, Safety, Travel.

CORRESPONDENCES: Fire, Summer, Sun.

SAMPLE APPLICATIONS: Pretzels are another snack food, but one that has some ancient ties as a solar symbol—it was served at many festivals that honored the sun (without the salt). Carrying a pretzel with you ensures providence and safe travel, while eating one after a ritual helps ground excess energy. If you like to bake and make your own dough, consider shaping your pretzel differently to correspond with various goals, like a heart that engenders a strong foundation for love (don't forget to share it with your loved one!).

RADISH

THEMES: Energy, Motivation, Protection, Success, Victory.

CORRESPONDENCES: Fire.

SAMPLE APPLICATIONS: About the only old lore concerning radishes is that eating the wild variety encouraged success, especially in battle. The hot taste and red coloring of this vegetable make it a good choice for inspiration, protection, and energy. Toss it with a traditional salad to stimulate the flow of magick!

RUBBER BAND

THEMES: Binding, Control, Cooperation, Organization, Resourcefulness, Unity.

CORRESPONDENCES: Water.

SAMPLE APPLICATIONS: The flexible yet binding nature of the rubber band makes it an excellent symbol of unity. Here you have a token that both draws things together *and* allows for elbowroom and adaptation. Since we often use rubber bands to put papers in order, they also represent organization. Carry a blessed, energized one in your pocket or wallet to encourage personal adaptability in situations that require thinking on your feet!

SCISSORS

THEMES: Banishing, Freedom, Gardening, Luck, Protection, Wishcraft.

CORRESPONDENCES: Fire.

SAMPLE APPLICATIONS: Around the turn of the century a few bits of lore emerged about scissors, specifically that receiving scissors as a gift brings bad luck or cuts off friendship, that when scissors accidentally fall and stick in the ground one should make a wish, and leaving an open pair beneath a bed (this looks like a cross) protects the sleeper from ghosts!

Today, there are a lot of ways a crafty witch can use scissors for magick. Bless a pair for working in your magickal garden, for example. Use a special pair when snipping paper for written spells. Clip ribbons or strings off yourself in spells for personal liberation, and perhaps carry a small pair that you've paid for yourself to encourage good fortune.

SHOWER

THEMES: Anxiety, Banishing, Beauty, Glamoury, Peace, Purification.

CORRESPONDENCES: Water.

SAMPLE APPLICATIONS: Akin to asperging with water, a shower gives you an opportunity to de-stress and cleanse away any unwanted energies lingering in your aura in perfect privacy. I like to hang a bundle of aromatic herbs in the shower stall. They release light scents when activated by the heat and moisture. Or I choose my soaps according to the type of energy I want to augment in the auric field, like heather for comeliness or lavender for peace.

STAR CHARTS

THEMES: Astral Realm, Awareness, Faith, Guidance, Hope, Knowledge, Prophecy, Vision.

CORRESPONDENCES: Spirit.

SAMPLE APPLICATIONS: The ancients used star charts to guide their way from one place to another. They also watched the sky's patterns for prophetic knowledge. Since we are on the threshold of a new millennium, we might wish to spiritually use this example and keep one (clip it from the newspaper) as a charm that inspires a positive vision of the future. Star charts also represent our ever growing awareness of the universe and our place within it. By looking to them, we can see that there is much more to life than what readily meets the eye.

SUGAR (REFINED)

THEMES: Blessing, Love, Money, Prosperity.

CORRESPONDENCES: Water.

SAMPLE APPLICATIONS: In Hawaii sugarcane has an associated deity that's believed to bring both blessings and love. For a long time sugar was quite expensive, so it's a fitting component to use in prosperity magick. Or you might sprinkle a bit around the sacred space for blessings and sweet love as long as you don't mind attracting a few ants too!

TELEPHONE

THEMES: Communication, Community, Congeniality, Fellowship, Friendship, Kindness, Kinship, Messages.

CORRESPONDENCES: Air.

SAMPLE APPLICATIONS: Put the name of the person or place with whom you want to open the lines of communication under the phone. Dab a little oil on the paper that fits the circumstances (rose for love, mint for healing, etc.). Hold both hands down over the phone and visualize light filling it and going out through the telephone line. Leave the paper in place until you connect with that individual or place.

TOILET

THEMES: Banishing, Communion, Meditation, Purification.

CORRESPONDENCES: Water/Earth.

SAMPLE APPLICATIONS: As one of the few places in your home where you can be assured of privacy, this is a great place for magick. Write your problems, bad habits, sicknesses and the like on toilet paper, and then flush them neatly down the drain. Or just close the door, put down the lid, and meditate quietly for a few minutes (no one need know what you're up to!).

TELEVISION

THEMES: Divination.

CORRESPONDENCES: Air/Fire.

SAMPLE APPLICATIONS: Although I'm sure you can think of magickal uses for your television, my personal opinion is that the best way to put this piece of furniture to use is to turn it off! Then focus on the screen while thinking of a question. Your mind already expects pictures to emerge here, so the likelihood of experiencing success increases. Make notes of what you see, and then interpret them as you might the results of crystal scrying.

VACUUM CLEANER

THEMES: Banishing, Luck, Purification.

CORRESPONDENCES: Air.

SAMPLE APPLICATIONS: The vacuum has much in common with its ancestor the broom in symbolic value. To get rid of the spiritual dirt in your home, sprinkle out some magickally prepared carpet freshener, let it absorb the negativity, then suck it up neatly, and throw it away! Move clockwise while you're vacuuming to draw in positive energy, or counter-clockwise to banish problems.

VETIVER

THEMES: Glamoury, Love, Money, Shapeshifting, Transformation.

CORRESPONDENCES: Earth.

SAMPLE APPLICATIONS: Though not seen much in ancient spells, vetiver has become a favored herb among Wiccans and shamans to use in shapeshifting and transformation magick. Why? Because it interacts with each individual's chemistry when dabbed on the skin, making a wholly unique scent. Additionally, carrying vetiver is said to draw both money and love into your life.

APPENDIX OF THEMES
AND CORRESPONDENCES

This list was assembled for those moments in life when you want to formulate a spell, ritual, or other magickal process for a specific goal. By looking up the theme or correspondence of your magick on this list, you can easily identify the components you have at hand and then choose from among them in designing the procedure. If you don't find the theme you're looking for right away, consider synonyms and related topics instead. For example, suitable components for relationship magick might be found under Aphrodite, Communication, Faithfulness, Kinship, Love, Sexuality, and/or Unity depending on the goals you have in mind!

ABUNDANCE Barbecue, Chalice, Corn, Frog, Horn, Kiwi, Lava Stone, Magnifying Glass, Milk, Oak, Oats, Orange, Primrose, Soil, Tides.

AIR Air Conditioner, Almond, Ant (flying ant), Balloons, Beans, Bee, Blender/Mixer/Food Processor, Book, Bubbles, Butterfly, Clover, Cross (eastern arm), Crow (Raven), Dandelion, Dental Floss, Eyeglasses, Feather, Honey, Intercom, Ivy, Kite, Leaf, Mail, Marjoram, Mica, Mint, Mistletoe, Owl, Paper, Parsley, Pine, Rice, Sage, Spider, Square (right side), Squirrel, Star, Telephone, Television, Tin, Vacuum Cleaner, Wand, White, Wind, Words, Yellow.

ANGER Air Conditioner, Ice.

ANTI-MAGICK Amber, Amethyst, Birch, Cat's Eye, Clover, Coral, Dandelion, Dill, Elder, Hawthorn, Holly, Iron, Key, Knife, Leaf, Mica, Nettle, Rowan, Tattoo, Walnut.

ANXIETY Balloons, Fluorite, Lettuce, Mint, Orange, Shower, Violet.

APHRODITE Apple, Bee, Copper, Dolphin, Fish, Marjoram, Parsley, Pearl, Rabbit, Rose, Shoes, Turtle (Tortoise).

APOLLO Bay, Crow (Raven), Dolphin, Hawk, Macaroni and Cheese, Meat, Mistletoe, Mustard, Olive, Snake (Serpent), Sun, Sunflower.

ARIES Bloodstone, Red.

ARTEMIS Almond, Arrow, Bear, Dog, Honey, Moon, Willow.

ARTS Dolphin, Honey, Mead, Runes.

ASTARTE Copper, Dog.

ASTRAL REALM Bear, Cross, Mirror, Mustard, Star Charts.

ATHENA Crow (Raven), Key, Oak, Olive, Owl, Spider.

AUTUMN Carrot, Corn, Oats.

AWARENESS Coffee, Dog, Eyeglasses, Fig, Hawk, Intercom, Lamp, Magnifying Glass, Marigold, Meat, Nutmeg, Silver, Star Charts, Tea.

BACCHUS Amethyst, Chalice, Glasses and Cups, Grapes, Ivy, Rose, Wine.

BALANCE Coasters, Cross, Duct Tape, Feather, Fluorite, Lotus, Onyx, Purple, Ring, Snake (Serpent), Triangle.

BANISHING Barbecue, Barley, Beans, Black, Correction Fluid, Cross, Dental Floss, Hammer/Gavel, Iron, Lamp, Marjoram, Mirror, Pine, Rosemary, Saliva, Salt, Scissors, Shower, Toilet, Triangle, Vacuum Cleaner, Woodruff, Words.

BAST Cat, Catnip.

BEAUTY Aloe, Amber, Amethyst, Egg, Heather, Lavender, Lotus, Mirror, Oats, Pearl, Primrose, Rosemary, Shower, Tansy, Water, Willow.

BINDING Brick, Concrete, Dental Floss, Duct Tape, Glue, Ice, Iron, Key, Knots, Mirror, Peanut Butter, Rubber Band, String, Words.

BLESSING Barley, Bread, Carnelian, Chocolate, Corn, Elder, Glasses and Cups, Gold, Holey Stones, Mint, Oak, Sugar (Refined), Sun, Water, Wine, Words.

BUDDHA Knots, Mirror, Rabbit, Turquoise, Umbrella.

CALLISTO Bear.

CERES Bread, Oats.

CHOICES Coins, Coupon, Cross, Door/Threshold, Fan, Fox, Hammer/Gavel, Shells.

CLARITY Air Conditioner, Camera, Carrot, Celery, Coffee, Coral, Crow (Raven), Eyeglasses, Fennel, Fire, Hawk, Magnifying Glass, Marjoram, Mouse, Nutmeg, Quartz.

CLEANSING Onion.

COMMUNICATION Agate, Beryl, Bloodstone, Camera, Carnelian, Computer, Crow (Raven), Dental Floss, Fan, Feather, Horn, Ink, Intercom, Mail, Mead, Paper, Pen, Runes, Spider, Telephone, Wind, Words, Yellow.

COMMUNION Costume, Dance, Ginger, Oak, Rattle, Statuary, Toilet.

COMMUNITY Ant, Bee, Computer, Dance, Tattoo, Telephone.

COMPREHENSION Barbecue, Cabbage, Coffee, Eyeglasses, Fire, Hawk, Lamp, Magnifying Glass, Nutmeg, Wind, Words.

CONCEALMENT Blacktop, Cat's Eye, Correction Fluid, Geode, Poppet, Snake (Serpent).

CONGENIALITY Beryl, Butter, Chestnut, Heater, Lotus, Macaroni and Cheese, Mint, Oven/Hearth, Salt, Tea, Telephone, Turquoise, Woodruff, Yellow.

CONSCIOUS MIND Amethyst, Coffee, Concrete, Coral, Eyeglasses, Fire,

Fluorite, Gold, Marjoram, Mint, Nutmeg, Rosemary, Sun, Walnut.

CONTROL Amethyst, Batteries, Duct Tape, Electricity, Glue, Gold, Ivy, Lava Stone, Rubber Band.

COOPERATION Bee, Blender/ Mixer/Food Processor, Doll, Glasses and Cups, Intercom, Pizza, Poppet, Rubber Band.

COURAGE Amber, Banana, Bear, Blood, Carnelian, Chestnut, Garlic, Nettle, Onion, Tattoo, Thyme, Words.

CREATIVITY Allspice, Ash, Bee, Bubbles, Dolphin, Honey, Lamp, Lotus, Mead, Moon, Runes, Silver, Spider, Turtle (Tortoise), Water, Wine, Yellow.

CRONOS Barley.

CYCLES Birch, Blender/Mixer/Food Processor, Circle, Coasters, Corn, Dolphin, Microwave, Moon, Pizza, Pretzels, Ring, Shells, Spider.

DANCE Costume, Drum, Rattle, Shells.

DEATH Apple, Basil, Beans, Black, Cinnamon, Clock (or Timer), Cross, Jade, Marigold, Parsley, Rose, Rosemary, Violet, Whale, White, Willow.

DEMETER Barley, Bee, Bread, Corn, Honey, Oats, Rose, Sunflower.

DEVOTION *See* Faithfulness.

DIANA Amethyst, Apple, Bear, Cat, Moon, Pearl, Silver, Willow.

DIONYSUS Fennel, Fig, Fox, Glasses and Cups, Grapes, Ivy, Milk, Mirror, Wine.

DIVINATION Almond, Arrow, Barbecue, Bay, Beans, Beryl, Book, Bubbles, Cabbage, Candle (Wax), Celery, Coal, Coffee, Coins, Costume, Coupon, Daisy, Dandelion, Dice, Drum, Egg, Feather, Fire, Incense, Ink, Knife, Lead, Mead, Mica, Mirror, Mistletoe, Numbers, Obsidian, Oven/Hearth, Peach, Pen, Quartz, Ring, Rowan, Runes, Shells, Shoes, Soil, Star, Statuary, Tea, Television, Turtle (Tortoise), Willow.

DREAMS Agate, Amethyst, Beer, Blue, Coral, Geode, Grapes, Holly, Marigold, Moon, Rosemary, Sage, Shoes, Silver, Thyme.

EARTH Agate (moss), Alfalfa, Ant, Barley, Bear, Black, Blacktop, Book, Box, Bread, Brick, Brown, Butter, Cat's Eye, Clock (or Timer), Coal, Coasters, Coins, Concrete, Coupon, Crackers, Cross (northern arm), Dice, Dill, Drum, Egg, Fingernails, Fluorite, Food-Storage Container, Geode, Glue, Green, Incense, Knots, Lead, Leaf, Macaroni and Cheese, Meat, Mouse, Oats, Paper, Peanut Butter, Potato, Potato Chips, Salt, Snake (Serpent), Soil, Spider, Square, Squirrel, String, Toilet, Turquoise, Turtle (Tortoise), Vetiver, Whale.

EAST Air Conditioner, Almond, Cross (right arm), Fan, Wind.

ELEMENTALS Bottle (Jar), Costume.

ELEMENTS Circle, Coasters, Cross, Drum, Square.

ENERGY Batteries, Blender/Mixer/ Food Processor, Blood, Bottle (Jar), Chamomile, Cinnamon, Coffee, Drum, Electricity, Fire, Food-Storage Container,

Ginger, Lamp, Lead, Leaf, Lodestone, Microwave, Nettle, Quartz, Radish, Red, Sun.

ENLIGHTENMENT Lamp, Rose, Sun, Tea.

EOS Butterfly.

EQUALITY Blender/Mixer/Food Processor, Circle, Duct Tape, Pizza, Ring.

EROS Bay, Rabbit, Rose.

FAIRIES Brown, Chrysanthemum, Clover, Dandelion, Geode, Green, Hawthorn, Iron, Marigold, Milk, Rose, Rosemary, Strawberry, Thyme.

FAITH Concrete, Mint, Mustard, Silver, Star Charts, Statuary, Yellow.

FAITHFULNESS Amethyst, Crow (Raven), Dog, Elder, Glue, Honey, Lemon, Lodestone, Orange, Ring, Square, Sunflower, Tea, Violet.

FATE Clock (or Timer), Chalice, Silver, Spider, Star, String.

FEAR Agate, Bloodstone, Salt, Thyme, Turquoise.

FELLOWSHIP Altar, Blacktop, Coffee, Mail, Telephone, Wine.

FERTILITY Amber, Ant, Apple, Banana, Basil, Bee, Bell, Cabbage, Catnip, Chalice, Coral, Cross, Drum, Egg, Fig, Fish, Frog, Grapes, Honey, Kiwi, Lettuce, Lotus, Milk, Moon, Moonstone, Oak, Oats, Olive, Orchid, Peach, Peanut Butter, Primrose, Rabbit, Rice, Shoes, Soil, Strawberry, Tansy, Tides, Walnut, Water, Wind, Yellow.

FIDES Bay, Corn, Olive.

FIRE Allspice, Amber, Ant (fire ants), Ash, Barbecue, Basil, Batteries, Bay, Bee, Beer, Blender/Mixer/Food Processor, Blood, Bloodstone, Brass, Candle (Wax), Carnelian, Carrot, Cedar, Celery, Chestnut, Chrysanthemum, Cinnamon, Coffee, Copper, Corn, Cross (southern arm), Daisy, Dandelion, Dill, Dog, Electricity, Eyeglasses, Fennel, Fig, Garlic, Ginger, Gold, Hammer/Gavel, Hawthorn, Heater, Honey, Incense, Iron, Knife, Lamp, Lava Stone, Magnifying Glass, Marigold, Mead, Microwave, Mustard, Nasturtium, Nettle, Nutmeg, Oak, Obsidian, Olive, Onion, Onyx, Orange, Oven/Hearth, Pen, Pepper, Pretzels, Radish, Red, Rowan, Scissors, Square (bottom), Star, Sun, Sunflower, Tattoo, Tea, Television, Triangle, Walnut, Wine, Woodruff, Yellow.

FOCUS Bell, Candle (Wax), Celery, Coffee, Copper, Costume, Cross, Drum, Electricity, Fire, Geode, Rattle, Ring.

FORGIVENESS Air Conditioner, Blacktop, Chalice, Chocolate, Correction Fluid, Glasses and Cups, Raspberry, Salve, Violet.

FREEDOM Butterfly, Dental Floss, Feather, Hammer/Gavel, Kite, Knots, Scissors, String.

FREY Cross, Primrose.

FREYJA Apple, Cat, Fish, Pearl, Primrose, Rabbit, Strawberry.

FRIENDSHIP Bread, Dance, Dog, Glue, Heater, Lemon, Macaroni and

Cheese, Mail, Orchid, Pizza, Ring, Rose, Telephone, Yellow.

GAIA Apple, Soil.

GARDENING Agate (moss), Chamomile, Chrysanthemum, Green, Jade, Mask, Moonstone, Oak, Oats, Scissors, Soil, Star.

GHOSTS *See* Spirits.

GLAMOURY Costume, Feather, Fox, Frog, Heather, Mirror, Shower, Snake (Serpent), Vetiver.

GOALS Cross, Kite, Pen, Pretzels, Turquoise, Wand.

GOD ASPECT Almond, Ash, Banana, Beans, Candle (Wax), Carrot, Chamomile, Doll, Gold, Jade, Knife, Orchid, Peanut Butter, Pepper, Star, Sun, Triangle.

GODDESS ASPECT Amber, Beans, Bell, Birch, Bottle (Jar), Candle (Wax), Chalice, Coral, Doll, Elder, Frog, Glasses and Cups, Holey Stones, Lotus, Milk, Moon, Peach, Pepper, Rabbit, Raspberry, Rowan, Salt, Shoes, Silver, Soil, Star, Tansy, Tides, Triangle.

GROUNDING Basil, Black, Brick, Concrete, Glue, Meat, Obsidian, Pizza, Potato Chips, Pretzels, Square, String.

GROWTH Green, Kiwi, Magnifying Glass, Moonstone, Soil, Sun, Sunflower, Triangle.

GUIDANCE Arrow, Barbecue, Crackers, Dolphin, Electricity, Geode, Star, Star Charts, String, Wind.

HAPPINESS Balloons, Basil, Blue, Bubbles, Butterfly, Catnip, Cat's Eye, Chocolate, Chrysanthemum, Daisy, Dandelion, Gold, Ivy, Lotus, Mail, Marjoram, Mint, Olive, Orange, Pine, Rose, Sun, Thyme, Vanilla, Water, Wine.

HATHOR Beer, Frog, Milk, Turquoise.

HEALING/HEALTH Agate, Almond, Aloe, Amber, Apple, Blood, Blue, Brass, Carnelian, Cherry, Chestnut, Clock (or Timer), Copper, Coral, Crackers, Dandelion, Fan, Frog, Ginger, Gold, Green, Holey Stones, Knots, Lava Stone, Lavender, Leaf, Lettuce, Marjoram, Mask, Mead, Milk, Mistletoe, Moon, Mustard, Numbers, Nutmeg, Olive, Oven/Hearth, Quartz, Pearl, Pine, Rosemary, Sage, Saliva, Salve, Soil, Snake (Serpent), Tansy, Tides, Water, Willow, Wind, Wine.

HECATE Almond, Cat, Cross, Dandelion, Garlic, Key, Moon, Willow.

HELIOS Arrow.

HEPHAESTUS Fire.

HERA Apple, Orange, Willow.

HESTIA Fire, Oven/Hearth.

HOPE Balloons, Bubbles, Hawthorn, Kite, Lamp, Mail, Marjoram, Star, Star Charts, Sun, Thyme.

HORAE Butterfly.

HORUS Hawk.

HOSPITALITY Chalice, Coffee, Door/Threshold, Mint, Oven/Hearth, Salt, Wine.

IMAGINATION Bubbles, Moon, Rabbit, Shells, Silver, Star.

IMITATIVE MAGICK Chocolate, Doll, Ice, Lemon, Mask, Poppet, Statuary, Turquoise.

INDRA Barley, Bee, Bread, Cross.

INSIGHT Catnip, Celery, Costume, Dance, Eyeglasses, Fennel, Silver.

ISHTAR Arrow, Bread, Key, Spider.

ISIS Beer, Carnelian, Dolphin, Frog, Heather, Lotus, Meat, Onions, Pearl, Rose, Shoes, Silver.

JANUS Door/Threshold.

JEALOUSY Barley, Carnelian, Mint, Violet.

JOY *See* Happiness.

JUNO Fig.

JUPITER Hawk, Oak, Walnut.

JUSTICE Ash, Hammer/Gavel.

KAMA Arrow, Bee.

KINDNESS Chocolate, Elder, Heater, Meat, Telephone.

KINSHIP Barbecue, Bread, Dance, Fire, Holly, Macaroni and Cheese, Mail, Orchid, Oven/Hearth, Tattoo, Telephone.

KNOWLEDGE Apple, Book, Computer, Eyeglasses, Fig, Rosemary, Star Charts, Triangle, Wind.

KRISHNA Bee.

LAKSHMI Basil, Lotus, Pearl.

LAW Beer, Beryl, Crow (Raven), Hammer/Gavel, Lotus, Sage.

LEADERSHIP Bear, Gold, Key, Purple, Ring, Shoes, Sun, Umbrella, Yellow.

LEARNING Beans, Beryl, Cherry, Coffee, Eyeglasses, Fluorite, Intercom, Lamp, Magnifying Glass, Mint, Nutmeg, Rosemary, Sun, Walnut, Wind.

LOKI Apple.

LONGEVITY Aloe, Apple, Bread, Cat, Chrysanthemum, Concrete, Coral, Food-Storage Container, Honey, Key, Lavender, Lotus, Mead, Mistletoe, Peach, Pine, Rabbit, Rice, Sage, Tansy, Turtle (Tortoise).

LOVE Amethyst, Apple, Barley, Basil, Bay, Beryl, Butterfly, Cabbage, Catnip, Chalice, Cherry, Chestnut, Chocolate, Cinnamon, Clover, Crow (Raven), Dill, Doll, Door/Threshold, Fingernails, Ginger, Glue, Hair, Heater, Honey, Ivy, Kiwi, Knots, Lavender, Lemon, Macaroni and Cheese, Marjoram, Mistletoe, Nutmeg, Onyx, Orange, Orchid, Oven/Hearth, Parsley, Pen, Pine, Raspberry, Ring, Rose, Strawberry, Sugar (Refined), Tattoo, Tomato, Vanilla, Vetiver, Willow, Wine.

LUCK Allspice, Aloe, Apple, Arrow, Ash, Banana, Basil, Beans, Bread, Butterfly, Carnelian, Cat, Cherry, Clover, Coal, Coins, Coral, Corn, Dice, Door/Threshold, Egg, Heather, Holey Stones, Holly, Ivy, Jade, Kiwi, Moon, Moonstone, Mouse, Nasturtium, Oak, Onion, Oven/Hearth, Parsley, Rabbit,

Red, Rice, Saliva, Scissors, Shoes, Spider, Tin, Vacuum Cleaner, White, Wind.

LUG Fire.

MAGICK Book, Cat, Circle, Ink, Key, Moon, Pen, Red, Rowan, Runes, Saliva, Shoes, Silver, Snake (Serpent), Wand, Whale, White, Willow.

MAIA Banana.

MANIFESTATION Batteries, Clock (or Timer), Dance, Dolphin, Electricity, Grapes, Ink, Lavender, Microwave, Paper, Poppet, Words.

MARI Fish, Shells, Water.

MEDITATION Amethyst, Blue, Drum, Fluorite, Geode, Incense, Rattle, Silver, Squirrel, Tea, Tides, Toilet.

MEMORY Clock (or Timer), Computer, Eyeglasses, Ice, Nutmeg, Paper, Pen, Rosemary, String, Words.

MESSAGES Air Conditioner, Bee, Camera, Crow (Raven), Doll, Drum, Electricity, Hawk, Horn, Intercom, Mail, Owl, Pen, Rabbit, Telephone, Turtle (Tortoise), Wind.

MIN Lettuce, Milk.

MIRACLES Bread, Duct Tape, Fish, Moon.

MITHRA Corn, Fig, Gold, Lotus, Water.

MONEY Agate, Alfalfa, Bee, Brass, Cat, Cedar, Coal, Coins, Coupon, Dill, Gold, Green, Hair, Kiwi, Lettuce, Moon, Mouse, Oats, Pepper, Salt, Spider, Sugar (Refined), Vetiver, Woodruff.

MOON Aloe, Beryl, Bubbles, Cabbage, Cat, Cat's Eye, Coins (silver), Dog, Duct Tape, Fox, Grapes, Horn, Lemon, Lettuce, Mica, Milk, Mirror, Moonstone, Mouse, Onion, Pearl, Purple, Rabbit, Ring, Rowan, Silver, Tin, White, Willow.

MOTIVATION Batteries, Beryl, Fan, Fire, Heater, Radish, Wind.

MUHAMMAD Carnelian, Garlic, Rose.

NORTH Cross (northern arm), Lodestone, Star.

OATHS Blood, Chalice, Concrete, Garlic, Onion, Pen, Ring, Rose, Saliva, Salt, Soil, Wine.

ODIN Apple, Ash, Beer, Cedar, Crow (Raven), Holey Stones, Mead, Oak.

OFFERING Altar, Barbecue, Beer, Blood, Bread, Cat's Eye, Egg, Ginger, Honey, Incense, Mead, Mint, Pepper, Rose, Statuary, White, Wine.

OMENS Bee, Clock (or Timer), Dolphin, Feather, Fingernails, Fish, Geranium, Hawk, Marigold, Moon, Mouse, Onion, Owl, Rose, Star, Wind.

OPPORTUNITY Bloodstone, Door/Threshold, Key.

ORACLES Oak, Shells, Star, Wind, Wine.

ORGANIZATION Ant, Bee, Eyeglasses, Food-Storage Container, Paper, Pen, Rubber Band, Square.

OSIRIS Bread, Heather, Ivy, Lotus, Salt, Sun.

PASSION Carrot, Celery, Cherry, Chocolate, Cinnamon, Fire, Heater, Honey, Mustard, Nutmeg, Onyx, Orchid, Peach, Pepper, Potato, Rabbit, Raspberry, Rose, Strawberry, Vanilla.

PATHWORKING Arrow.

PEACE Agate, Aloe, Amethyst, Basil, Blacktop, Bloodstone, Blue, Carnelian, Coral, Fig, Lavender, Lettuce, Lotus, Mistletoe, Olive, Pizza, Rabbit, Shower, Water.

PELE Lava Stone.

PERSISTENCE Bee, Duct Tape, Hammer/Gavel, Squirrel.

PERSPECTIVE Camera, Crow (Raven), Feather, Fluorite, Fox, Glasses and Cups, Hawk, Magnifying Glass, Potato.

PLAYFULNESS Allspice, Balloons, Bubbles, Catnip, Fox, Squirrel.

POPPET MAGICK Doll, Potato, Statuary.

POSEIDON Ash, Olive, Pearl, Pine, Salt, Shells, Water.

POTENTIAL Batteries, Beans, Electricity, Geode, Green, Magnifying Glass, Moon.

POWER Batteries, Bear, Bell, Blood, Chrysanthemum, Dance, Electricity, Fingernails, Gold, Hair, Key, Pen, Purple, Red, Ring, Saliva, Umbrella, Wand, Words.

PRAYER Barbecue, Bell, Incense, Jade, Rose, Tea.

PRODUCTIVITY Primrose, Rabbit.

PROPHECY Bell, Bloodstone, Brass, Cedar, Crow (Raven), Dance, Dolphin, Moonstone, Star, Star Charts, Statuary.

PROSPERITY Bread, Butter, Cat's Eye, Cedar, Fish, Frog, Grapes, Lotus, Meat, Peach, Sugar (Refined), Tides.

PROTECTION Agate, Aloe, Arrow, Ash, Banana, Basil, Bay, Bear, Bell, Beryl, Birch, Bottle (Jar), Box, Brick, Cat, Cat's Eye, Cedar, Coasters, Copper, Correction Fluid, Cross, Dill, Dog, Doll, Door/Threshold, Drum, Elder, Fire, Food-Storage Container, Garlic, Geranium, Hair, Hawthorn, Holey Stones, Holly, Horn, Ice, Intercom, Iron, Key, Knife, Knots, Lava Stone, Lead, Leaf, Marjoram, Mica, Mirror, Mistletoe, Nettle, Olive, Onyx, Parsley, Peach, Pearl, Pepper, Poppet, Radish, Raspberry, Rattle, Red, Rice, Ring, Rowan, Runes, Scissors, Shells, Silver, Snake (Serpent), Soil, Sun, Tattoo, Turquoise, Umbrella, Violet, White, Woodruff, Words.

PROVIDENCE Alfalfa, Barbecue, Corn, Crackers, Fish, Food-Storage Container, Horn, Milk, Oats, Oven/Hearth, Pretzels, Rice, Soil, (Tortoise), Willow.

PSYCHISM Amethyst, Beans, Cinnamon, Clover, Dandelion, Dog, Fennel, Geode, Mica, Nutmeg, Purple, Rowan, Silver, Star, Whale.

PURIFICATION Barbecue, Beer, Cedar, Cinnamon, Fan, Fennel, Fire, Incense, Lavender, Lemon, Onion, Pine, Purple, Red, Rosemary, Sage, Salt, Shower, Tansy, Thyme, Toilet, Vacuum Cleaner, Water.

PURITY Chrysanthemum, Daisy, Gold, Lead, Lodestone, Lotus, Orange, Rose, White.

RA Bee, Beer, Hawk, Honey.

REINCARNATION Bear, Butterfly, Circle, Hawk, Rose, Salt, Snake (Serpent), Star, Tansy, Whale.

RESOURCEFULNESS Batteries, Coupon, Crackers, Food-Storage Container, Mouse, Primrose, Rabbit, Rubber Band, Squirrel.

REST Black.

SAFETY Amethyst, Ash, Coins, Elder, Garlic, Olive, Pretzels, Shoes, Square, Tattoo, Turquoise, White, Willow.

SATURN Black, Corn, Lavender.

SEXUALITY Drum, Fig, Fire, Lodestone, Orchid, Potato, Shoes, Snake (Serpent), Vanilla.

SHAPESHIFTING Blacktop, Crow (Raven), Doll, Fox, Frog, Moon, Rosemary, Snake (Serpent), Spider, Vetiver.

SLEEP Coral, Lavender, Violet.

SOUTH Candle (Wax), Cross (southern arm), Fire, Gold, Red.

SPELLCRAFT Almond, Amber, Bloodstone, Book, Clock (or Timer), Coasters, Lead, Leaf, Moon, Paper.

SPIRIT Agate, Altar, Camera, Circle, Coasters, Corn, Costume, Cross, Drum, Duct Tape, Fire, Key, Pizza, Quartz, Spider, Star Charts, White, Wind.

SPIRITS Beans, Camera, Candle (Wax), Chestnut, Chrysanthemum, Copper, Costume, Dance, Dandelion, Geode, Heather, Iron, Jade, Lead, Mask, Mirror, Mistletoe, Oak, Parsley, Pen, Rowan, Star, Violet, Wind.

SPIRITUALITY Bear, Brown, Fig, Fluorite, Key, Lotus, Mint, Owl, Peach, Purple, Silver, Squirrel, Whale.

SPRING Agate (blue lace), Ant, Birch, Butterfly, Clover, Green, Kite, Marjoram, Purple, Rabbit, Woodruff.

STRENGTH Amber, Ash, Blood, Bloodstone, Brick, Concrete, Dill, Duct Tape, Feather, Fig, Garlic, Hammer/ Gavel, Lodestone, Mead, Nettle, Onion, Pine, Saliva, Squirrel, Sun, Tattoo, Thyme, Turtle (Tortoise), Yellow.

STRESS Chamomile.

SUCCESS Amber, Bay, Bloodstone, Chamomile, Grapes, Kite, Radish, Rosemary, Silver, Sun, Tattoo.

SUMMER Air Conditioner, Ant (fire), Barbecue, Chamomile, Daisy, Fan, Fire, Lavender, Pretzels, Sun.

SUN Amber, Ant (fire), Ash, Bay, Brass, Carnelian, Cedar, Chamomile, Chrysanthemum, Cinnamon, Coins (gold), Copper, Daisy, Electricity, Fire, Gold, Hawk, Honey, Lamp, Lotus, Marigold, Mistletoe, Oven/Hearth, Pretzels, Ring, Rosemary, Umbrella, Walnut, Yellow.

TENACITY Ant, Batteries, Bear, Coffee, Duct Tape, Glue, Peanut Butter, Tides, Turtle (Tortoise).

THOR Bear, Birch, Daisy, Nettle, Oak, Tin, Wine.

TRANSFORMATION Blacktop, Blender/Mixer/Food Processor, Crackers, Fan, Microwave, Moon, Poppet, Shells, Snake (Serpent), Tides, Vetiver, Wand.

TRAVEL Blacktop, Bread, Coins, Crackers, Mead, Pretzels, Tin, Turquoise, Wind, Yellow.

TRUTH Bloodstone, Blue, Intercom, Lamp, Magnifying Glass, Mirror, Owl, Peach, Square, Sunflower.

UNITY Altar, Chalice, Computer, Drum, Geode, Glasses and Cups, Hair, Holly, Knots, Lodestone, Oven/Hearth, Rubber Band, Tattoo, Umbrella, Wine.

URANUS Allspice.

USIL Arrow.

VENUS Aloe, Apple, Blue, Cinnamon, Heather, Parsley, Raspberry, Rose.

VICTORY Agate, Ivy, Meat, Nasturtium, Pine, Radish, Words.

VISHNU Basil, Knots, Lotus, Rose, Turtle (Tortoise).

VISION Carrot, Dance, Eyeglasses, Fennel, Hawk, Lamp, Marigold, Obsidian, Potato, Quartz, Saliva, Star Charts.

VULCAN Fire.

WATER Agate (blue lace), Aloe, Amethyst, Apple, Banana, Beer, Birch, Blue, Bubbles, Cabbage, Catnip, Celery, Chalice, Cherry, Chocolate, Coffee, Copper, Coral, Correction Fluid, Cross (western arm), Dolphin, Elder, Fish, Fluorite, Frog, Geranium, Glasses and Cups, Grapes, Heather, Holey Stones, Horn, Ice, Ink, Ivy, Jade, Kiwi, Lemon, Lotus, Mead, Milk, Moon, Moonstone, Orchid, Peach, Pearl, Pen, Purple, Quartz, Raspberry, Rice, Rose, Rubber Band, Saliva, Salt, Shells, Shower, Silver, Square (left side), Strawberry, Sugar (Refined), Tansy, Tea, Thyme, Tides, Toilet, Tomato, Turquoise, Turtle (Tortoise), Vanilla, Violet, Willow, Wine.

WEATHER MAGICK Amethyst, Bay, Bell, Bloodstone, Bread, Cross, Fan, Frog, Jade, Knots, Leaf, Magnifying Glass, Mask, Pearl, Quartz, Rattle, Squirrel, Turquoise, Water.

WEST Cross (western arm), Glasses and Cups, Shells.

WINTER Drum, Quartz, White.

WISDOM Almond, Ant, Blue, Book, Coupon, Dog, Fig, Fox, Gold, Lamp, Olive, Owl, Purple, Sage, Snake (Serpent).

WISHCRAFT Agate, Apple, Balloons, Barbecue, Bay, Bottle (Jar), Cat, Coins, Crackers, Daisy, Dandelion, Kite, Paper, Runes, Sage, Scissors, Shells, Star, Walnut, Wind.

WORSHIP Altar, Dance, Incense, Mask, Oak, Shoes, Statuary, Walnut.

YOUTHFULNESS Balloons, Bubbles, Daisy, Green, Kite, Macaroni and Cheese, Rosemary.

ZEAL Bee, Coffee, Microwave.

ZEUS Almond, Apple, Bay, Bear, Bee, Daisy, Fire, Milk, Oak, Olive, Orange, Sage, Snake (Serpent), Violet, Walnut, Wind.

GLOSSARY

AMULET: An object worn for protection from evil or negative energies, including those generated by sickness. Traditionally amulets were made during auspicious astrological periods from natural, durable materials that could be easily worn or carried.

BELTANE: Known as May Day on the modern calendar, Beltane began in Rome with a festival called Floralia, which celebrates earth's renewal, vitality, and all the positive things associated with spring.

CABBALISM: An ancient form of Hebrew mysticism still practiced today as a form of witchcraft.

CASTING: A way of tossing small objects like stones or seeds on a surface in order to foretell the future from the resulting patterns.

CHAKRA: The word *chakra* means wheel. In Eastern thought, small spinning power centers are located in the human body, each of which has a specific function. The "heart" chakra, located aptly over the heart (for example), indicates a person's emotional accessibility. If a person's heart chakra spins clockwise and is large, that would indicate a big-hearted individual. The "third eye" chakra, located on a person's forehead between the eyebrows, indicates a person's psychic openness, and so forth.

CHARGING: The New Age term for putting power into an object, similar to charging a battery. Rather than electricity, the energy being put into an item comes from nature—sunlight and moonlight being the most popular energy boosters. You can, for example, place a stone in sunlight to accent conscious, masculine, logical energies or in moonlight to accent psychic, feminine, intuitive energies. Other popular media for charging are soil, which provides foundations, and water, which cleanses and improves energy "flow." An example of charging that requires nothing other than you is given in Chapter 2, "Charging an Object Through Visualization."

CHARM: A verbal incantation meant to evoke a specific result, often in connection with love or another heartfelt desire, or a small object (like those seen on charm bracelets) that is energized and worn in the hopes of improving life's circumstances. Usually the object represents the desired goal, such as a four-leaf clover carried for luck.

COMPONENT: An ingredient for making magick. Each component in a ritual or spell is carefully chosen for its symbolic, metaphysical value to the overall working.

CONSTRUCT: A magickal means and/or method. Constructs are the main focus through which the magick is created and directed.

CUNNING FOLK: An old name for wise people, village seers, and witches.

DIVINATION: The art of gaining information and insights through mystical means. Although this can mean looking into the future, as we expect from a fortune-teller, it also means looking at the here and now to better understand what's happening in both the seen and unseen realms. Most diviners use a specific tool, such as a tarot deck or a crystal ball, to gather information, but some people can do this without the aid of any outside implements. Some of the components listed in this book include instructions on how to use them for divination yourself.

DRUID: A natural wizard who works with and venerates the earth and all its living inhabitants.

ELEMENTAL ENERGIES: The energies and symbols generated by the four main elements in nature, namely, earth, air, fire, and water.

FETISH: A meaningful natural or created item that the bearer believes possesses a spirit or power that can be utilized for specific goals. Some fetishes are made for one-time use, during which their "spirit" is released to its task immediately by burning, burying, tossing in water, or carrying them to a designated location. Other fetishes are designed for long-term use, like those one might keep at home for peace and happiness.

GLAMOURY: In folklore witches learned the art of glamoury, or magical illusion, from fairies. Basically, glamoury changes a person's aura in small ways to create a temporary energy shift, often to bolster personal energy or project a certain "air" such as confidence or trust.

GRIMOIRE: An older term used to describe a collection of spells and other folk magicks, often called a Book of Shadows today.

INCANTATION: Any set of words (often rhythmic, rhyming, and/or repetitive) that expresses a magickal desire or is meant to evoke magickal energy through its recital. Words have power, and the incantation uses that power to focus the magick being created. Note, however, that if you cannot recite an incantation out loud, you can *think* it. Thoughts equate to energy patterns: they are words uttered inwardly and as such can work just as effectively.

INVOCATION: An invitation to a specific power, such as the god/dess or the elemental beings, to join you in your magickal effort. Think of it as a prayer with a distinct purpose.

KARMA: The idea that whatever we do in life, good or bad, eventually comes back to us in this life or the next.

MAGICK CIRCLE: Any protected magickal space (not necessarily round, although it often is); any area that's been set aside for mystical work by cleansing and blessing that region and invoking the Sacred Powers of earth-air-fire-water-spirit to act as guardians in that space. A circle was chosen as the optimum design for magickal sacred space, because it represents continuance, cycles, and the earth and the fact that everyone within the circle is equally important to the success of the magick being created.

MEDITATION: Thinking deeply about something. In a magickal construct, meditation is used to quiet our minds and turn our thoughts away from the mundane long enough to focus on spiritual matters, specifically prevalent issues, questions, or study topics.

PAGAN: A member of one portion of the magickal community with polytheistic overtones and a strong emphasis on living in harmony with nature.

PENDULUM: A type of divinatory system in which an object is suspended by string and its movements observed for interpretive values.

POWER POUCH: A small bundle into which various tokens are placed to provide the bearer with specific types of energy.

PSYCHISM: The natural ability (latent or otherwise) that all people have to "sense" things beyond the normal levels of awareness.

RITUAL: One means of building and directing power. A ritual is comprised of a series of sacred words and actions with a specific goal, usually in the construct of a magick circle. Seasonal rituals and those for specific deities are often "traditional," that is, performed in much the same manner as they have been for decades or centuries. Other personal rituals can, and do, change to suit the prevalent circumstances of the individual(s).

SACRED SPACE: Any region in which the powers of the elements have been called upon to protect and guide whatever is happening within that space. In considering what constitutes true sacred space, remember this: Sacredness is determined as much by attitude as actions (*see also* magick circle).

SCRYING: The word *scrying* comes from an Old English word meaning "discover" and it's used to describe a type of divination. Here, a person looks at the flames of a fire, the surface of a crystal, a reflective surface, or the like, and watches for specific visions to appear. Many students of this art believe the intense staring leads to a self-induced trance that heightens awareness so the symbolic imagery can appear for interpretation.

SHAMAN: An original priest of nature, who goes to the spirits who abide in that realm for power and insights into daily living. Shamanism has many varieties, as any other form of magick, and is among the most popular of the modern magickal schools because of its reverence for the earth. Like pagans and Wiccans, shamans see the earth as a living, vital organism that is very important to our spiritual progress as well as our physical and mental well-being.

SHAPESHIFTING: Shapeshifting is a type of glamoury but with a different effect. The process transforms the magic user's outlook, perceptions, and understanding to that of the animal, plant, or person they're mimicking. Sometimes this auric transformation can be sensed by people around the magick user, but the ultimate goal of shapeshifting is not a literal one. Instead, the hope is to "walk in something else's shoes" to learn and grow from the experience.

SPELL: A mini-ritual in which magick is raised and directed toward a specific goal.

SUMMERLAND: The dwelling place of spirits after death.

TALISMAN: A portable magickal object that's created during auspicious astrological times to help with a specific goal or meet a need.

VISUALIZATION: The forming of empowered, creative mental images designed to augment meditation and magickal focus.

WICCAN: The name given to anyone who follows the religion of Wicca (note that one may be a witch without being a Wiccan).

WITCH: Someone who uses spells, conjurations, and other occult/magickal methods to raise and direct energy.

SELECTED BIBLIOGRAPHY

Well over one hundred books were used to compile the information in *Magick Made Easy*. This bibliography reflects the books most helpful to me and those I believe will be most useful to students who wish to delve into specific topics in more detail.

Aldington, Richard, trans. *New Larousse Encyclopedia of Mythology*. Middlesex, England: Hamlyn Publishing, 1973.

Ann, Martha, and Dorothy Myers Imel. *Goddesses in World Mythology*. New York: Oxford University Press, 1995.

Arrien, Angeles. *The Four-Fold Way*. New York: HarperCollins, 1993.

Beyerl, Paul. *Herbal Magick*. Custer, WA: Phoenix, 1998.

Bruce-Mitford, Miranda. *Illustrated Book of Signs and Symbols*. New York: DK Publishing, 1996.

Budge, E. A. Wallis. *Amulets and Superstitions*. Oxford, England: Oxford University Press, 1930.

Cavendish, Richard. *A History of Magic*. New York: Taplinger, 1979.

Cooper, J. C. *Symbolic and Mythological Animals*. London: Aquarian Press, 1992.

Cunningham, Scott. *Crystal, Gem and Metal Magic*. St. Paul, MN: Llewellyn, 1995.

———. *Encyclopedia of Magical Herbs*. St. Paul, MN: Llewellyn, 1988.

———. *Magic in Food*. St. Paul, MN: Llewellyn, 1991.

Davison, Michael Worth, ed. *Everyday Life Through the Ages*, Pleasantville, NY: Reader's Digest Association, 1992.

De Grandis, Francesca. *Be a Goddess! A Guide to Celtic Spells and Wisdom for Self-Healing, Prosperity, and Great Sex*. San Francisco: Harper San Francisco, 1998.

Gordon, Leslie. *Green Magic*. New York: Viking, 1977.

Gordon, Stuart. *Encyclopedia of Myths and Legends*. London: Headline Book Publishing, 1993.

Hall, Manly P. *Secret Teachings of All Ages*. Los Angeles: Philosophical Research Society, 1977.

Jordan, Michael. *Encyclopedia of Gods*. New York: Facts on File, 1993.

Kowalchik, Claire, and William Hylton, eds. *Rodale's Illustrated Encyclopedia of Herbs*. Emmaus, PA: Rodale, 1987.

Kunz, George Frederick. *Curious Lore of Precious Stones*. New York: Dover, 1971.

Leach, Maria, ed. *Standard Dictionary of Folklore, Mythology, and Legend*. New York: Harper & Row, 1984.

Leach, Marjorie. *Guide to the Gods*. Santa Barbara, CA: ABC-Clio, 1992.

Loewe, Michael, and Carmen Blacker, eds. *Oracles and Divination*. Boulder, CO: Shambhala, 1981.

Lurker, Manfred. *Dictionary of Gods and Goddesses, Devils and Demons*. New York: Routledge and Kegan Paul, 1995.

Matthews, John, ed. *The World Atlas of Divination*. New York: Bullfinch Press, 1992.

Miller, Gustavus Hindman. *Ten Thousand Dreams Interpreted*. Chicago: Donohue and Company, 1931.

Opie, Iona, and Moira Tatem. *A Dictionary of Superstitions*. New York: Oxford University Press, 1989.

Sargent, Denny. *Global Ritualism*. St. Paul, MN: Llewellyn, 1994.

Spence, Lewis. *The Encyclopedia of the Occult*. London: Bracken, 1988.

Steiger, Brad. *Totems*. San Francisco: Harper San Francisco, 1996.

Telesco, Patricia. *Futuretelling*. Freedom, CA: Crossing Press, 1997.

———. *The Herbal Arts*. Secaucus, NJ: Citadel Books, 1997.

———. *Kitchen Witch's Cookbook*. St. Paul, MN: Llewellyn, 1994.

———. *The Language of Dreams*. Freedom, CA: Crossing Press, 1997.

———. *Witch's Brew*. St. Paul, MN: Llewellyn, 1995.

Walker, Barbara. *The Woman's Dictionary of Symbols and Sacred Objects*. San Francisco: Harper & Row, 1988.

Waring, Philippa. *The Dictionary of Omens and Superstitions*. Secaucus, NJ: Chartwell, 1978.

FINAL WORDS

Magick is an ever growing, ever changing spiritual tradition. Like Dorothy's yellow brick road, there are bound to be twists, turns, upsets, challenges, and amazing victories along the way. Even so, when you at last click your heels together and make the magick happen, it will lead you back home—to your own heart and soul. That is how it should be. As long as you remain responsible to your path and your power, never violating morals, another's free will, or the earth's sacredness, you will rarely go astray (Glinda will be downright proud!).

As a side note, what I've presented in this book is but one way of many to practice magick successfully. So when you see others approaching their magick differently, revel in that diversity and talk about the variations. You'll likely both benefit from the experience, gaining insights and ideas from the exchange.

May you always live and *be* the magick!

In service,

Trish

www.loresinger.com
clubs.yahoo.com/clubs/folkmagickwithtrishtelesco